IMAGES
of America

SACRAMENTO'S SOUTHSIDE PARK

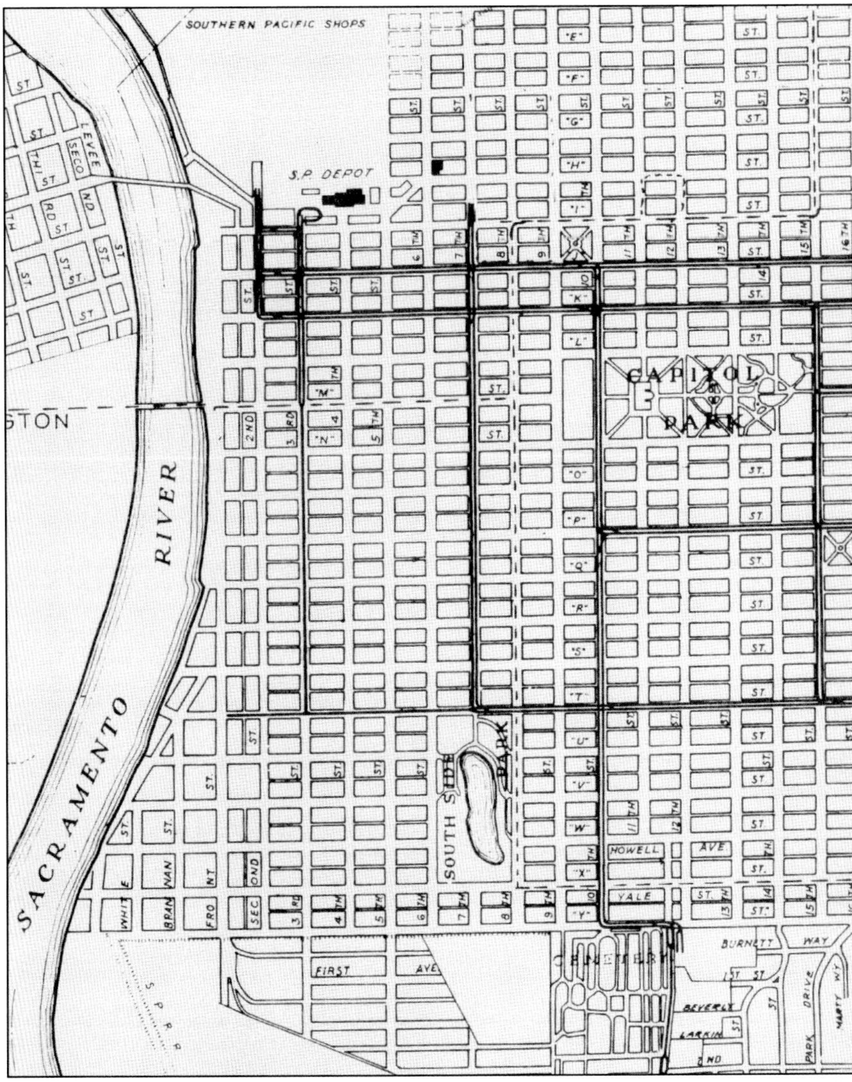

The boundaries of the Southside Park neighborhood have varied over time. The modern boundaries are from Interstate 5 to Twelfth Street and from R Street to Highway 50. However, these highways did not exist when Southside was first defined, and the neighborhoods north of R Street were considered part of Southside prior to their demolition. The Southside Improvement Club considered anyone who lived south of K Street and north of Broadway, between the river and Fourteenth Street, to be a Southsider, and the City of Sacramento once considered the neighborhood to stretch as far as Twenty-first Street. The Southside Park Historic Preservation District includes structures from Third to Nineteenth Street, with irregular boundaries but generally South of R Street. (Author's collection.)

ON THE COVER: This photograph of the Lincoln School graduating class captures the cultural diversity of Southside Park. In his book *Barrio Boy*, author Ernesto Galarza wrote: "At Lincoln, making us into Americans did not mean scrubbing away what made us originally foreign. . . . It was easy for me to feel that becoming a proud American, as she [the teacher] said we should, did not mean feeling ashamed of being a Mexican." (Sacramento Archives and Museum Collection Center.)

IMAGES
of America

SACRAMENTO'S SOUTHSIDE PARK

William Burg

ARCADIA
PUBLISHING

ISBN 978-0-7385-4796-1

Published by Arcadia Publishing
Charleston SC, Chicago IL, Portsmouth NH, San Francisco CA

Printed in the United States of America

Library of Congress Catalog Card Number: 2007925812

For all general information contact Arcadia Publishing at:
Telephone 843-853-2070
Fax 843-853-0044
E-mail sales@arcadiapublishing.com
For customer service and orders:
Toll-Free 1-888-313-2665

Visit us on the Internet at www.arcadiapublishing.com

Contents

ACKNOWLEDGMENTS

During an earlier project, Al Balshor suggested that I write a book about Southside Park, and I wish to thank him the most. He introduced me to the Southside Improvement Club, shared his memories and photographs, and encouraged others to participate. Equally important was the help of Paul Trudeau, president of the Southside Park Neighborhood Association. He provided research material and leads and introduced me to longtime neighborhood residents who were willing to share their stories and photographs. Both of these gentlemen embody the community spirit and genuine love of neighborhood that I have found in Southside Park and hope to capture in this book.

Photographs and documents from many archives and libraries were used to create this book. My thanks go to the staff of the Sacramento Room of the Sacramento Public Library, the Sacramento Archives and Museum Collection Center, the California State Library's California Room, Sacramento State University's Special Collections and University Archives, the University of Southern California (USC) Archives, and the Western Railway Museum Archives.

Dolores Silva Greenslate, historian of the Portuguese Cultural and Historical Society of Sacramento, provided many photographs and helped fact-check the Portuguese history section. Bill Cerrutti and Tony Plescia of the Italian Cultural Society of Sacramento provided photographs and background on Sacramento's Italian community. Ed Carroll provided research information on baseball and the Fong Mansion.

Oral history interviews, background information, and photographs were provided by Tony Lopez, Ed Mores, Gene Plecas, Al and Marie Balshor, Clarence Kunz, Steve Morgan, Steve Silva, Ed Kanelos Jr., Billie Kanelos, Imam Ibrahim Hamdani, the Pompei family, Ronny King, Georgina Montrond, Manuel Viera, Dora Bazan, Ginger Rutland, Mike Pryor, and Marjorie Hollins.

Finally, thanks to all the members of the Southside Improvement Club for welcoming me at their meetings and sharing their memories. They still meet regularly, and membership is still 25¢ a month.

INTRODUCTION

As the Gold Rush slowed and the Sacramento Valley filled with farms, Sacramento became the regional hub for processing and shipping agricultural products. At the junction of two rivers and served by railroads, Sacramento was the transportation nexus for the region. Sacramento's population in the wake of the Gold Rush provided labor for processing agricultural goods, and by the 1860s, Sacramento was the home of grain and lumber mills and canneries. The completion of the transcontinental railroad in 1869 increased Sacramento's importance as a transportation and industrial processing center. In addition to agricultural products, Sacramento's premier industry was the railroad itself, as the Central Pacific General Shops became the largest industrial facility in the western United States.

All of this industry created a massive demand for labor. As elsewhere in the United States, primarily immigrants met this demand. Sacramento's early industries hugged the waterfront, from the massive railroad shops complex to the north of downtown to the industries alongside the railroad levee on R Street. In an era when nearly everyone traveled to work on foot, laborers sought homes within walking distance of their work. Thus, many workers settled in the blocks just east of the river between downtown and R Street.

This neighborhood was already inhabited by many of Sacramento's wealthiest citizens, like E. B. Crocker, Leland Stanford, and August Heilbron. As the 19th century progressed and the neighborhood grew, many of these wealthy residents departed. The introduction of the horse-drawn streetcar allowed middle-class families to live farther from the factory smoke and crowded neighborhoods downtown. Working people stayed closer to the river and their jobs. The streetcar may have only cost a nickel, but a loaf of bread also cost a nickel, and families must be fed.

As the 19th century progressed, the Sacramento River levee system was improved and the depression known as Burns' Slough was filled, making more land in the southern part available for use. Development progressed past the R Street railroad levee to the Y Street levee and the city limits.

New waves of immigrants came to Sacramento seeking work and homes. By the dawn of the 20th century, Sacramento's Southside neighborhood was growing rapidly. While much of Sacramento's growth followed the electric streetcar lines eastward on J and K Streets, and outward beyond the city limits into Highland Park and Oak Park, working people still remained close to Front Street. As the R Street industrial corridor grew eastward, workers' homes went up along the trackside.

Immigrant laborers formed their own communities within Sacramento. Bound together by common bonds of language and culture, immigrants created their own support networks to welcome countrymen and help the needy within their community. These communities grew into ethnic neighborhoods centered on churches and mutual aid societies. As time went on, ethnic communities relocated or spread into different parts of town, and new waves of immigrants moved in to take their place.

In addition to its proximity to workplaces along the waterfront, Southside Park became an important destination for immigrants in the early 20th century because nonwhites were not prevented by racial covenants from living there. Many of Sacramento's early suburban developments, including Land Park, Curtis Park, and East Sacramento, prohibited nonwhites from purchasing land. Some of these neighborhoods remained exclusively white by force of law until the 1960s. The Southside neighborhood had no such restrictions. The neighborhood's population became a diverse mix of Portuguese, Italians, Slavs, Japanese, Chinese, Mexicans, Russians, and other ethnic groups. During World War II, many African Americans moved to the Sacramento area seeking wartime employment. At about the same time, immigrants from India, in the region that is now Pakistan, moved to Sacramento and established the oldest mosque in the western United States.

Some residents of Southside Park were moved against their will. During the Second World War, Japanese Americans living in Sacramento were relocated to internment camps for years. Many lost their homes and businesses. This would not be the last displacement for Sacramento's Japanese neighborhood. In the 1950s and 1960s, urban redevelopment projects in Sacramento, including multiple freeways and the construction of state buildings along Capitol Avenue, destroyed many blocks of homes and businesses.

At the same time, Sacramento as a whole was changing. The automobile and publicly funded highway systems were transforming the way American cities were built, and millions of middle-class Americans moved to new homes in the suburbs. While suburban growth was a national trend throughout the 20th century, city planners originally assumed that suburban residents would still come downtown to work, to shop, and to seek recreation. The suburban shopping mall and the dispersal of industry and commercial districts away from downtown left many suburban residents with little reason to come downtown, and many stopped coming altogether.

Downtown's response to suburban decentralization, both in Sacramento and around the country, was an effort to attract middle-class and wealthy people back to the downtown core. This was often done in conjunction with federal programs intended to improve conditions in inner-city slums, principally the Housing Act of 1949. These programs were interpreted and administered at the local level.

City governments hoped to use redevelopment to increase revenue from property taxes. Downtown business leaders hoped to utilize the tools of redevelopment to expand central business districts into adjacent neighborhoods. However, many of these neighborhoods did not qualify as slums in their own right. Many were older residential neighborhoods, occupied by working people and ethnic communities, like Southside Park. In order to justify the legal proceedings necessary to acquire these neighborhoods, urban planners used a new term to describe them: blight. Under the banner of blight eradication, whole city blocks in Southside Park were razed for government buildings, commercial structures, and parking lots.

In addition to these challenges, residents of central city neighborhoods like Southside Park faced other difficulties. The Federal Housing Administration (FHA), whose loan programs made new homes in the suburbs possible for millions of Americans, instituted the policy of redlining risky neighborhoods. Neighborhoods were designated as risky if they were occupied by nonwhites or even considered likely to attract nonwhite residents. Loans for property in redlined neighborhoods were far harder to obtain and had higher interest rates. This made home purchases, loans for improvement, or new construction impossible. As loans became harder to obtain, people were less able to improve their homes and neighborhoods became more dilapidated. As the neighborhood fell into disrepair, many of those who could afford to relocate did so, and landlords were less inclined to maintain or improve their rental properties.

At the same time, people displaced from downtown neighborhoods affected by redevelopment began moving into Southside Park. This included prostitutes, who had previously operated along J and K Streets. By the mid-1960s, the corner of Fourth and T Streets became notorious for prostitution and drug dealing and known as "Hooker Hollow."

Despite the many problems that caused Southside Park's decline, many in the neighborhood simply refused to give up hope. In the 1970s and 1980s, activists formed self-help organizations to combat prostitution in the neighborhood, which met with great success. Progress in civil rights eliminated racial covenants and banned redlining, which removed some of the economic barriers to neighborhood improvement and contributed to a greater sense of cultural awareness among the ethnic communities of Southside Park. In the 21st century, Southside Park has maintained its identity as a diverse, inclusive neighborhood.

One

The Arizona District

The oldest part of Southside Park, between M Street and R Street, was an early residential district with varied uses. Closest to the river were riverfront warehouses for transferring cargo between railroad cars and riverboats. Various early industries were located between Front and Second Streets. To the east were a variety of stately homes, ranging from Gold Rush–era structures shipped around Cape Horn to the stately mansions of E. B. Crocker, August Heilbron, and Leland Stanford.

The land south of the R Street railroad levee was swampy marsh, with a slough that ran south in the vicinity of Seventh Street. The city sewer main, a 30-inch cement pipe, ran along Sixth Street, ending in a drainage ditch south of the city limits, near the old city cemetery. From the time that the original Sacramento street plan was laid out, land speculators held and traded parcels sporadically, but few structures were built. Some of the land was used for gardens and small-lot farming, but homes were sparse until about 1900. While the neighborhood south of K Street began to be known as "Southside," the portion of Southside south of R Street was known as the "Arizona District" after the Arizona Gang that resided there.

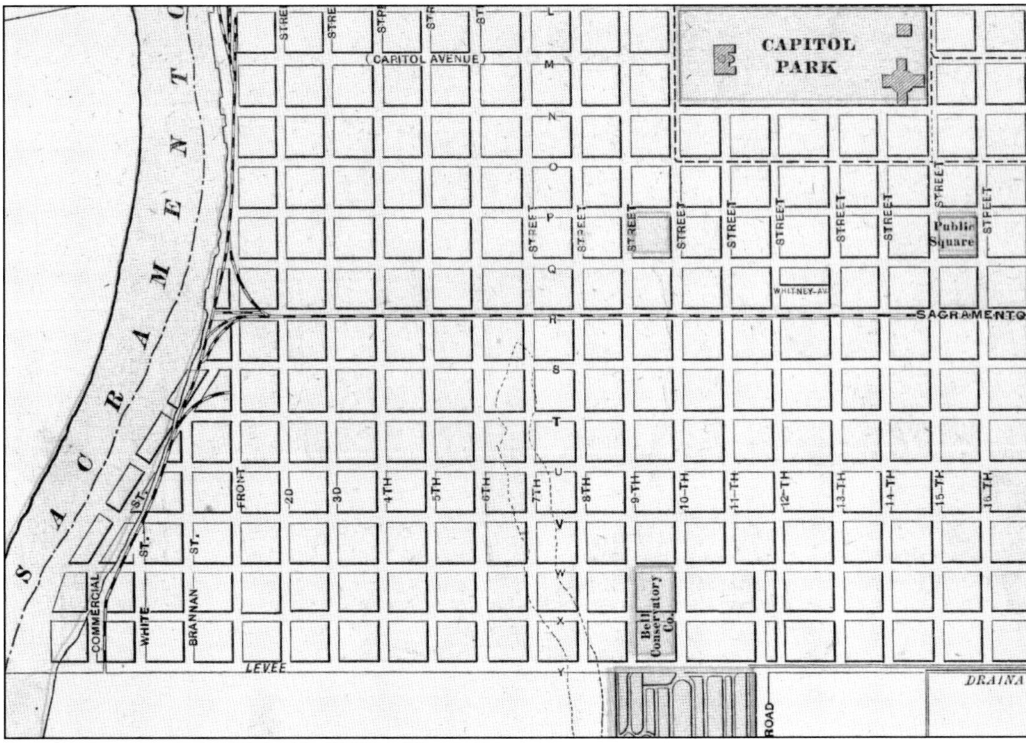

This map shows the southwestern corner of Sacramento in about 1895, clearly showing downtown Sacramento's grid pattern. The railroad tracks along R Street marked the southern boundary of the original residential neighborhood. The long slough, indicated on the map by an irregular dotted line between Sixth and Eighth Street, eventually became the site for Southside Park. South of the city limits at Y Street is the Old City Cemetery. The cemetery was originally sited closer to X Street on lower ground, but it was found to be susceptible to flooding. (Sacramento Public Library, Sacramento Room.)

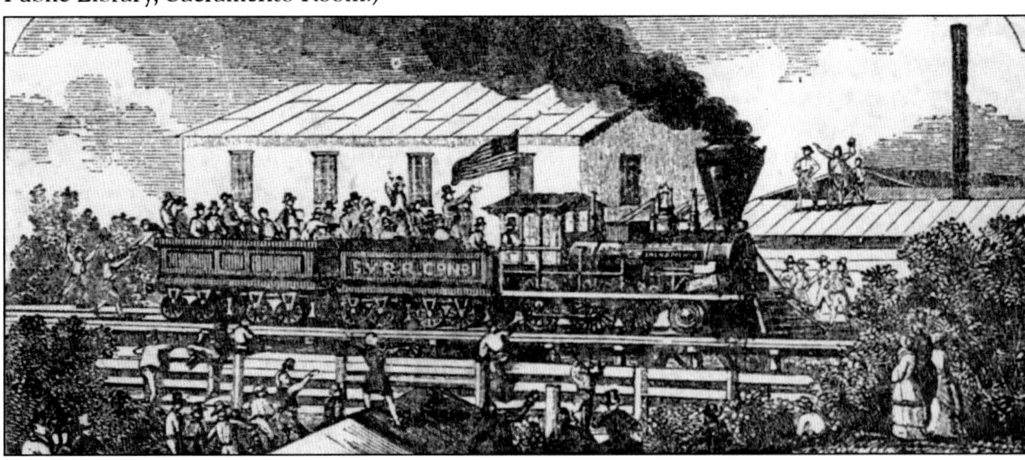

The Sacramento Valley Railroad (SVRR), completed in 1856, was the first steam railroad in California. The route was planned by engineer Theodore Judah and was intended to carry goods from the waterfront to mining camps around Folsom. Because Sacramento was still very vulnerable to flooding when the SVRR was completed, the tracks along the western end of R Street were elevated on wooden trestles, visible under the locomotive in this illustration. (California State Library.)

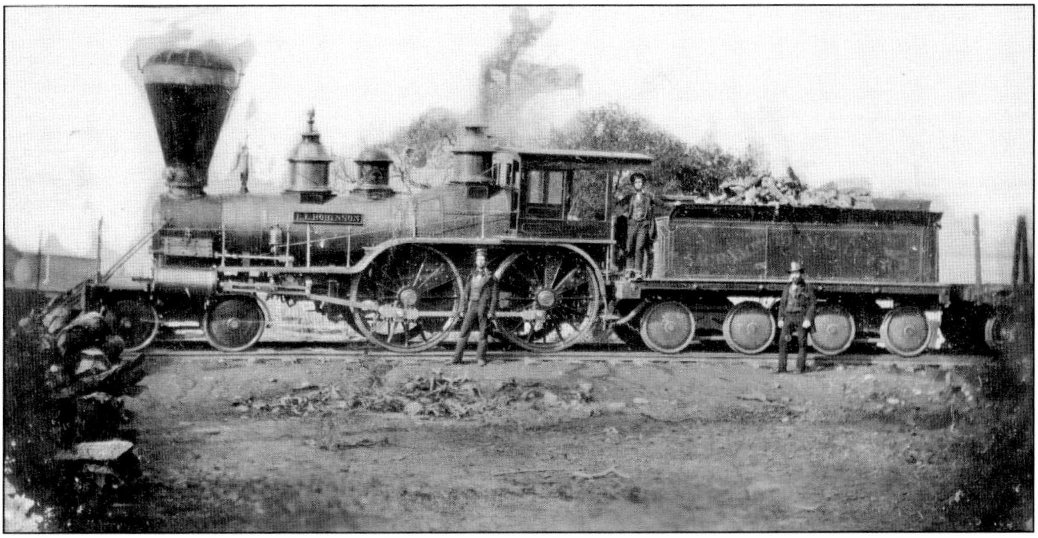

The SVRR used wood-burning steam locomotives like this one, the *L. L. Robinson*. Because there were not yet any heavy foundries on the West Coast, locomotives had to be ordered from the East Coast. Because there were not yet any railroads spanning the country, these locomotives had to be shipped to California around Cape Horn. The *L. L. Robinson* was one of the first such locomotives to make the journey. (USC Archives.)

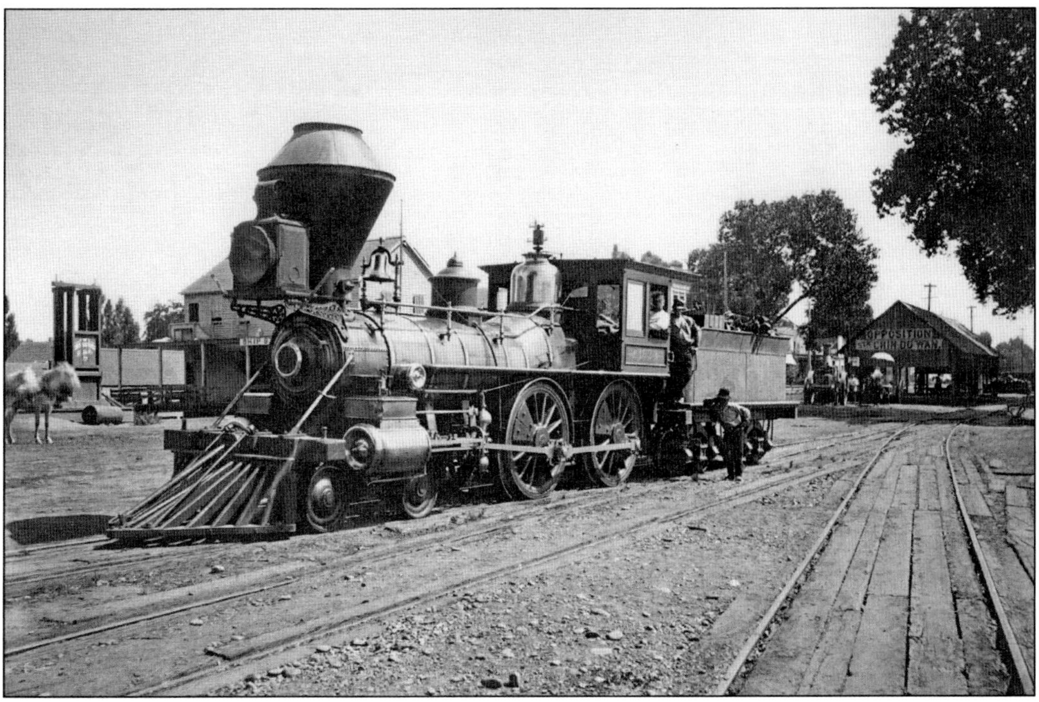

In 1863, the Central Pacific Railroad began construction with the more dramatic goal of sending a railroad line east across the Sierra Nevada. Central Pacific also hired Theodore Judah away from the SVRR and purchased the SVRR outright in 1865. In 1869, the transcontinental railroad was completed, giving Sacramento a direct railroad route to the eastern United States. (California State Library.)

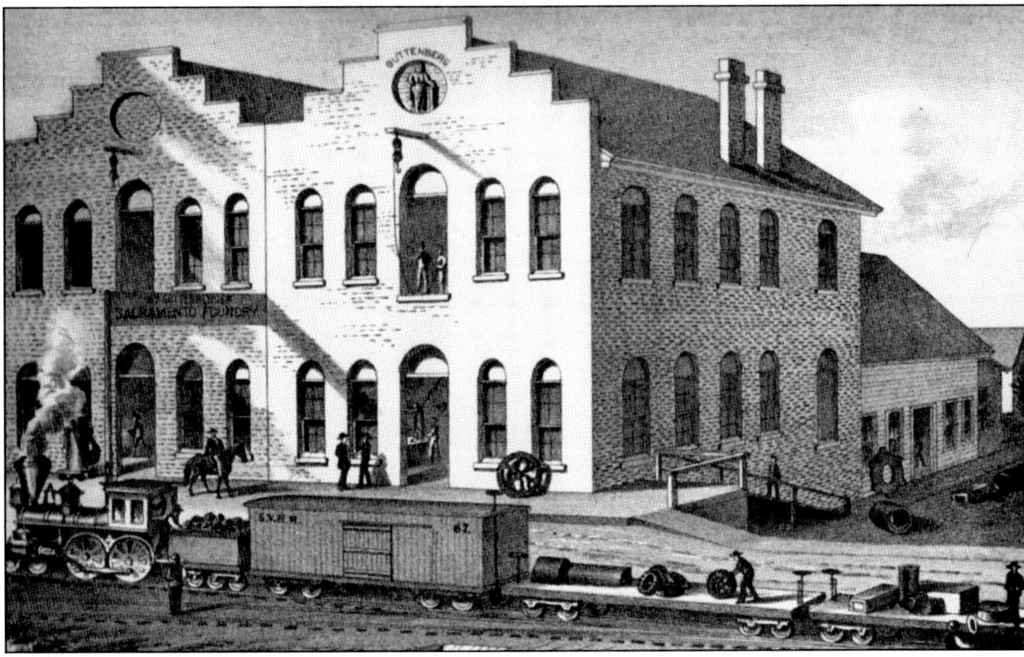

Located at Front and N Streets, the Sacramento Foundry was one of the few industries on Front Street in early Sacramento not dedicated to agricultural processing or transportation. Every industry of the era had some call for metalwork, however, and the foundry provided metal goods to other industries on the waterfront. (Sacramento Public Library, Sacramento Room.)

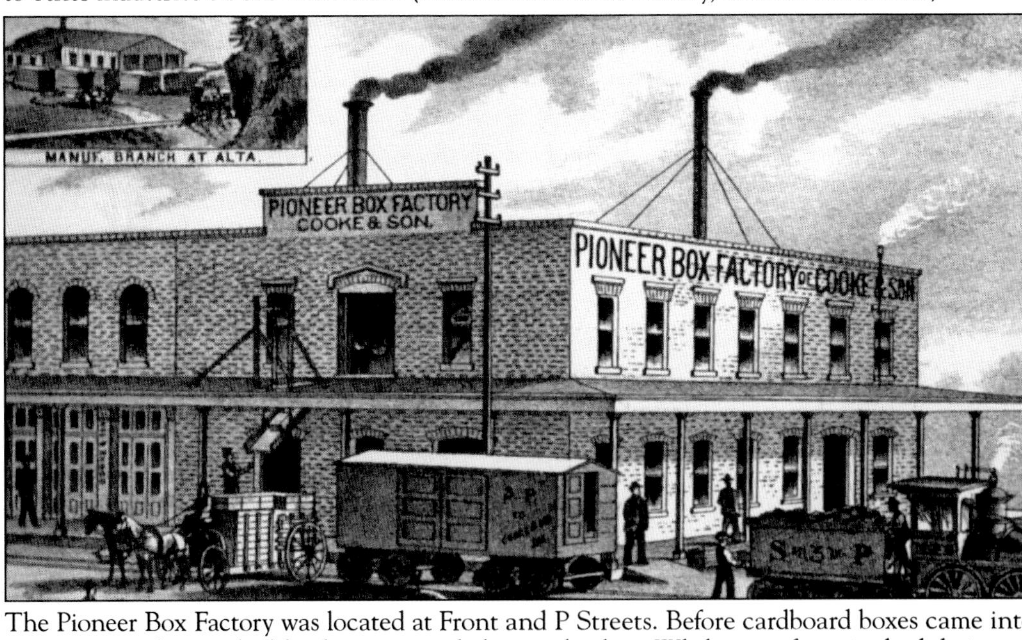

The Pioneer Box Factory was located at Front and P Streets. Before cardboard boxes came into use, every product packed for shipping needed a wooden box. While some factories had their own facilities for creating packing boxes, Pioneer created boxes for other businesses to fill. Located directly on the SVRR mainline, their products could be shipped out by rail or via a stake-sided delivery wagon, one of which can be seen to the left of the boxcar in this illustration. (Sacramento Public Library, Sacramento Room.)

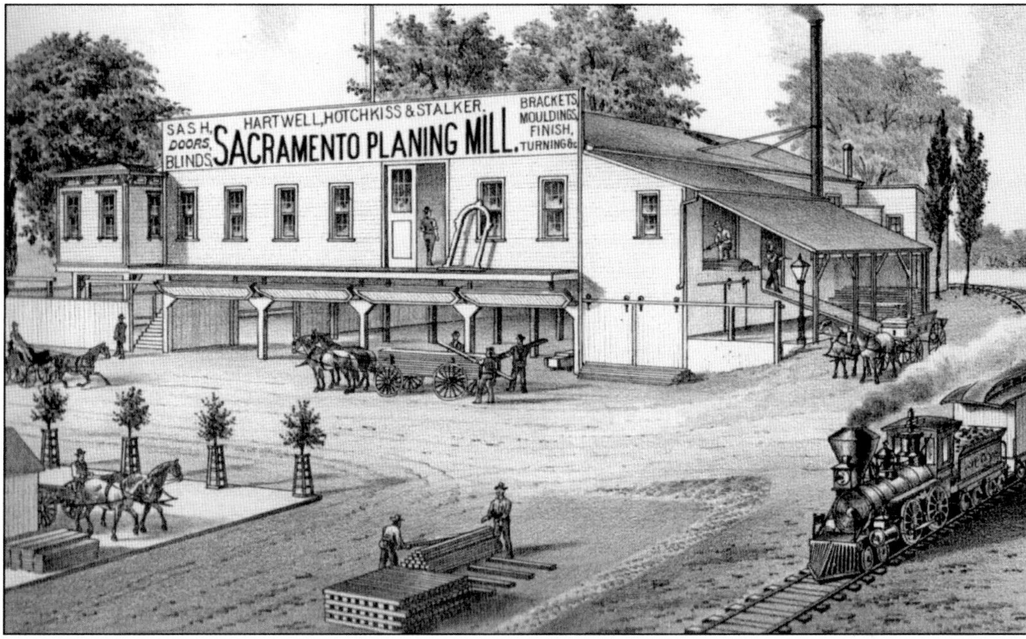

Mills like the Sacramento Planing Mill were an essential step in the transformation of cut lumber to finished molding, doors, and other fine woodwork. Logging operations all over California sent lumber to Sacramento via the railroads or by ship. While many of Sacramento's earliest buildings were shipped as prefabricated kits from the East Coast, the demand for wood for homes and the development of California's logging industry made locally produced lumber far more economical. (Sacramento Public Library, Sacramento Room.)

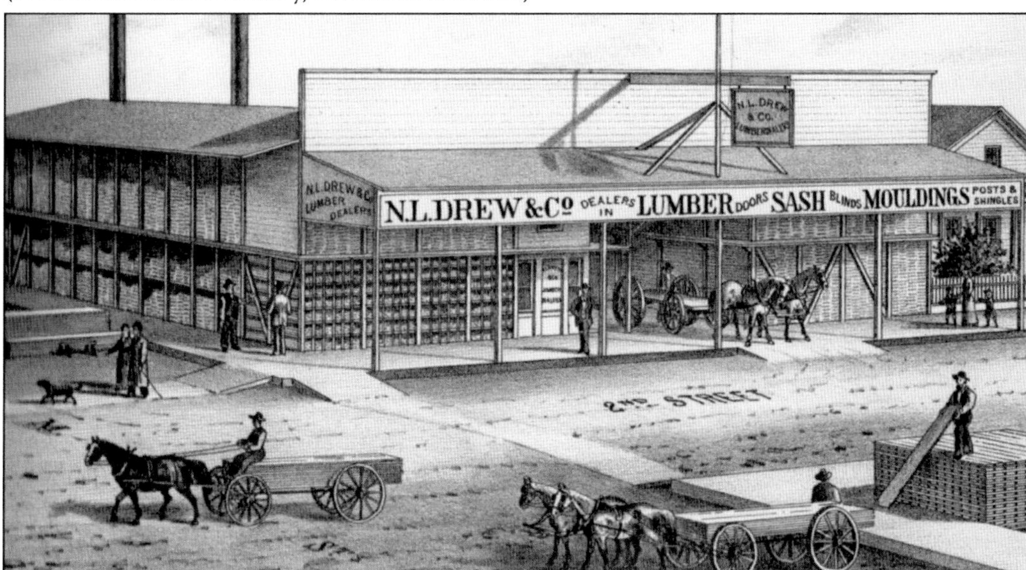

The N. L. Drew lumberyard sold finished wood products to the general public. Advancements in milling technology made the elaborate architectural styles of the late 19th century possible. Like many developing Western cities, home builders in Sacramento copied contemporary Eastern styles in order to promote their city's image as a cosmopolitan place. (Sacramento Public Library, Sacramento Room.)

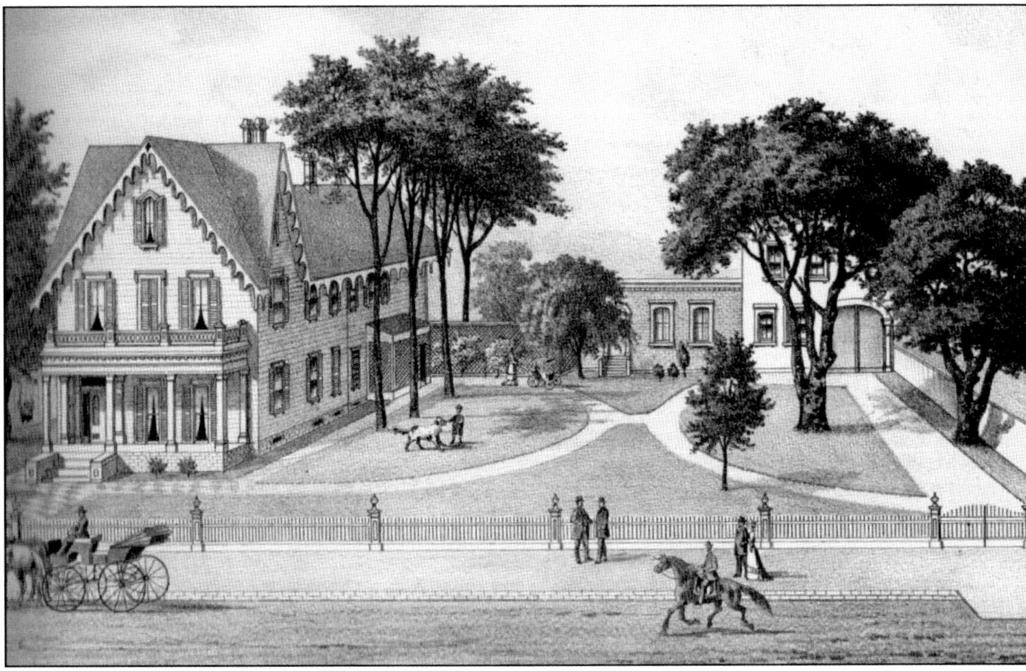

George Cadwalader came to Sacramento as a forty-niner in search of gold. In 1855, he became an attorney and was joined by his brother Edward, a stock and real estate broker. George's home at 720 N Street is shown here. (Sacramento Public Library, Sacramento Room.)

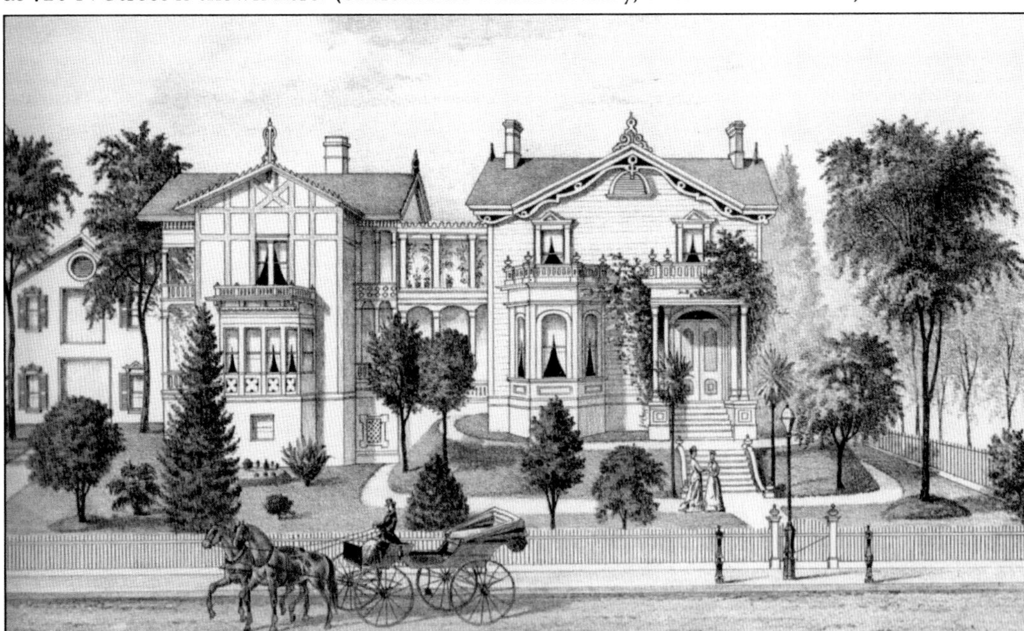

The residence of William R. S. Foye was located at Third and O Streets. Foye was a chief salesman of Huntington and Hopkins Hardware. That firm's founders, Collis P. Huntington and Mark Hopkins, were two of the "Big Four" who built the Central Pacific Railroad. Foye was one of several employees who were made full partners in Huntington and Hopkins when the founders went into the railroad business. (Sacramento Public Library, Sacramento Room.)

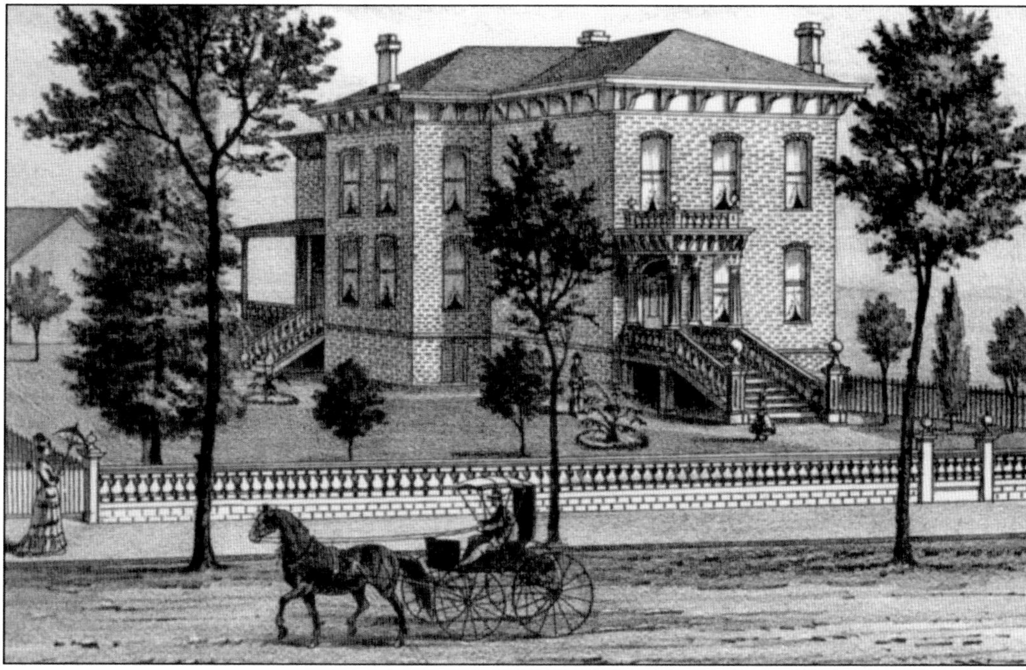

This home of John C. Ryan was constructed in 1878 and was located on Q Street between Tenth and Eleventh Streets. Ryan came to California in 1852 to mine for gold. Two years later he came to Sacramento and founded the city's first brickyard. Ryan's brickyard provided many of the bricks used in the raising of Sacramento's downtown streets. Appropriately his home was made of brick. (Sacramento Public Library, Sacramento Room.)

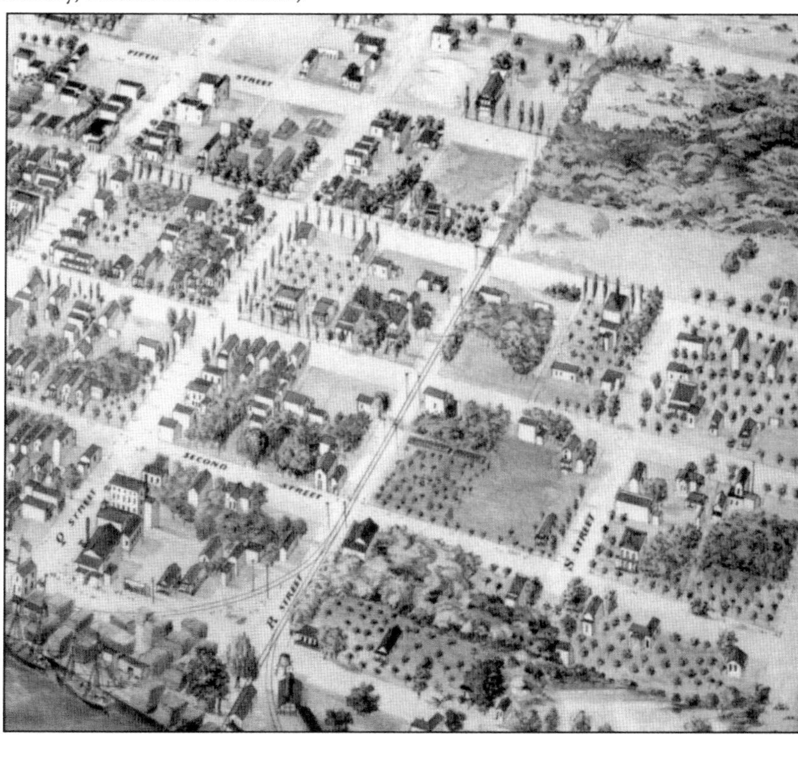

This perspective map of Sacramento from the 1870s shows the area around R Street near the waterfront. The area north of the tracks is already starting to fill with homes and with larger structures indicating industry along the waterfront, while much of the land to the south is still open and undeveloped or is cultivated garden plots. (California State Library.)

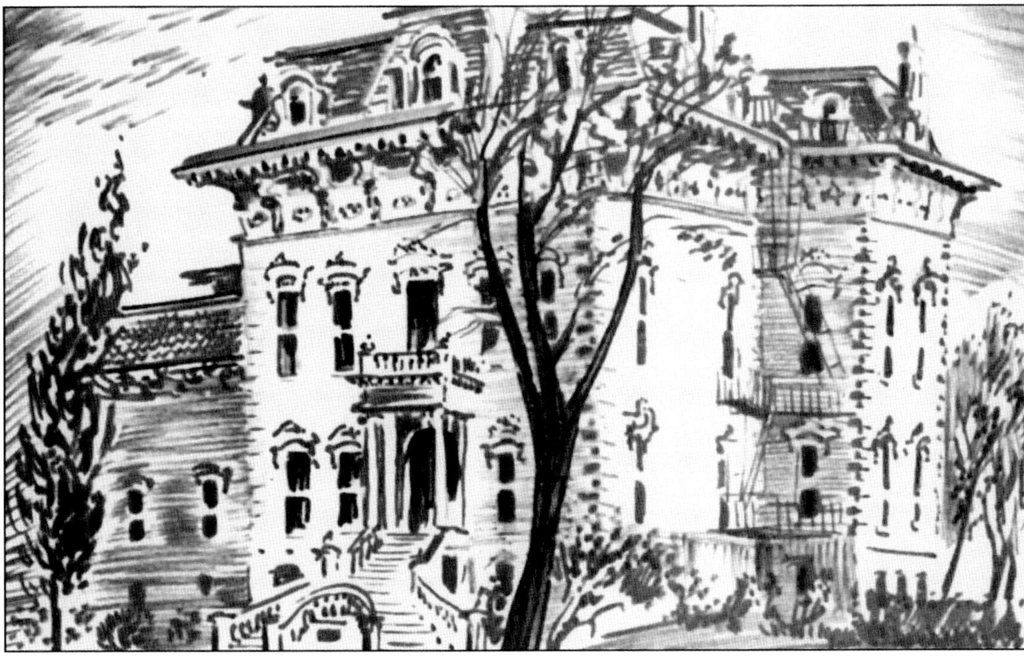

Leland Stanford's home at Eighth and N Streets was originally built for Shelton C. Fogus in 1857. Stanford purchased the house in 1861 after being elected governor of California. Stanford greatly expanded the structure in 1871. His widow, Jane Stanford, gave the house to the Catholic diocese in Sacramento for use as an orphanage in 1900. Stanford was also one of the Big Four. (Author's collection.)

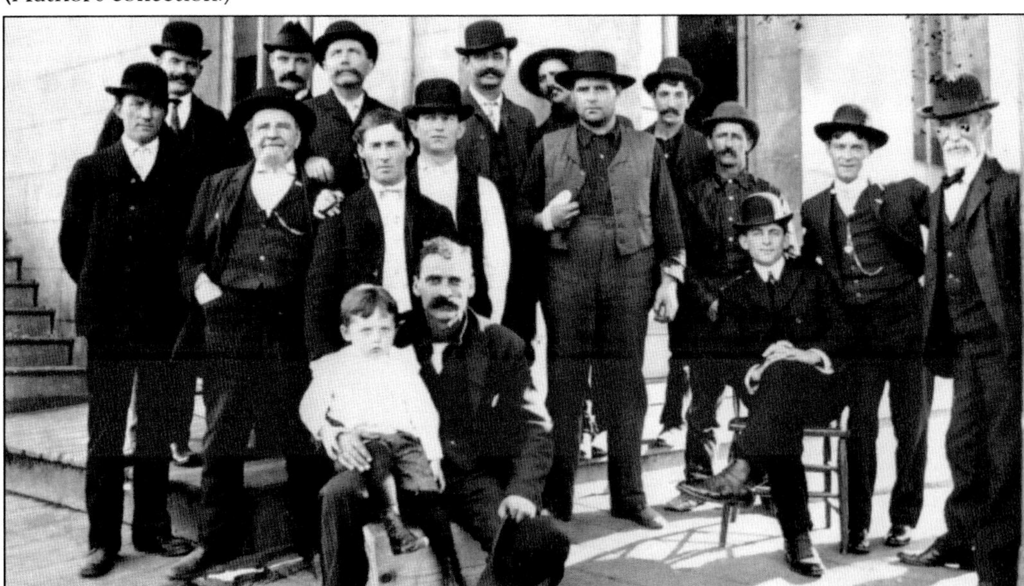

The Ryan family owned this brick building at the corner of Tenth and S Streets. Unrelated to the brick maker, whose home is pictured on page 15, family patriarch Thomas Ryan was the captain of the Sacramento Transportation Company steamboat *Flora*. His sons George and Arthur briefly worked on the riverboats as well, before George became a grocer and Arthur a police officer. (Kanelos family collection.)

The Crocker mansion, on Third and O Streets, was built in several stages. The oldest portion of the house was built by John Bay in 1854. A new structure was built onto the house for banker B. F. Hastings in 1859. In 1868, the house was sold to Judge E. B. Crocker. Crocker was legal counsel for the Central Pacific Railroad and brother of Charles Crocker, one of the Big Four. From 1900 to 1913, the Crocker mansion served as a home for unwed mothers. (Author's collection.)

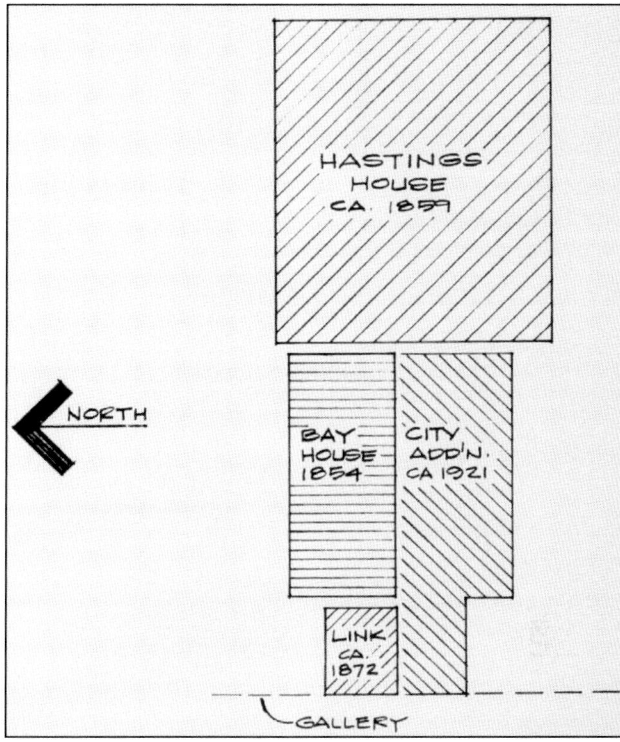

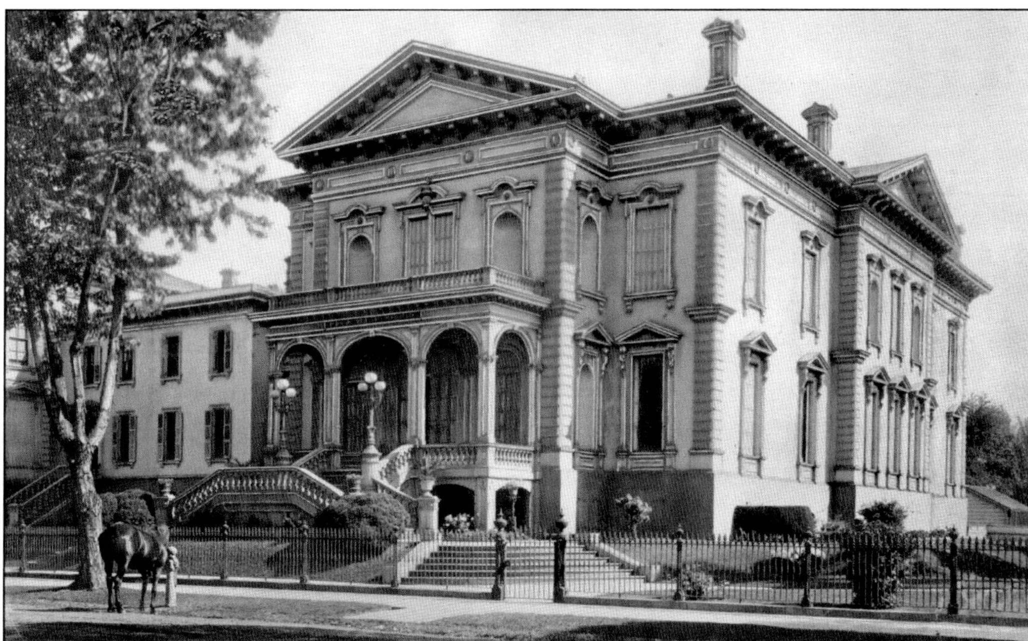

In 1873, the Crocker family completed another expansion: an art gallery larger than the rest of the house. The gallery was intended to hold the Crocker family's extensive art collection. E. B. Crocker died in 1875, shortly after the gallery's completion. Today known as the Crocker Art Museum, it is the oldest continuously operating art museum in the western United States. (USC Archives.)

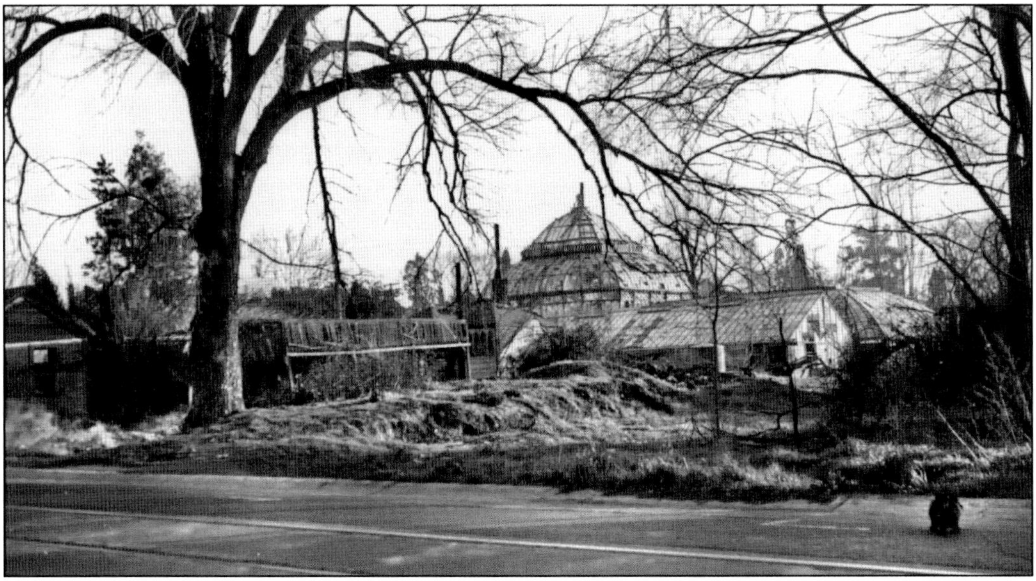

The Bell Conservatory was constructed in 1878 on the block bounded by X, Y, Ninth, and Tenth Streets. Margaret Crocker provided $38,000 for its construction. Flowers grown here were for use in funerals at the cemetery across the street. This 1955 photograph was taken not long before the conservatory was demolished to make way for a supermarket. (Sacramento Archives and Museum Collection Center.)

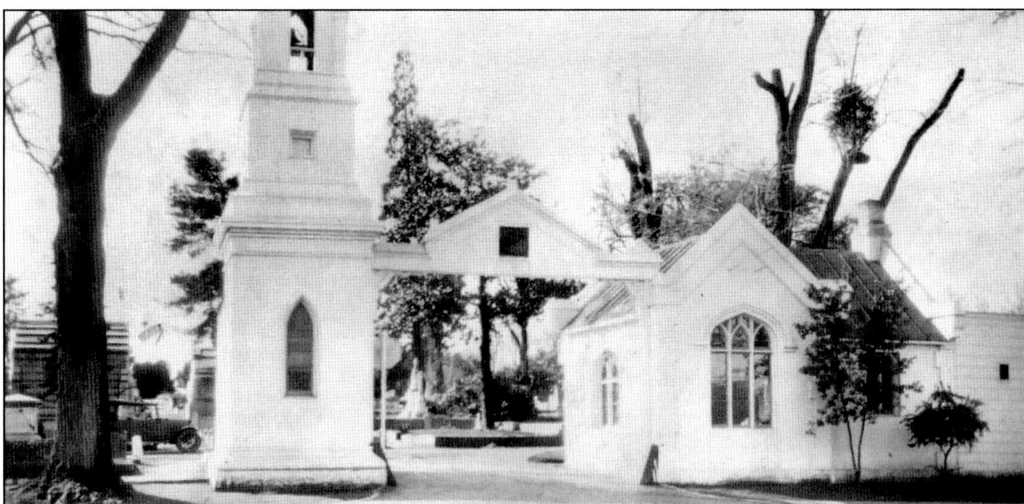

Sacramento's Old City Cemetery was established in 1849 on land provided by Capt. John Augustus Sutter. It replaced an earlier cemetery near Sutter's Fort. Many of Sacramento's first settlers and notable citizens are buried here, including E. B. Crocker, John Sutter Jr., and over 600 victims of Sacramento's 1850 cholera epidemic. This photograph shows the original cemetery entrance, demolished in 1949 to widen Broadway. (Sacramento Archives and Museum Collection Center.)

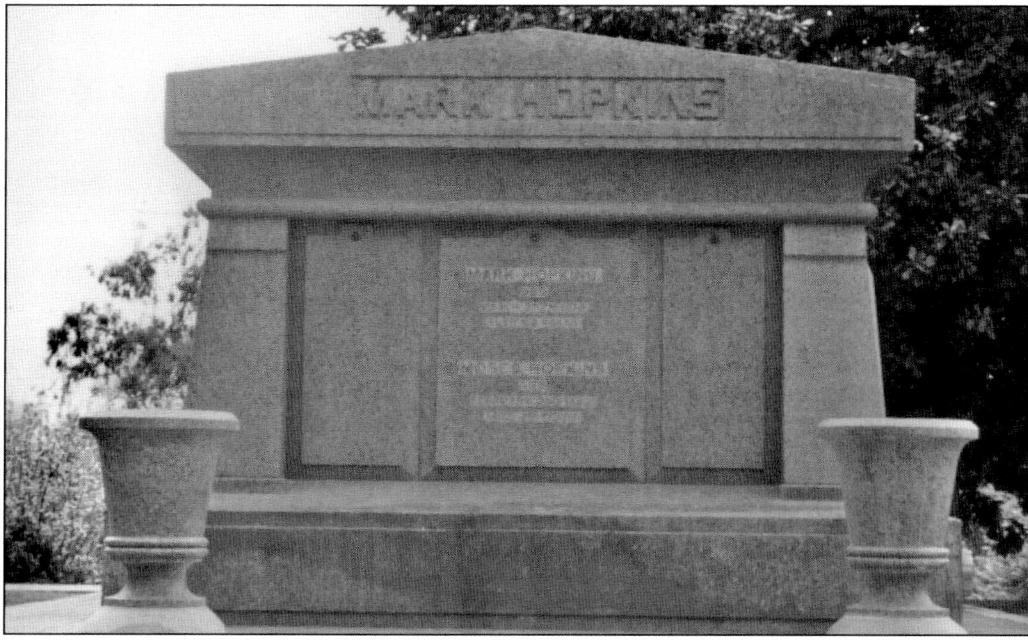

Mark Hopkins came to California in 1849 and opened a general merchandise store in Placerville. In 1855, he became Collis P. Huntington's partner at Huntington and Hopkins Hardware. He became one of the Central Pacific's Big Four and was treasurer of the railroad. Hopkins died in 1878 aboard his private railroad car in Yuma, Arizona. His mausoleum is one of the largest in the Old City Cemetery. (Author's collection.)

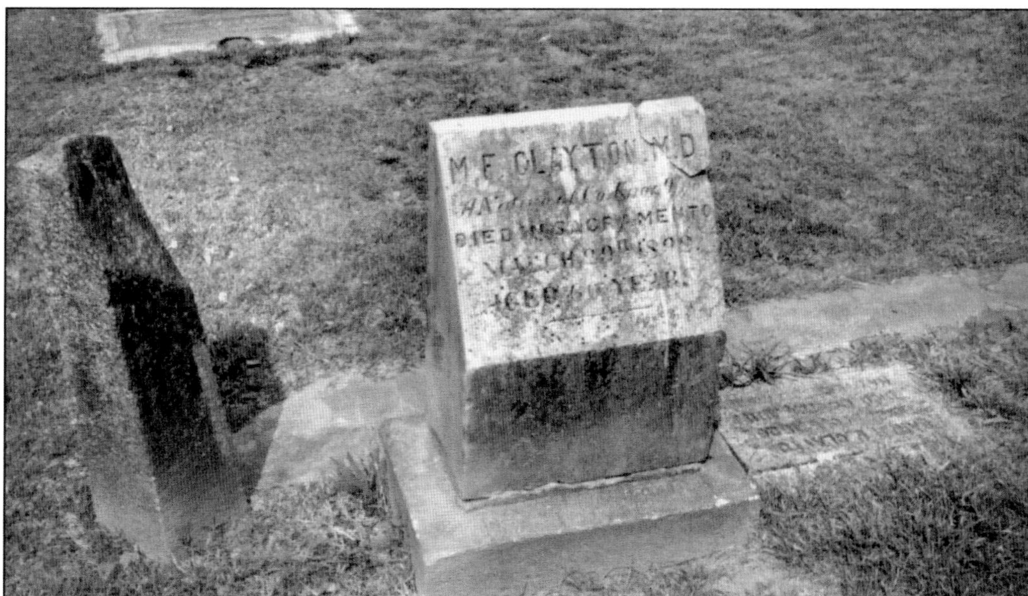

Dr. Marion Clayton and his wife, Sarah, came to Sacramento after the Civil War. Dr. Clayton founded the Pacific Water Cure clinic at Seventh and L Streets. Sarah helped relocate the Sacramento County hospital from Tenth and L Streets to the current site of UC Davis Medical Center and also helped found the Sacramento Foundlings' Home. Their graves are located in the Old City Cemetery. (Author's collection.)

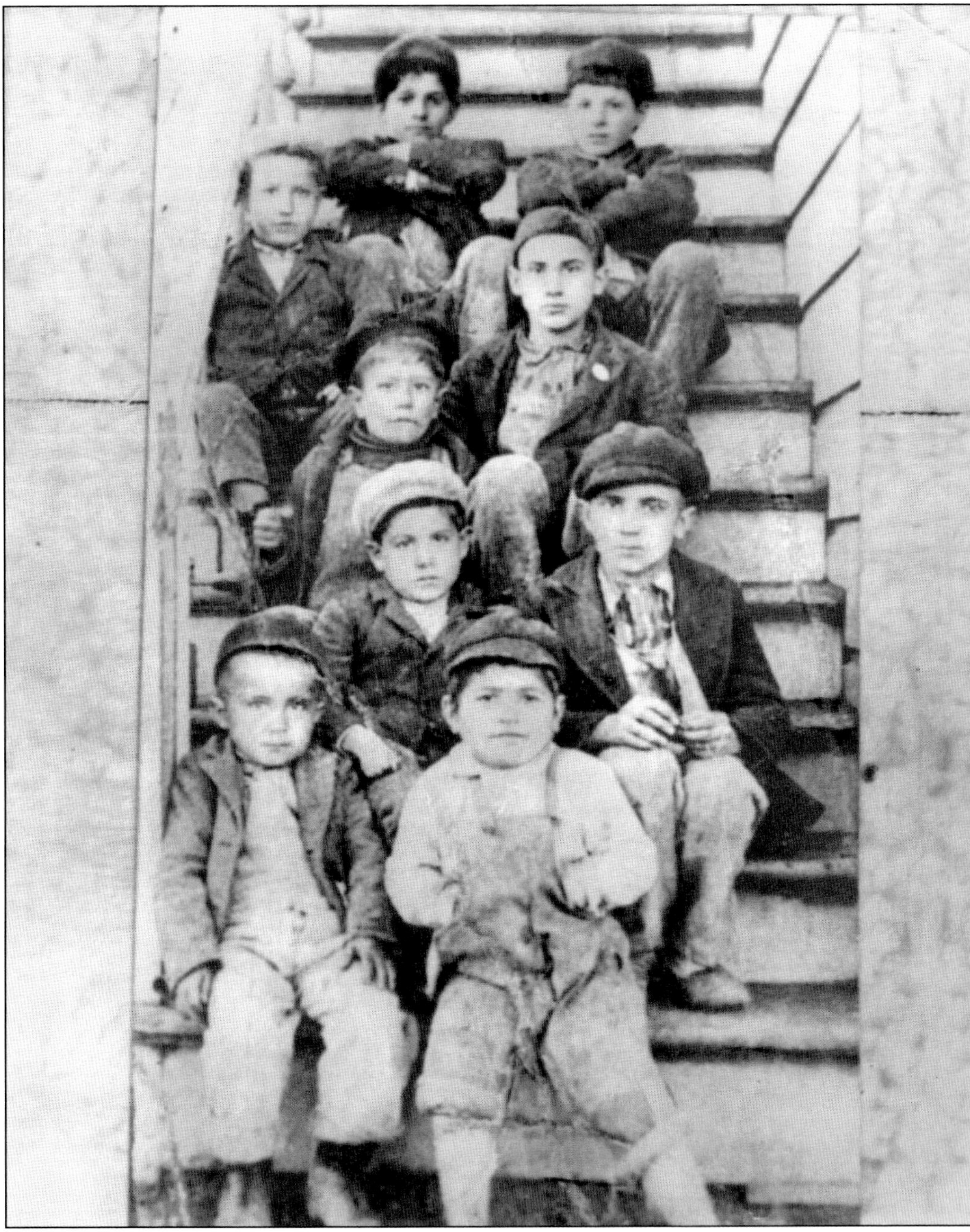

In the late 19th century, the neighborhood south of R Street was known as "The Arizona District." The source of this name is the subject of some debate, but the most likely answer is that the name refers to a group of young men known as "The Arizona Gang." Aside from a handful of newspaper articles, little is known about the Arizona Gang, and this is the only known photograph of this legendary group, probably taken in about 1880. In the top row on the right is Manuel Vierra, but the rest of this dangerous-looking bunch are still unidentified. (Manuel Viera collection.)

Two

Down in Southside Park

The bell's gonna ring
The cat's gonna sing
The dog's gonna bark
Down in Southside Park.

—song traditionally sung by Steve Morgan and his friends just before the bell signifying the end of recess was rung at Holy Angel School, about 1930

At the dawn of the 20th century, many of the wealthy residents in the old mansions north of R Street had moved on, often to homes farther from the river and the bustling waterfront. As flood control improved and Sacramento was less frequently flooded, the land south of the R Street levee began to fill with homes. When Sacramento's streets were originally laid out, several blocks were designated as park spaces, but none were located in Southside. A group of neighborhood citizens formed an organization called the Southside Improvement Club in order to lobby for civic improvements. Their first goal was to eliminate the R Street levee that disconnected Southside from the rest of town. This was achieved in 1902. Their second goal was to convince the city to build a park in Southside. In 1906, the city responded to the club's demands and began land assembly for the public park that would become the neighborhood's namesake.

At the time, much of the neighborhood was still open land. The site selected for Southside Park had previously been used as a peach orchard, a vegetable garden, and an open sewage channel. At least one landowner, G. O. Hayford, was eager to sell his parcel for use in the park. In a May 1905 letter to the city, he explained that "having learned since that time that public spirited Citizens are projecting the establishment of a small lake or body of water for recreation purposes. . . . This lot is nearly always under water, so but little excavation will be needed."

Architect R. A. Herold and city engineer George N. Randle designed the park, with consultation by John McLaren of Golden Gate Park. The park was designed around a large lake with two islands and occupied eight city blocks between T and X Streets and Sixth and Eighth Streets. The park also featured a rose garden, a playground, tennis courts, and baseball and football fields.

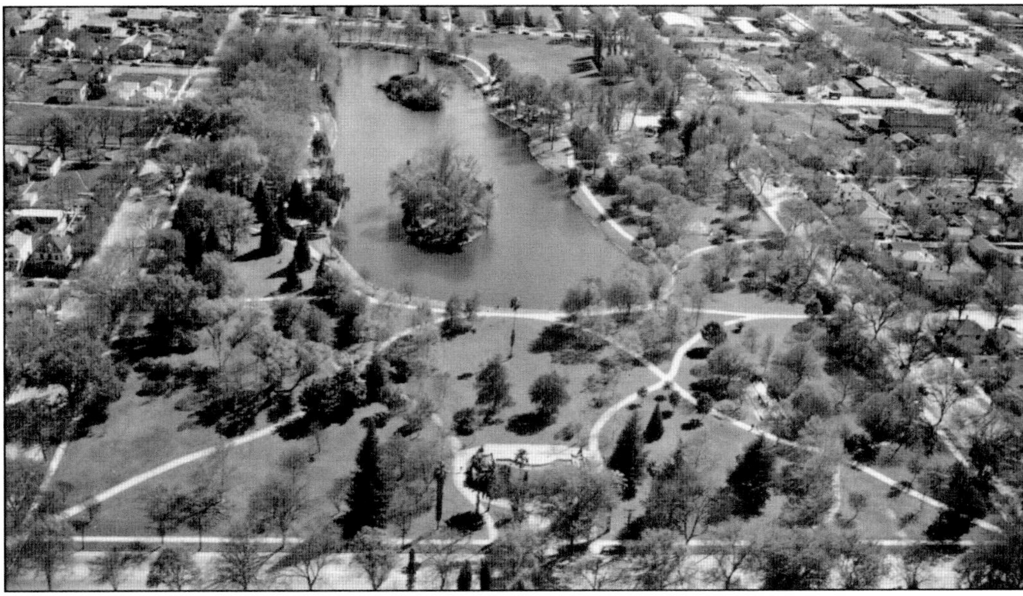

Southside Park originally covered eight city blocks, from T Street to X Street between Sixth and Eighth Streets. The clubhouse was located near the corner of Sixth and X Streets, to the upper right. Along Sixth Street were tennis courts and a football field. The Robert E. Callahan Memorial Bandstand and Outdoor Theater, completed in 1934, sits along T Street at the bottom edge of the photograph. (Sacramento Archives and Museum Collection Center.)

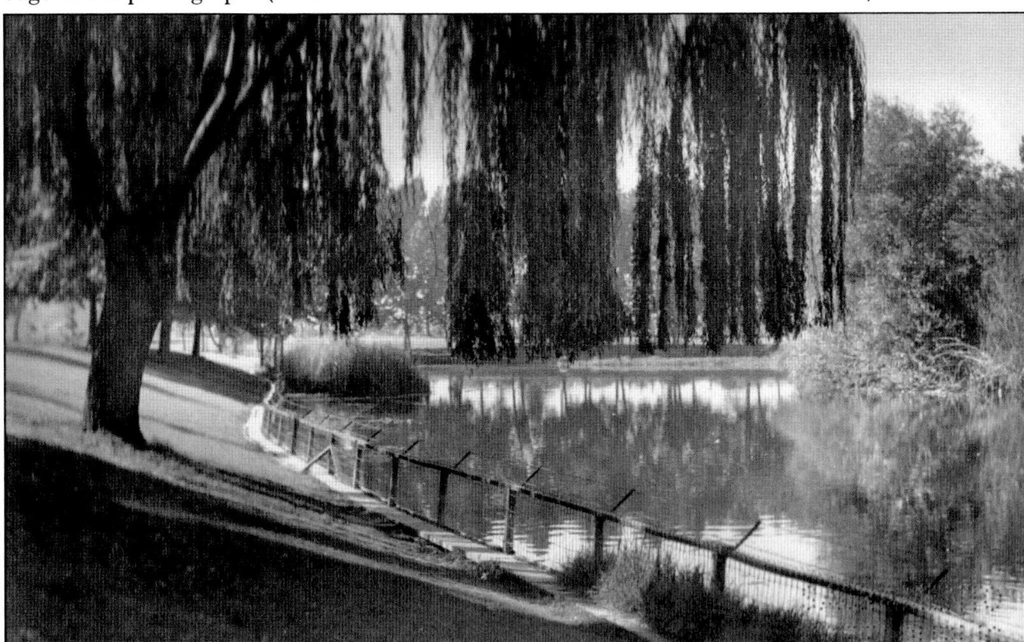

When the park was built, boats were available free for public use. Later the parks department charged a dime for boat rental. According to Tom Irion, the city used an old streetcar fare box as a collection box at the boat rental station. Southside Park's lake was stocked with fish by the city. Annual fishing competitions were held, with prizes going to those who caught the largest fish—and the smallest. (Sacramento Public Library, Sacramento Room.)

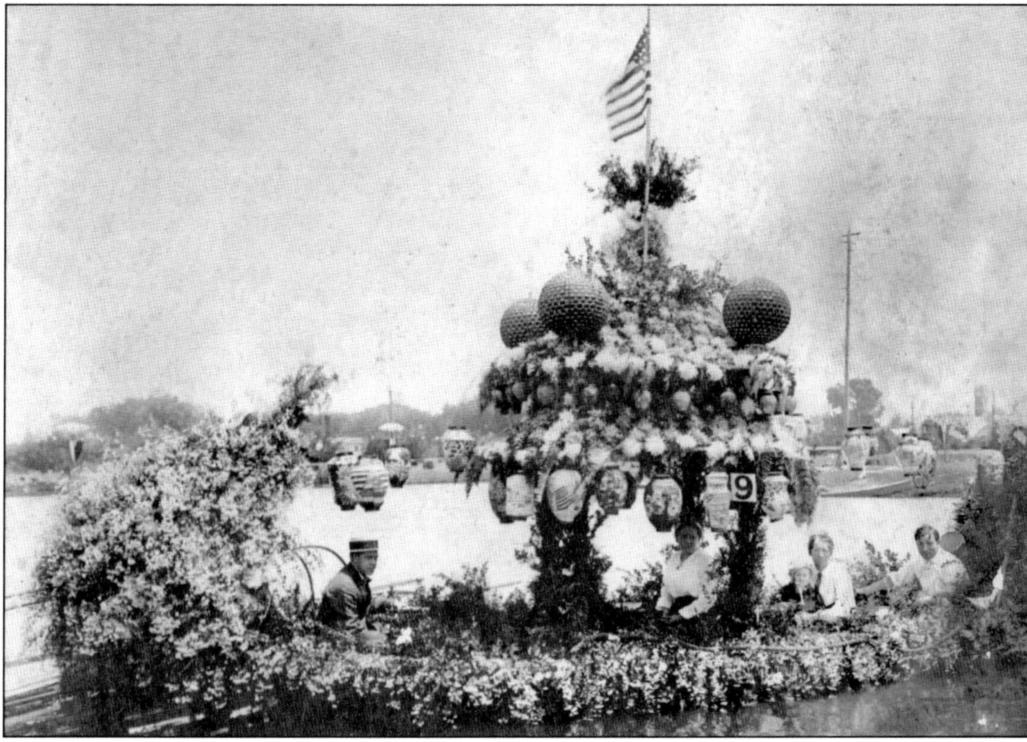

On May 30, 1914, Sacramento held a water festival that included boat races along the American River and an "Oriental Night" at Southside Park, featuring a parade of boats carrying electrified Japanese lanterns. This gaily decorated boat, complete with lanterns, may be from the 1914 festival. (Al Balshor collection.)

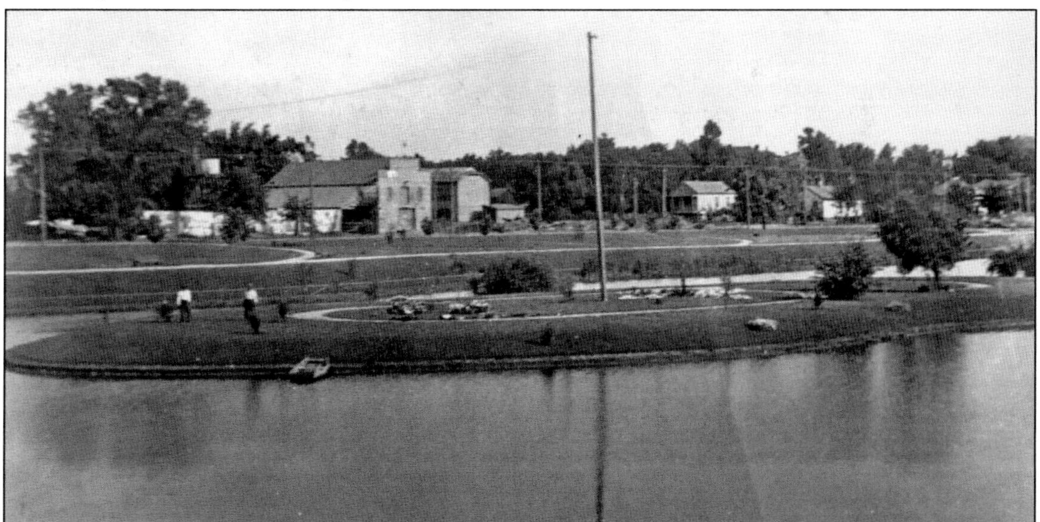

This 1912–1914 photograph was taken shortly after the park's construction. Despite its lowland location and frequent flooding, the artificial lake required extensive dredging. In 1908, the *Sacramento Union* reported that the pneumatic dredger was equipped with an electrolytic sluice box. This device was intended to gather gold dust from the sand and sediment from the bottom of the lake. (Portuguese Historical and Cultural Society.)

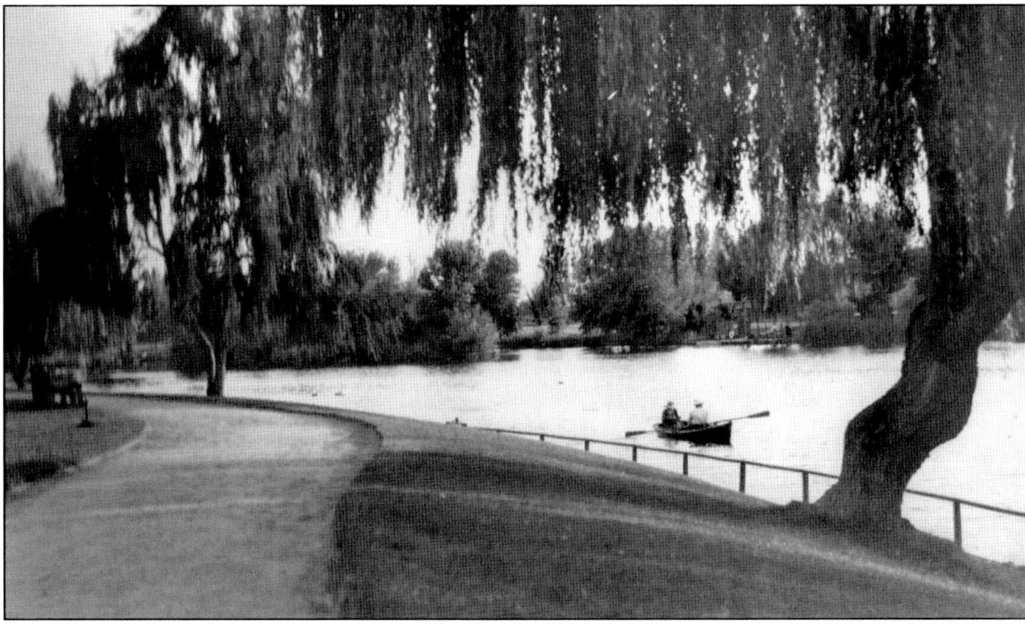

The park was described in a 1921 park report: "There is in this park a well kept rose garden, an exceptionally attractive comfort station, and nearby a large picnic grove sheltered by sycamore trees. The broad expanse of turf, attractive tree and shrub groups, and the view of the water from every side makes this park a delightful spot the year around. South Side Park, at present the only developed park area in the southern part of the city, has served as a much-needed breathing spot in this locality." (Sacramento Public Library, Sacramento Room.)

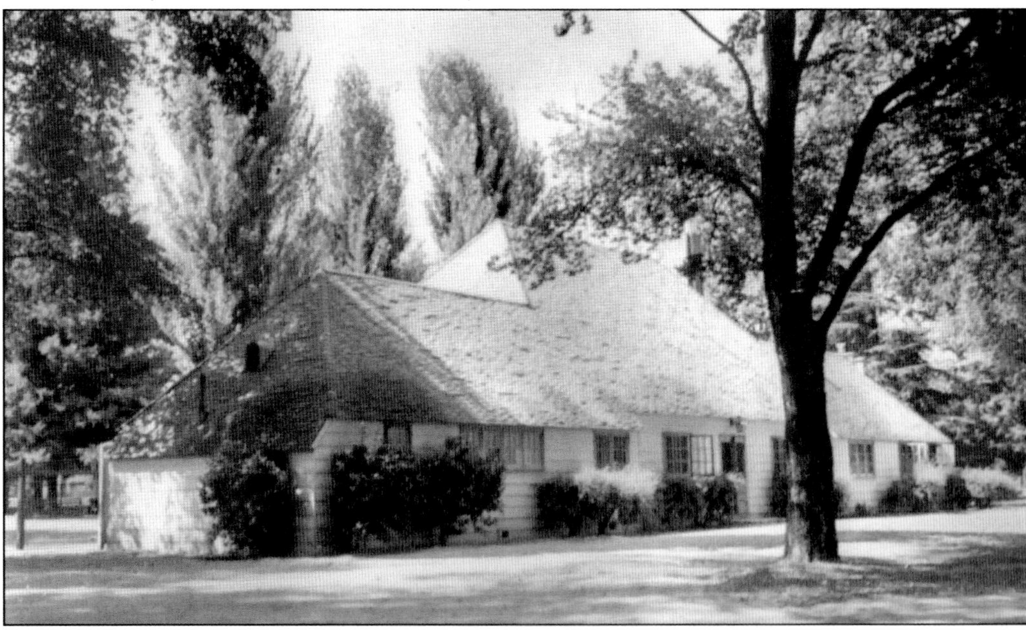

The Southside Park clubhouse was a multipurpose building. It served as a meeting place for community organizations and a headquarters for local parks and recreation staff. James Mangan, caretaker of the park, worked here and was well liked by the neighborhood kids. Today there is a park in south Sacramento named for Mangan. (Sacramento Archives and Museum Collection Center.)

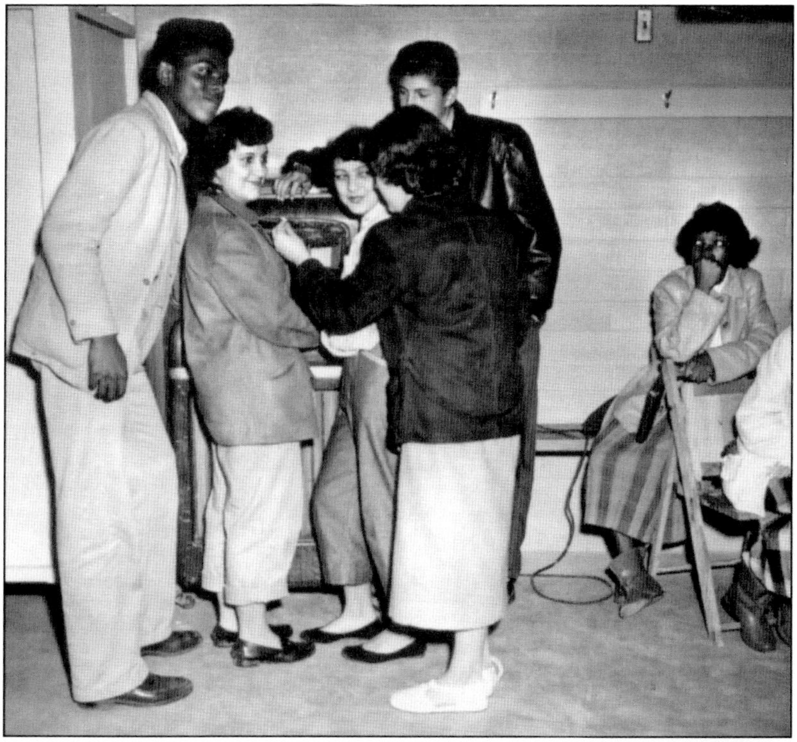

The Southside Park clubhouse was also used as a social gathering place for local young people. Here a group of teenagers gathers around the jukebox. The building was razed when two square blocks of the park were removed to make way for the W/X Freeway. (Sacramento Archives and Museum Collection Center.)

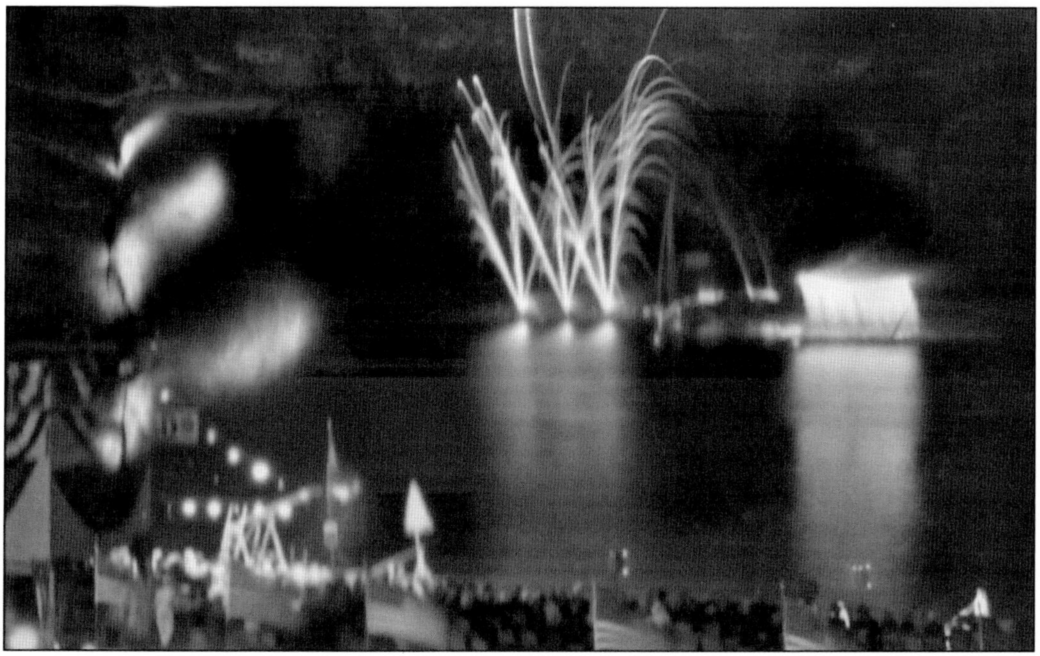

Fireworks in Southside Park were a hallmark of Sacramento's Fourth of July, and people from all over the city flocked to the park to view them. The Southside Improvement Club sponsored the event and sold beer. Neighborhood kids made extra money selling bags of peanuts to park visitors, and some made more extra money on July 5, searching the park for wallets and change accidentally dropped the previous night. (Sacramento Public Library, Sacramento Room.)

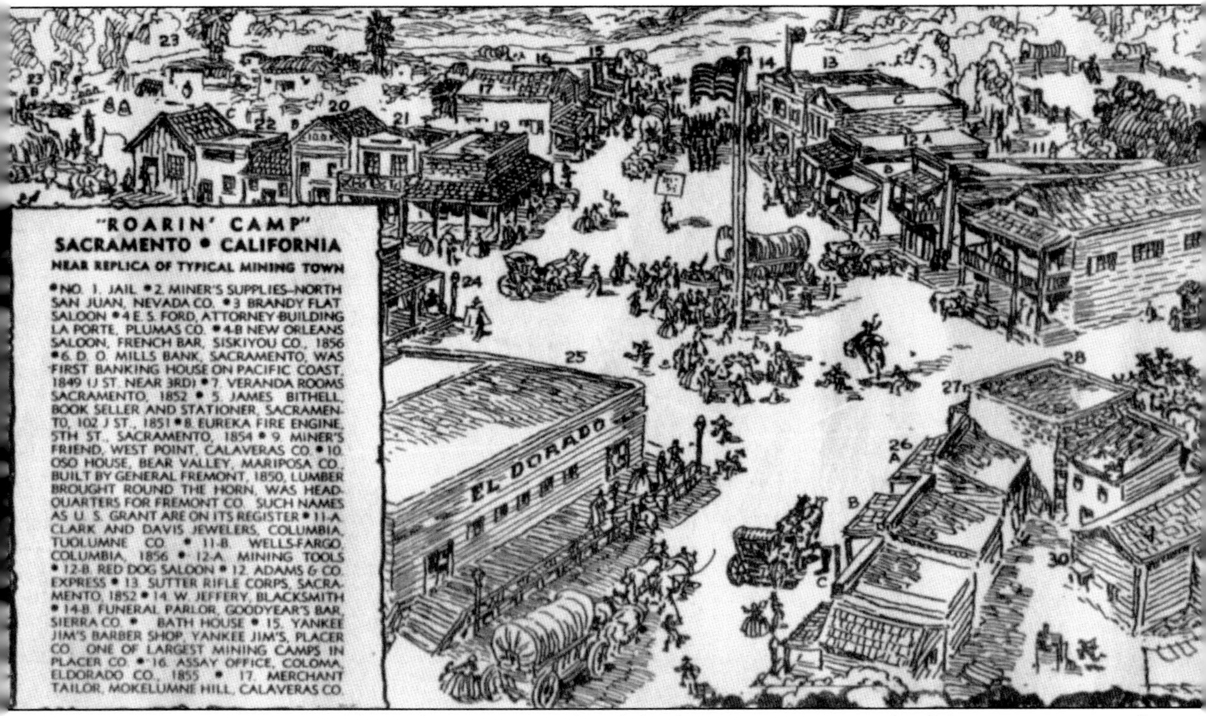

In 1939, California celebrated its centennial. While there were centennial celebrations organized by many California cities, Sacramento held a three-month celebration in Southside Park called Roaring Camp. From May until August, the southern end of Southside Park became a California

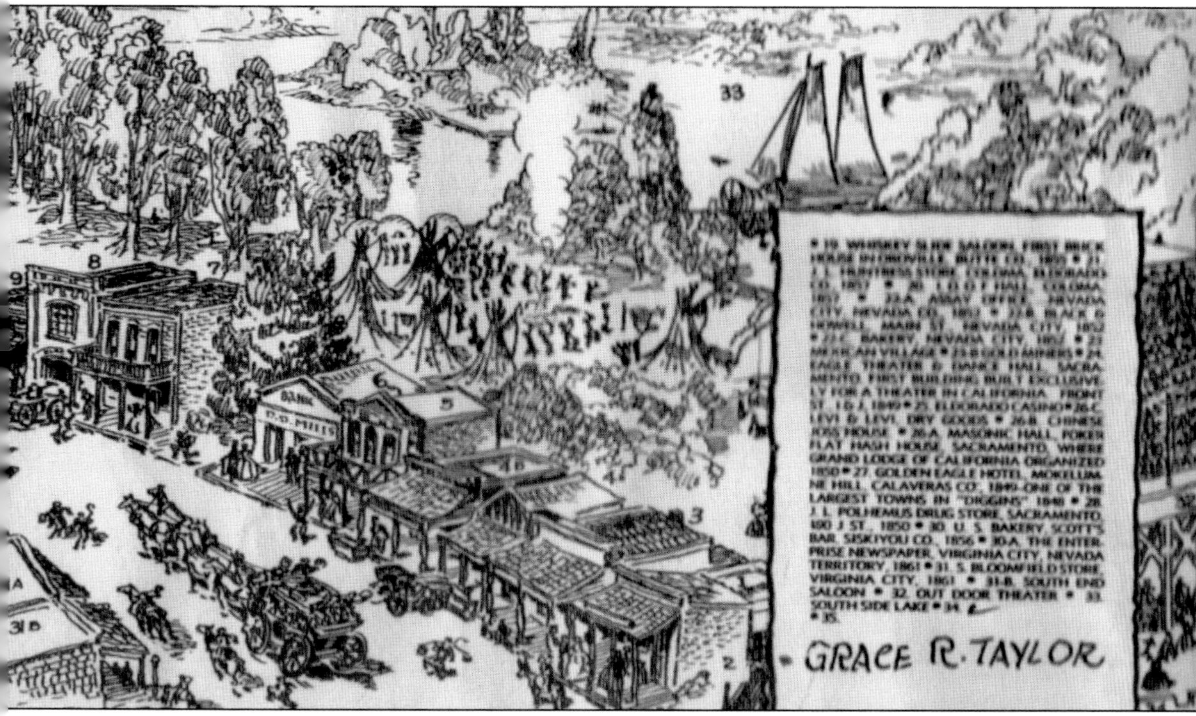

mining town. More than 50 structures constructed especially for Roaring Camp were built, many based loosely on actual buildings located in Sacramento or other California cities. (Sacramento Public Library, Sacramento Room.)

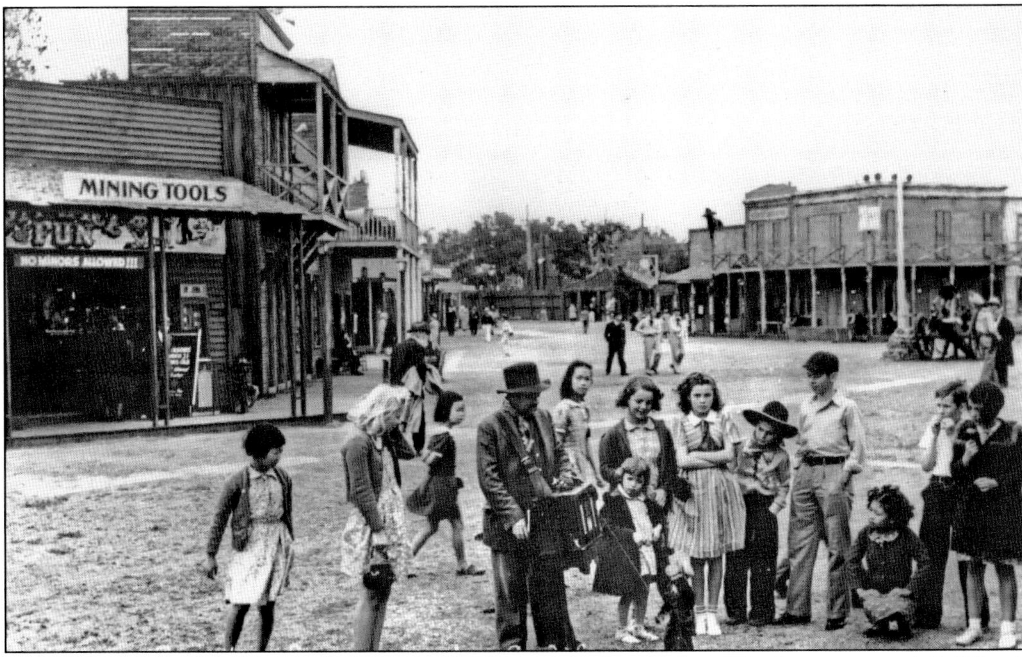

In many ways, Roaring Camp owed more to Western movies and novels than to actual California history. The display of a typical Native American village featured teepees and headdresses utterly unlike those used by the Nisenan tribes who lived near Sacramento, and the large wooden Eagle Theater looked nothing like the original canvas structure on Front Street. Despite this, Roaring Camp was very popular, attracting visitors from all over California. (Al Balshor collection.)

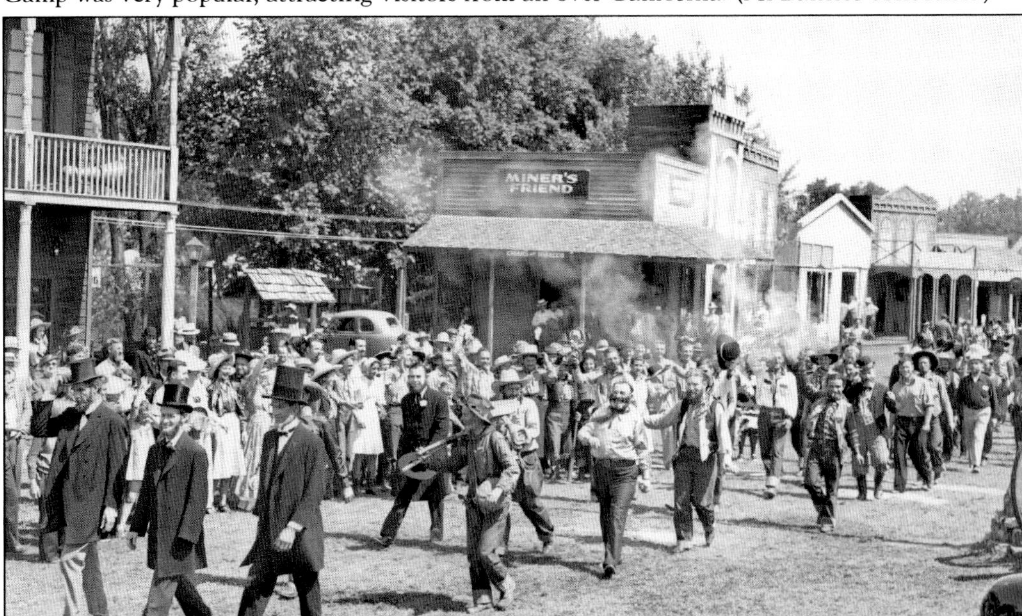

The Whiskerinos were participants in a citywide beard-growing contest. Clean-shaven men who came to Roaring Camp risked being thrown in the camp's jail. The Sacramentan with the finest whiskers was awarded a prize of $100, with $75, $50, and $25 prizes going to runners-up. Here a parade of Whiskerinos marches through Roaring Camp's main street. (USC Archives.)

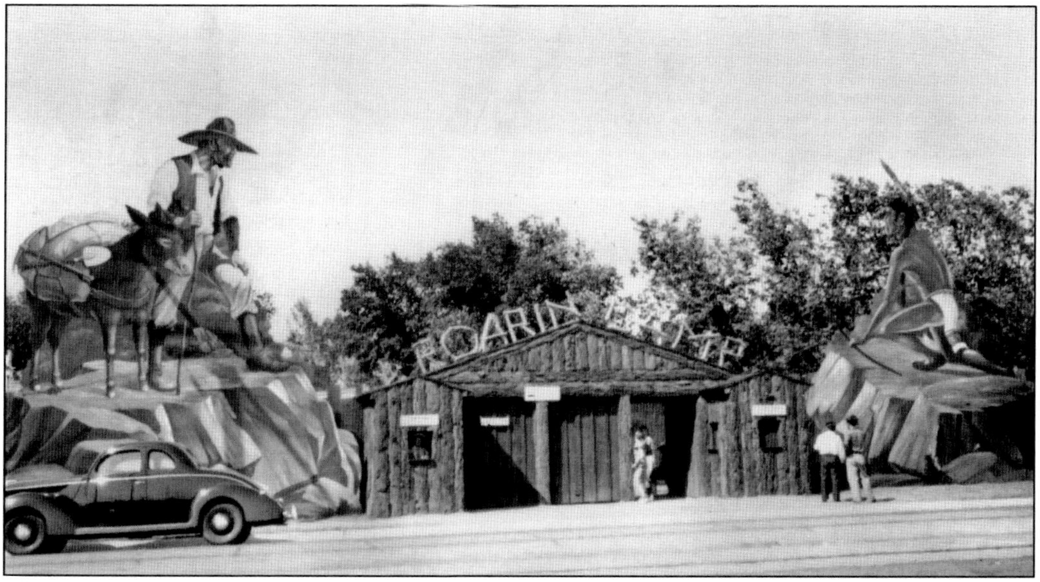

This was the entrance to Roaring Camp. Admission cost 50¢, but enterprising neighborhood kids willing to take a risk found ways to sneak in through the back fence. Inside there were dances, educational displays, food and drinks, and a daily stagecoach robbery. (Sacramento Archives and Museum Collection Center.)

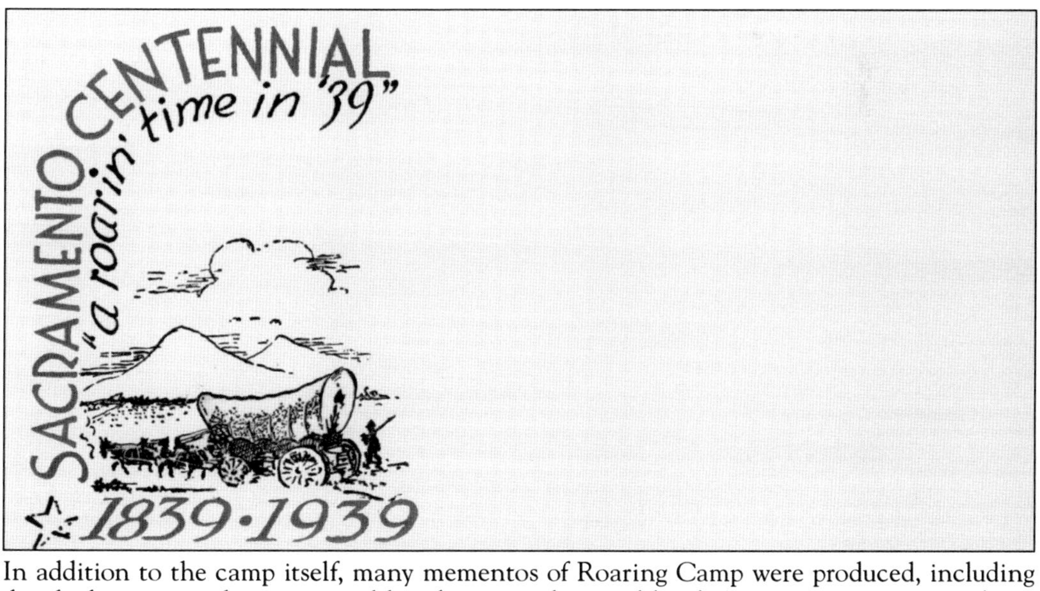

In addition to the camp itself, many mementos of Roaring Camp were produced, including decals, banners and promotional brochures, and items like this commemorative envelope. (Author's collection.)

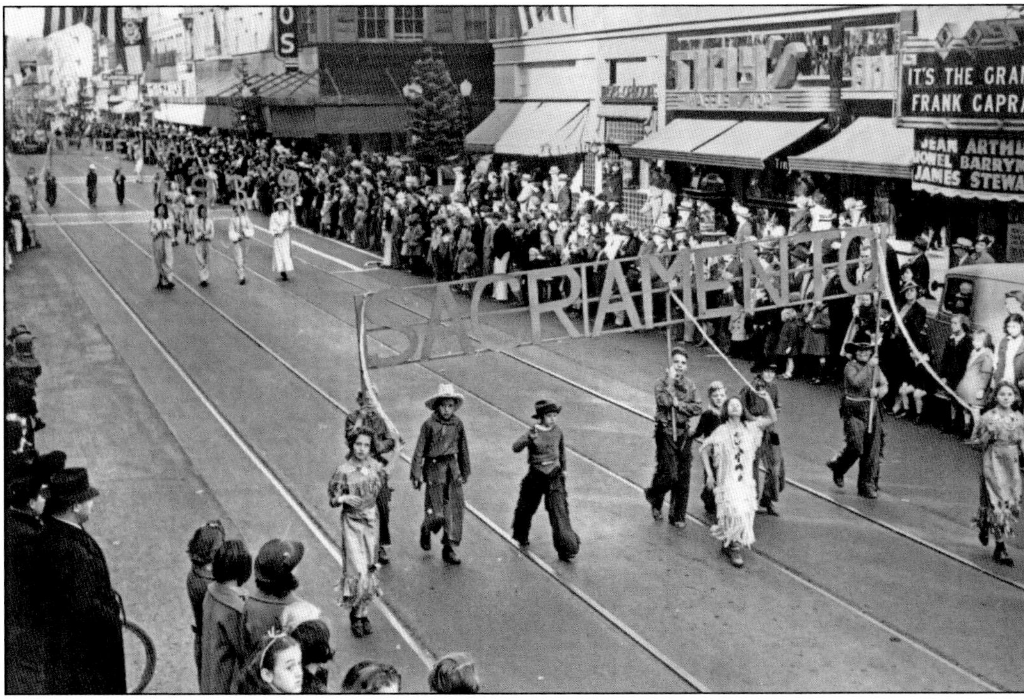

Centennial festivities extended throughout Sacramento. The California State Fair featured a centennial theme, and parades were held on K Street, pictured above. Manuel Viera, grandson of the Arizona Gang member on page 22, worked as a page in the state capitol in 1939. He and the other pages dressed in cowboy attire during the summer of Roaring Camp, not unlike that of the children pictured in this K Street parade. (Sacramento Archive and Museum Collection Center.)

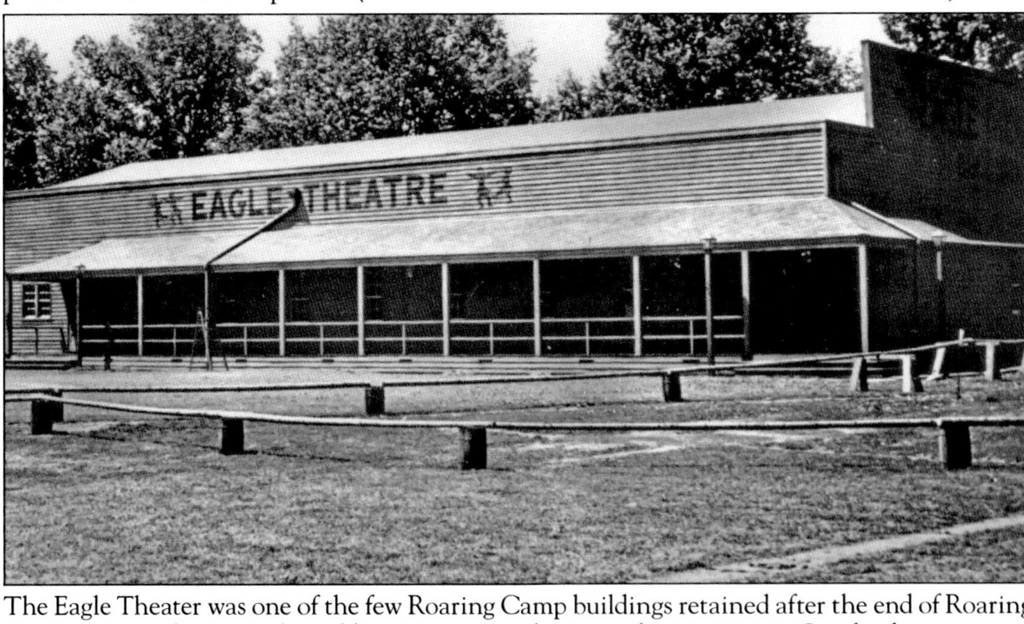

The Eagle Theater was one of the few Roaring Camp buildings retained after the end of Roaring Camp. During the Second World War, it was used as an induction center. Southsiders receiving draft notices reported to this building for physical examination prior to being shipped out to basic training. (Sacramento Archives and Museum Collection Center.)

Three

League of Nations

Residents of Southside Park often described their neighborhood as a "League of Nations." Immigrants often settled into neighborhoods occupied by those of similar ethnic background. Common bonds of shared language, culture, and religion encouraged the growth of these enclaves. As these small communities grew, they became a way station for later immigrants. Churches and cultural societies provided social and religious centers and community support and maintained cultural traditions.

However, life in Southside was by no means segregated or exclusive. Immigrant children attending school at William Land, Holy Angel, or Lincoln School would encounter fellow students from a dozen different countries, many of whom were not yet fluent in English. Second-generation children of immigrants learned the traditions and languages of their parents but were raised in a broad international milieu. Friendships made through school and play often crossed racial and ethnic lines. Ron King commented, "[It] seemed like it didn't make any difference in those days. If he was your friend, he was your friend."

King also mentioned that sometimes being a Southsider meant facing a certain stigma. "I sold a jacket to afford a date with this girl. I walked all the way to her house and her mother asked where I was from. I said 'Southside' and she said 'Goodbye! My daughter isn't going out with anyone from Southside!' "

Ernesto Galarza, upon arriving in Sacramento in the early 20th century, described the major ethnic neighborhoods:

The lower quarter was not exclusively a Mexican *barrio* but a mix of many nationalities. Between L and N Streets two blocks from us, the Japanese had taken over. Their homes were in the alleys behind shops, which they advertised with signs covered with black scribbles. . . . The Portuguese and Italian families gathered in their own neighborhoods along Fourth and Fifth Streets southward toward the Y Street levee. The Poles, Yugo-Slavs, and Koreans, too few to take over any particular part of it, were scattered throughout the *barrio*. Black men drifted in and out of town, working the waterfront. It was a kaleidoscope of colors and languages and customs that surprised and absorbed me at every turn.

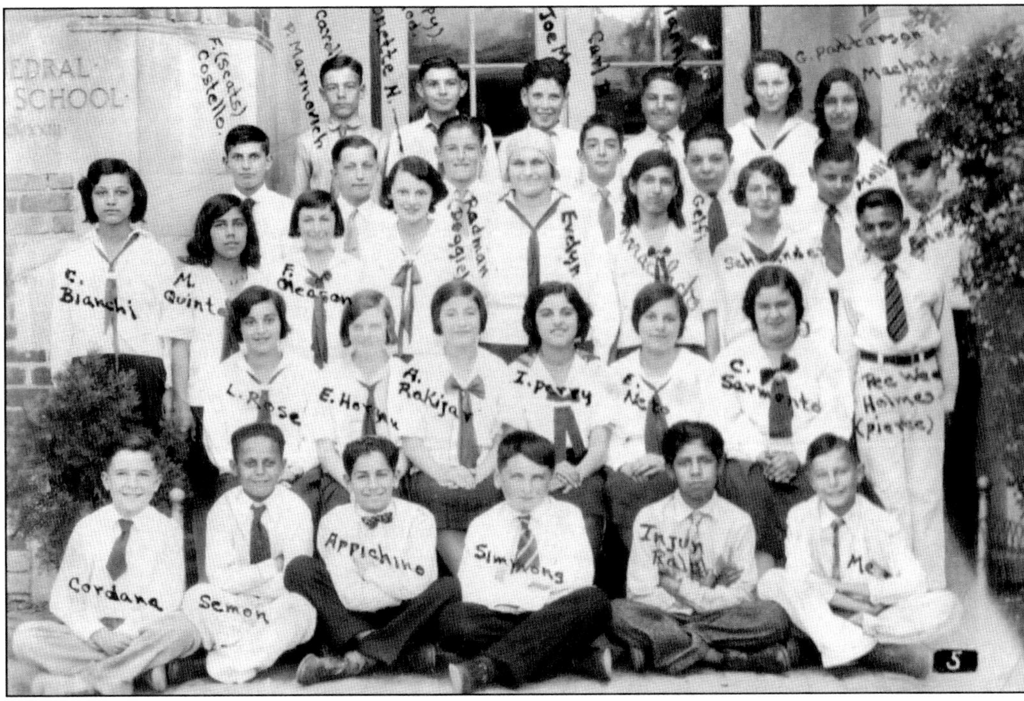

Holy Angel School was located on the corner of Eighth and S Streets. This photograph shows the seventh-grade class of 1932, including Steve Morgan (first row, far right). His father, Joseph Brïzich, changed his name to "Morgan" after emigrating from Austria. In the first row, far left, is George Cordano, who later became a priest and Franciscan friar. Ralph Sotelo (first row, second from right) became a fire chief. (Steve Morgan collection.)

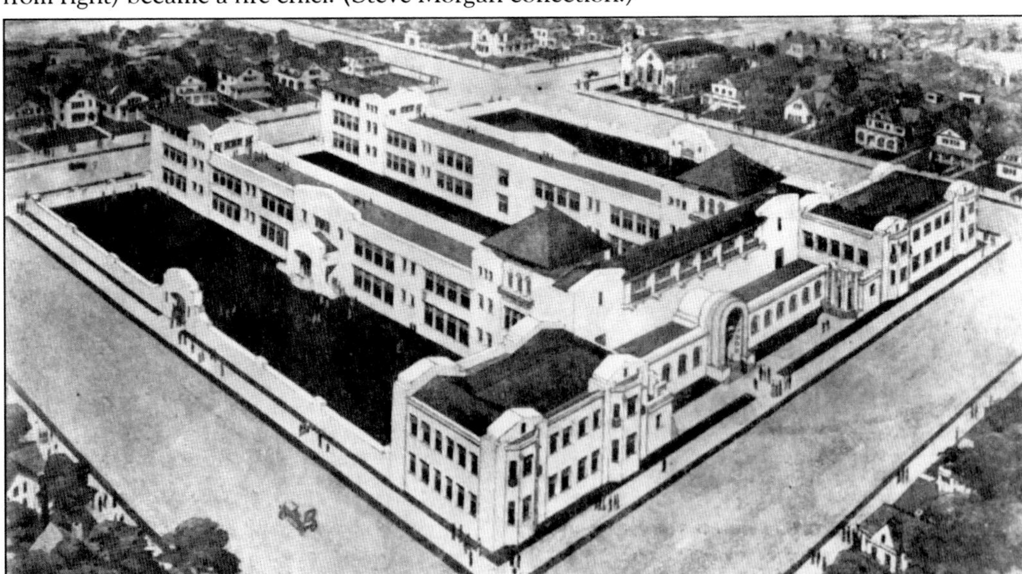

This illustration of William Land School shows the building that stood at Twelfth and V Streets from about 1917 until the 1980s. It was replaced by a modern structure because of concerns about earthquake safety. (William Land School.)

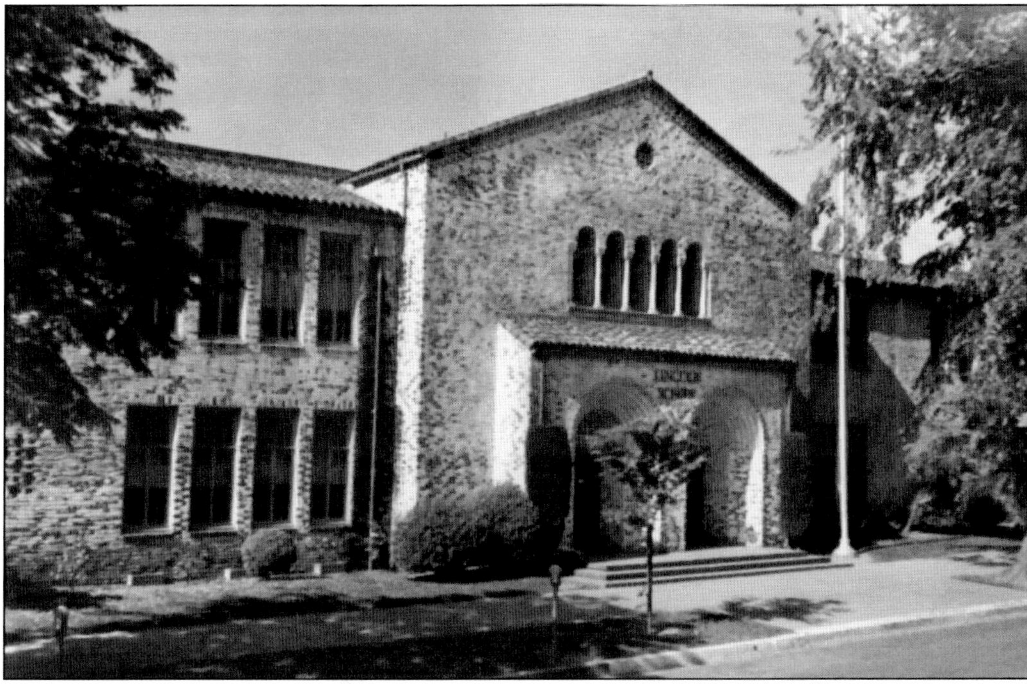

The Lincoln School was located on Q Street between Third and Fifth Streets. Classes began in 1857, and a larger two-story building was erected in 1867. The school expanded in the 1870s after purchasing a half-block from E. B. and Margaret Crocker. By 1927, Lincoln School was the largest school in Sacramento. The land was purchased by the California Public Employees' Retirement System (CalPERS) in 1980, and the school was leveled in 1981. (Al Balshor collection.)

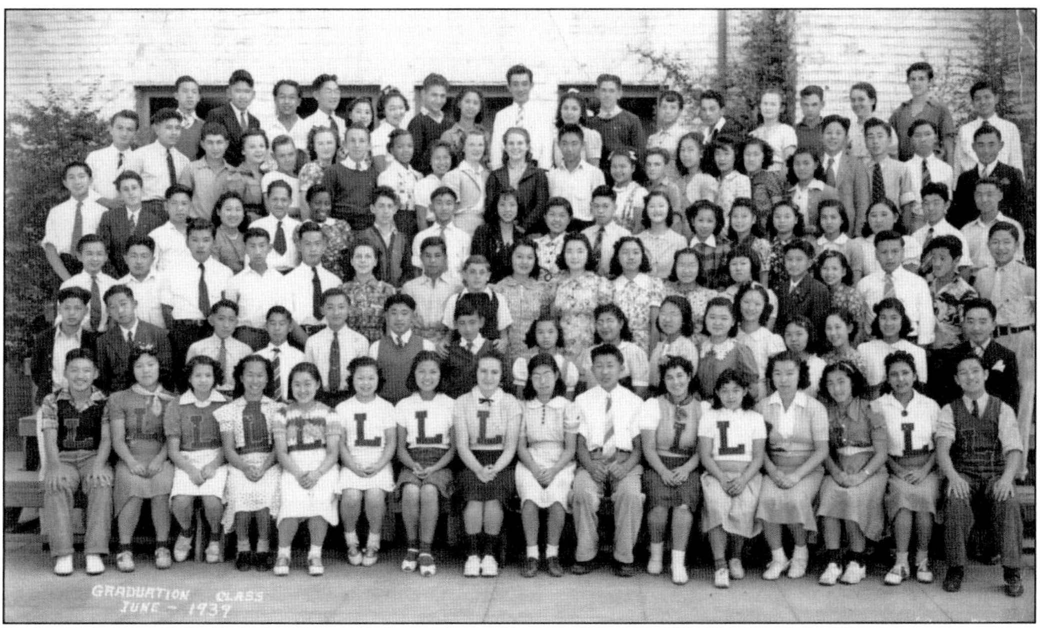

The 1939 graduating class of Lincoln School is shown here. By this time, Lincoln School was a junior high school. There was no high school in Southside Park, so these students had to take the bus or streetcar to Sacramento High School in the fall of 1939. (Al Balshor collection.)

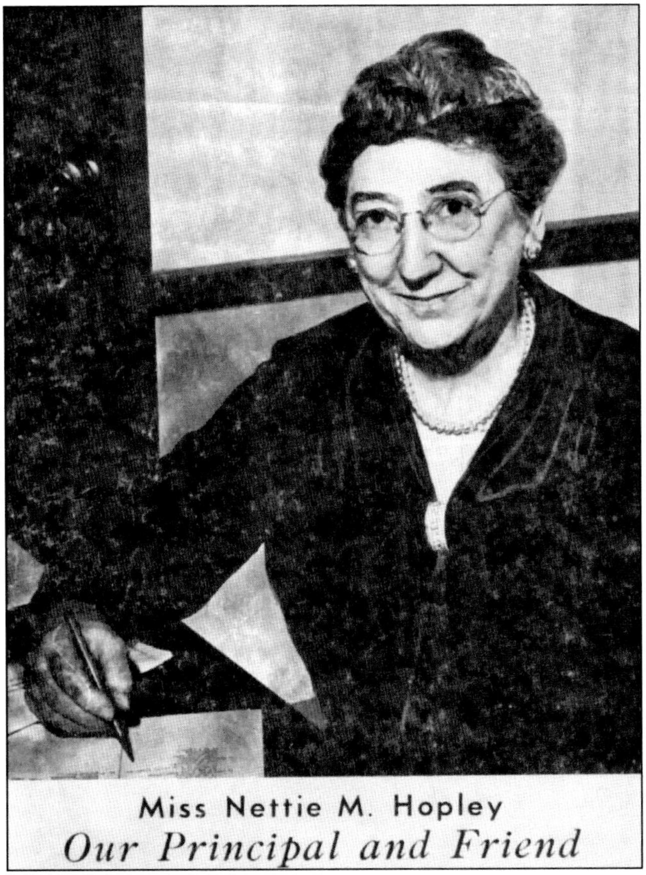

Nettie Hopley, a graduate of Sacramento High School's class of 1885, was principal of Lincoln School for many years. Ernesto Galarza said of her: "The lower part of town was a collage of nationalities in the middle of which Miss Nettie Hopley kept school with discipline and compassion." (Al Balshor collection.)

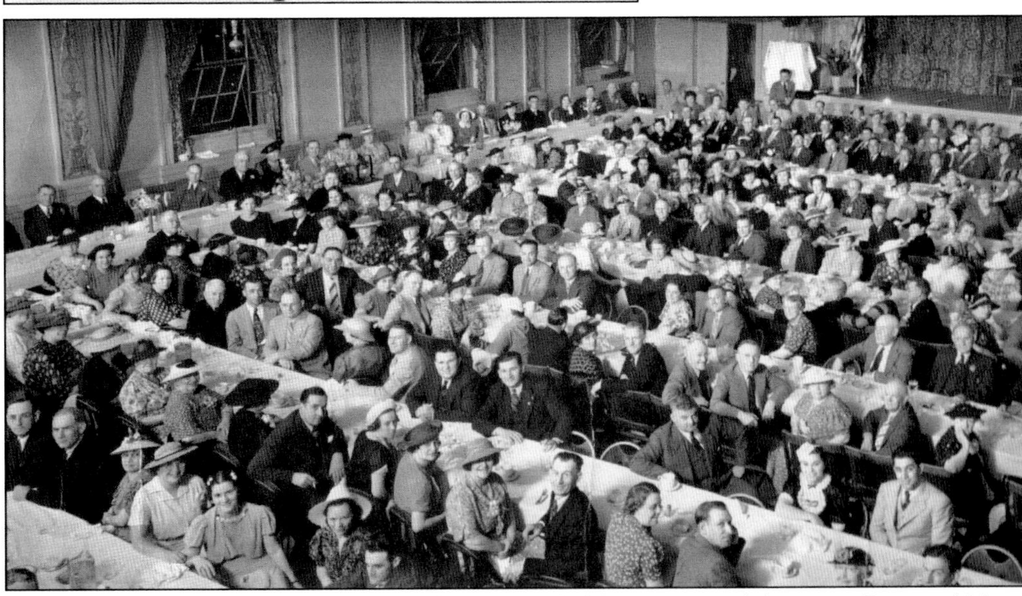

On May 21, 1938, the Southside Improvement Club held a testimonial dinner in Principal Nettie Hopley's honor. Many of the club members were once students at Lincoln School during her tenure. (Al Balshor collection.)

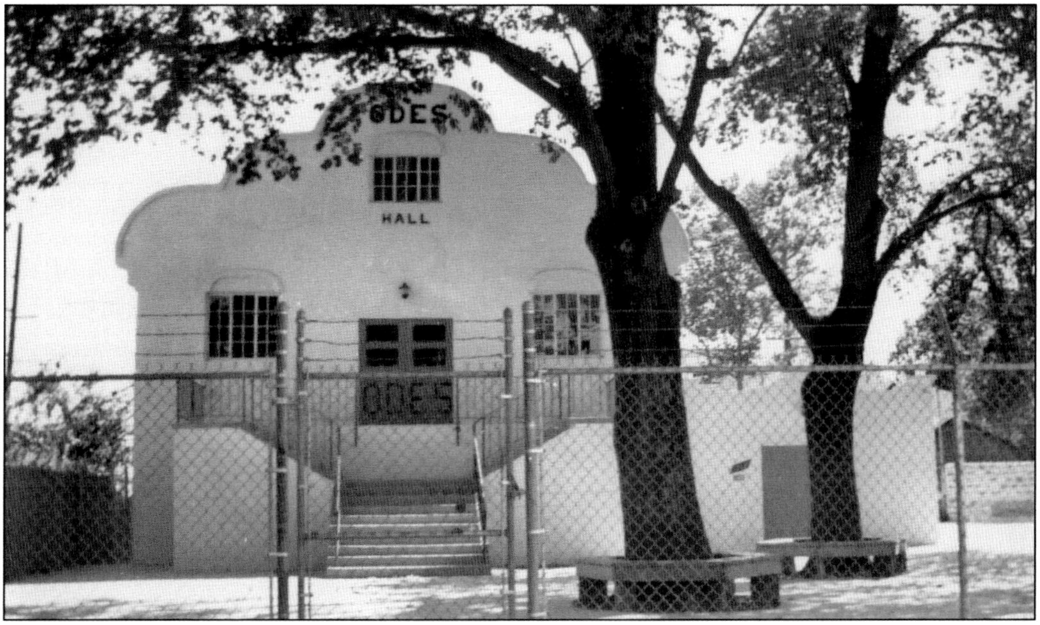

One of the earliest ethnic communities in Southside was the Portuguese neighborhood, centered on Fourth and T Streets and stretching several blocks in all directions. Portuguese immigrants came from mainland Portugal or from several island chains in the Atlantic that were under Portuguese dominion, such as the Azores, Madeira, or the Cape Verde Islands. The ODES (*Ordem do Divino Espirito Santo* or Order of the Divine Holy Spirit) hall, located at 514 W Street, was the site of local Portuguese cultural activities. (Portuguese Historical and Cultural Society.)

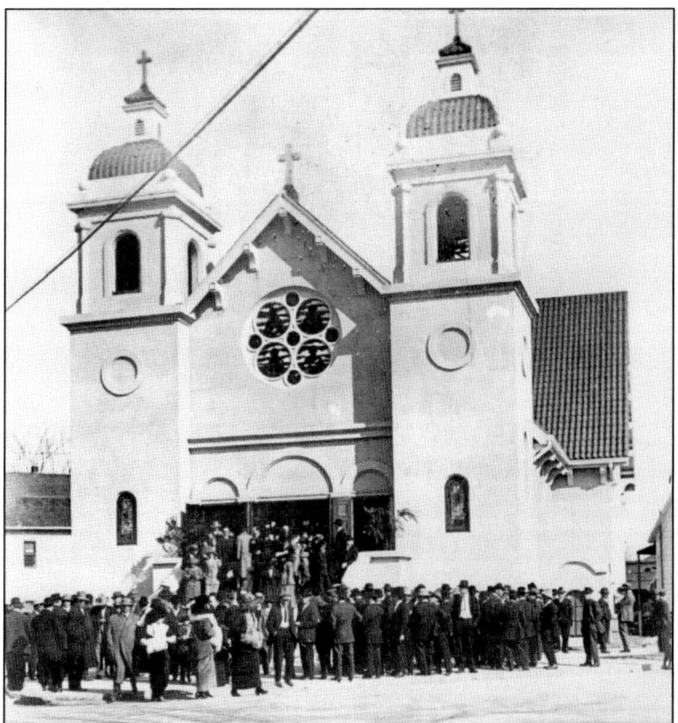

The center of Portuguese spiritual life in Southside Park was St. Elizabeth's Church, dedicated on February 2, 1913. The church was one of the first reinforced concrete buildings in Sacramento and is the oldest Portuguese National Church in the western United States. Services here were in Portuguese. (Portuguese Historical and Cultural Society.)

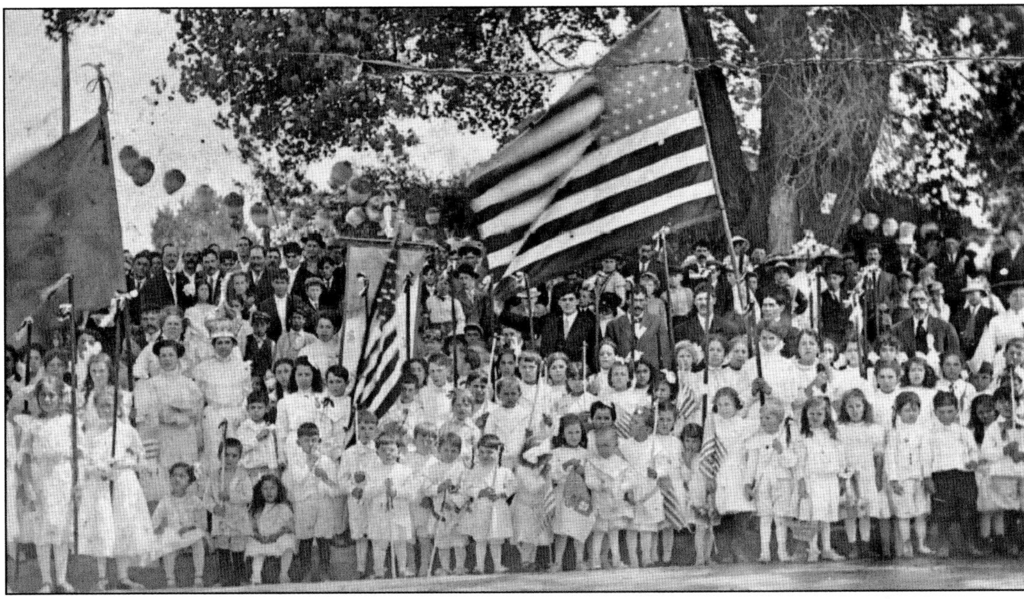

The Festa do Espirito Santo, or Festival of the Holy Spirit, was very important in the Portuguese community. This *festa* took place in 1909. The event took place on an empty lot at Fourth and U Streets, which belonged to Manuel Jacinto. In 1907, a small one-story hall was built on W Street between Fifth and Sixth Streets, later the site of the ODES hall, seen the previous page. (Portuguese Historical and Cultural Society.)

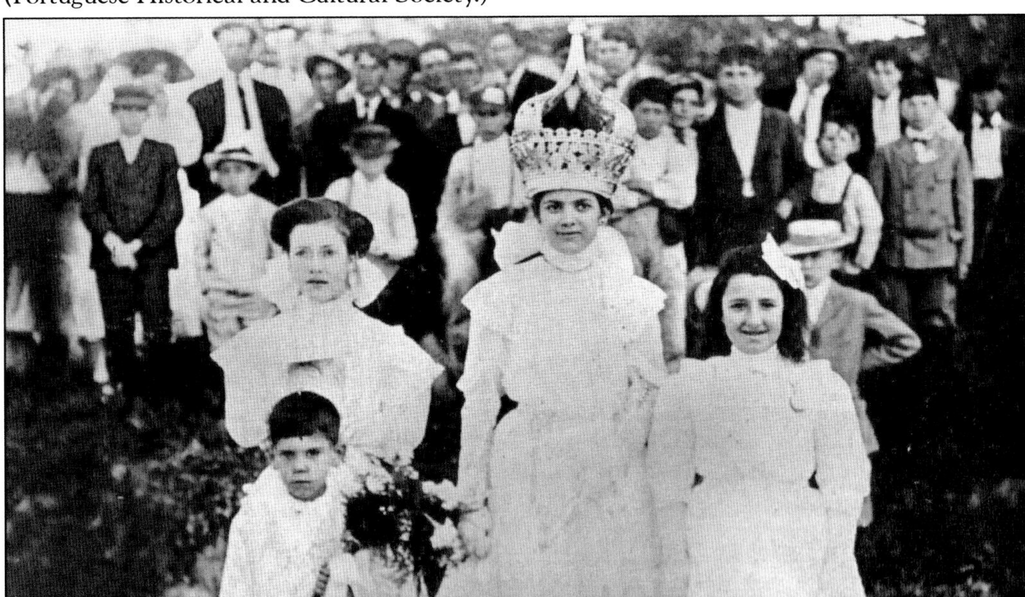

The Festa do Espirito Santo celebrates the miracle of Queen St. Elizabeth, who sold her jewels and incurred the wrath of the king to feed her people during a great famine. This celebration was held in different ways in continental Portugal and the various Portuguese island groups. At the Southside Park *festa*, an adolescent girl was chosen as the queen, a position considered to be a great honor. Pictured here is Laura Semas, queen of the *festa* in 1909. (Portuguese Historical and Cultural Society.)

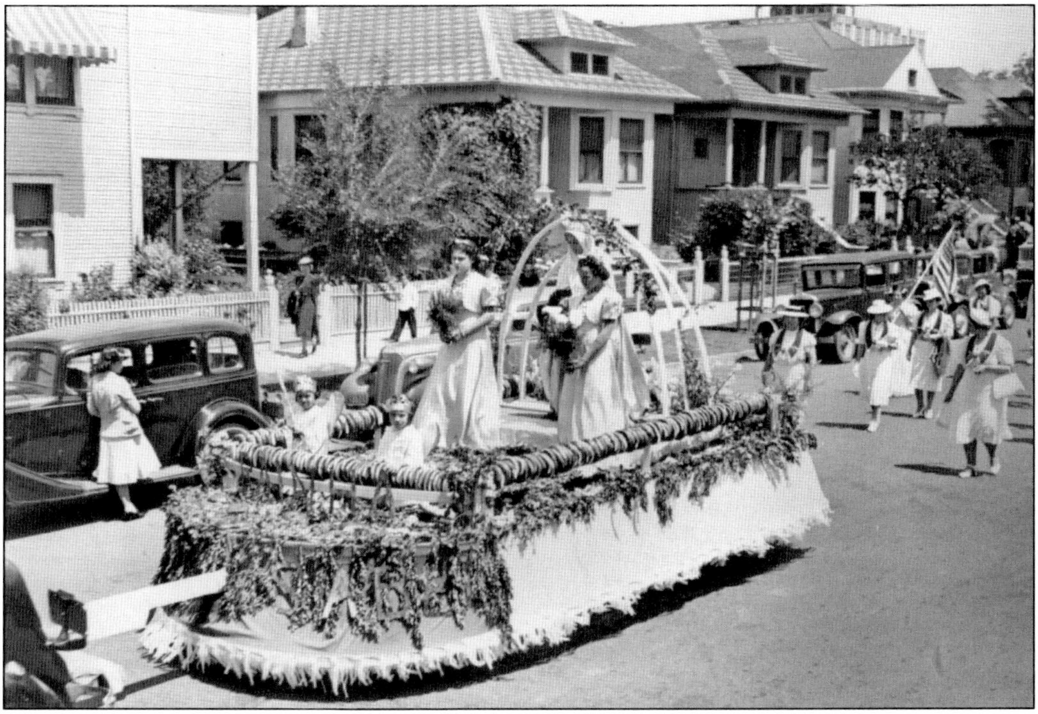

After the dedication of St. Elizabeth's Church in 1913, the *festa* began at the ODES hall with a parade to the church. After mass and the crowning of the queen, the parade returned to the hall. Dolores Nevis, Queen St. Elizabeth of the 1940 *festa*, rides on a float with her attendants down S Street. (Portuguese Historical and Cultural Society.)

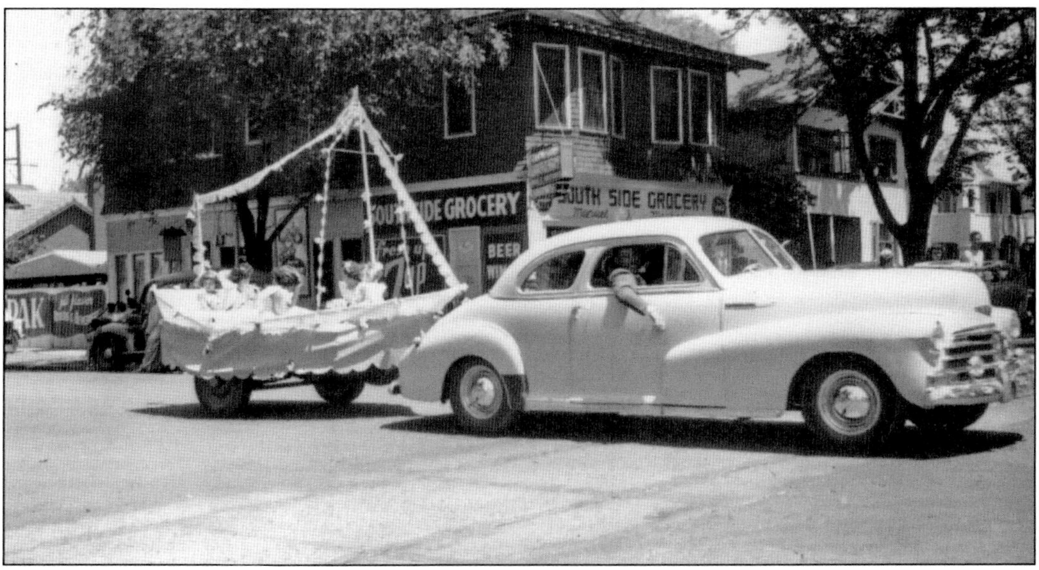

In addition to the queen, often a little queen was also selected. The queen was typically a teenager or young adult, while the little queen was a much younger child. Both selected attendants to accompany them. Here the little queen's float is passing the corner of Sixth and T Streets at the edge of Southside Park. Machado's Grocery can be seen in the background. (Portuguese Historical and Cultural Society.)

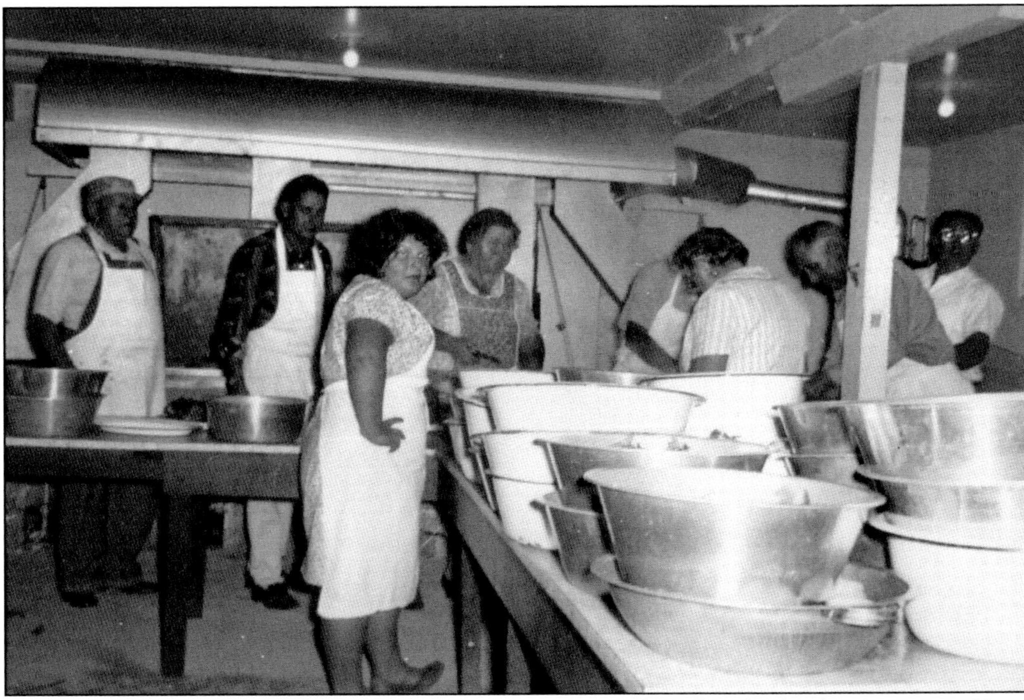

At the end of the parade, a traditional feast of *sopas e carne*, bread with a hot beef gravy and beef, was shared. Keeping with St. Elizabeth's tradition of feeding the hungry, the meal was served without charge. A decorated box for donations was located in the hall. (Portuguese Historical and Cultural Society.)

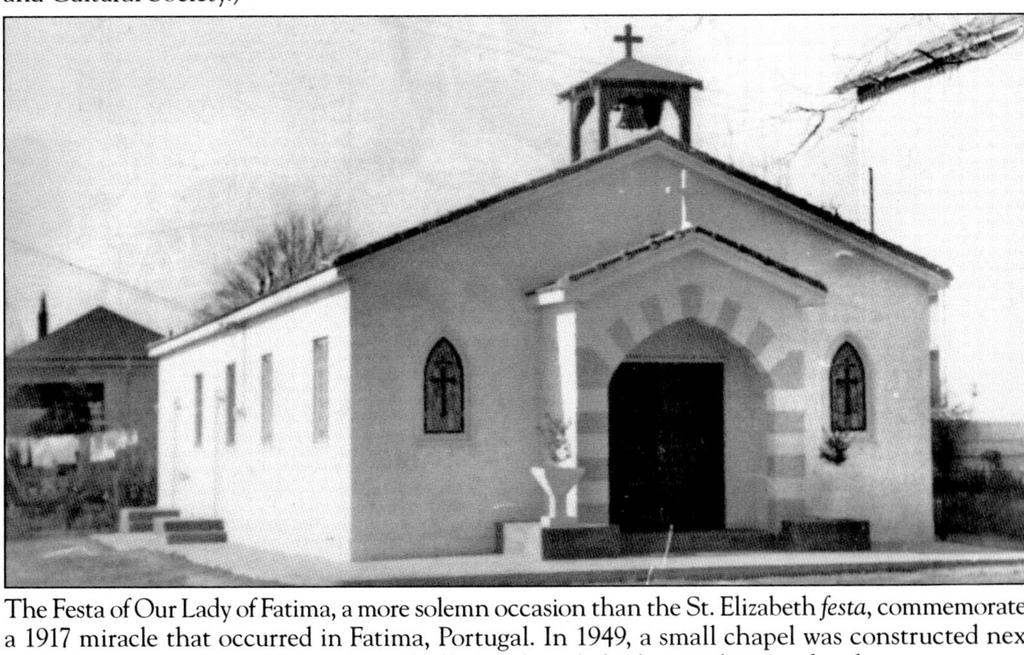

The Festa of Our Lady of Fatima, a more solemn occasion than the St. Elizabeth *festa*, commemorates a 1917 miracle that occurred in Fatima, Portugal. In 1949, a small chapel was constructed next to the ODES hall. When the main hall was demolished to make way for the construction of the W/X Freeway, the Fatima chapel was moved to a new location on Fifth Street. (Al Balshor collection.)

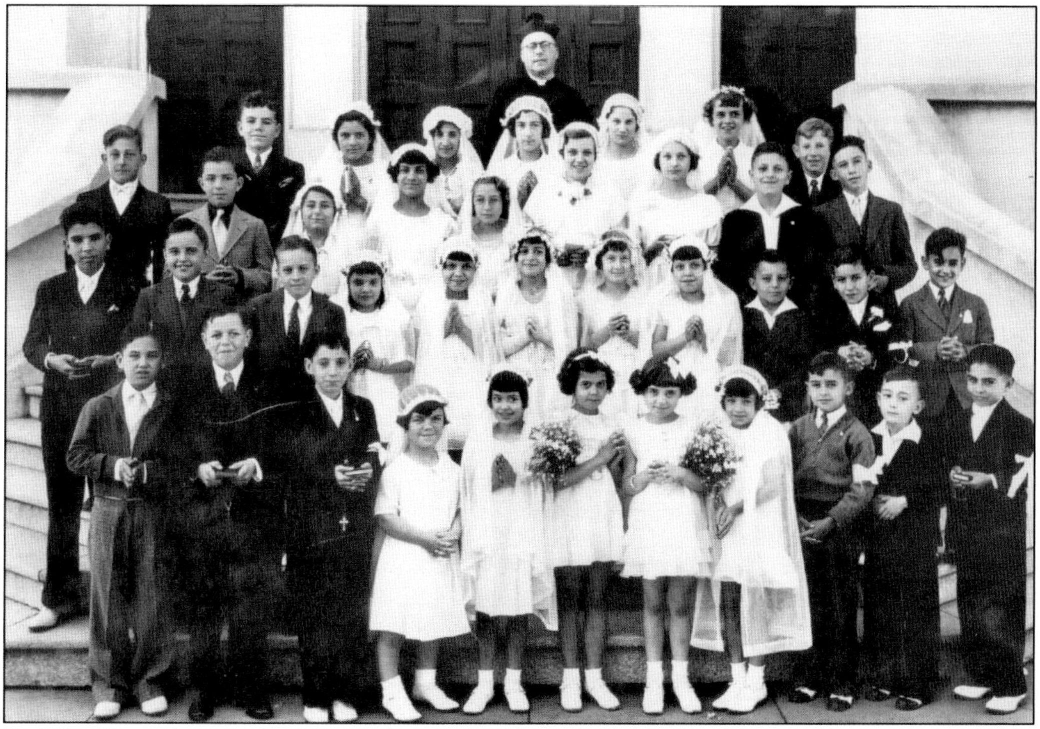

Fr. John Azevedo was the first pastor of St. Elizabeth's Church. He was ordained in 1904 and started the Sacramento parish on October 24, 1909. He retired in 1955, and St. Elizabeth's associate pastor, Fr. Valdemiro Fagundes, took his place. (Portuguese Historical and Cultural Society.)

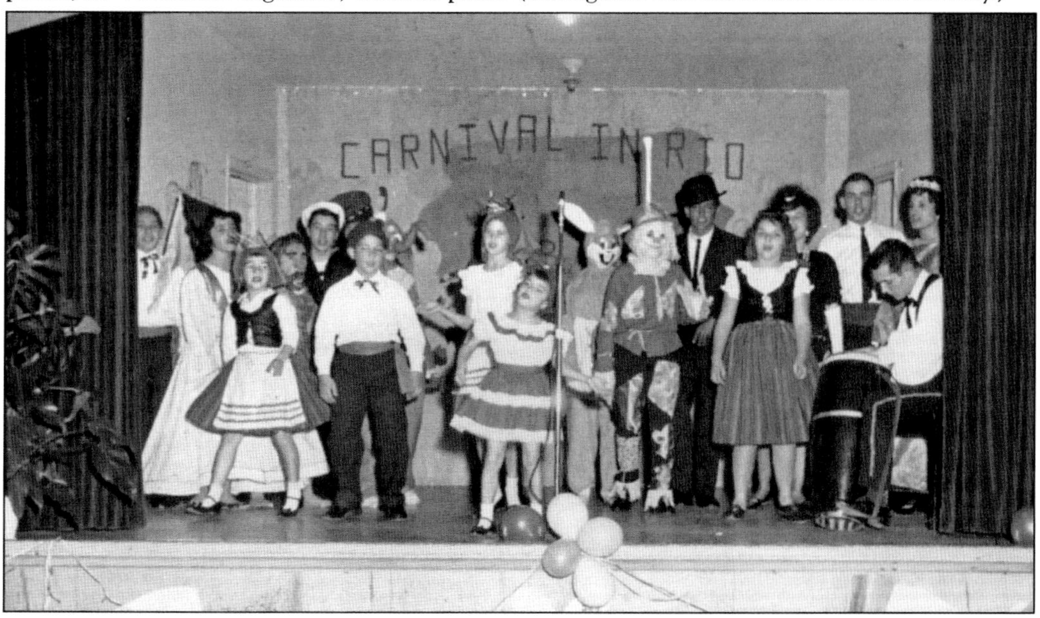

The ODES hall was used for many community events not related to the church. This "Carnival in Rio" event from the 1930s included a play with singing, dancing, and a wide variety of costumed characters and featured Southside Park's local talent. (Portuguese Historical and Cultural Society.)

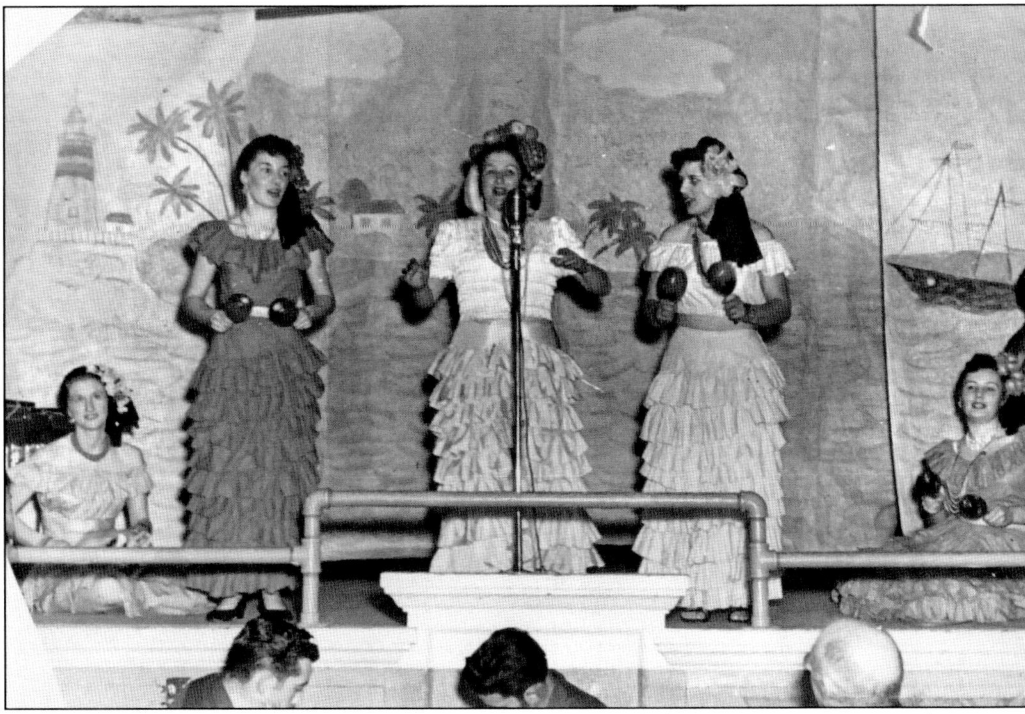

In the 1940s, tropical themes were still popular at the ODES hall's community events. The singing trio pictured here are (left to right) Alice Silva, Teofla Silva, and Alveda Silva. (Portuguese Historical and Cultural Society.)

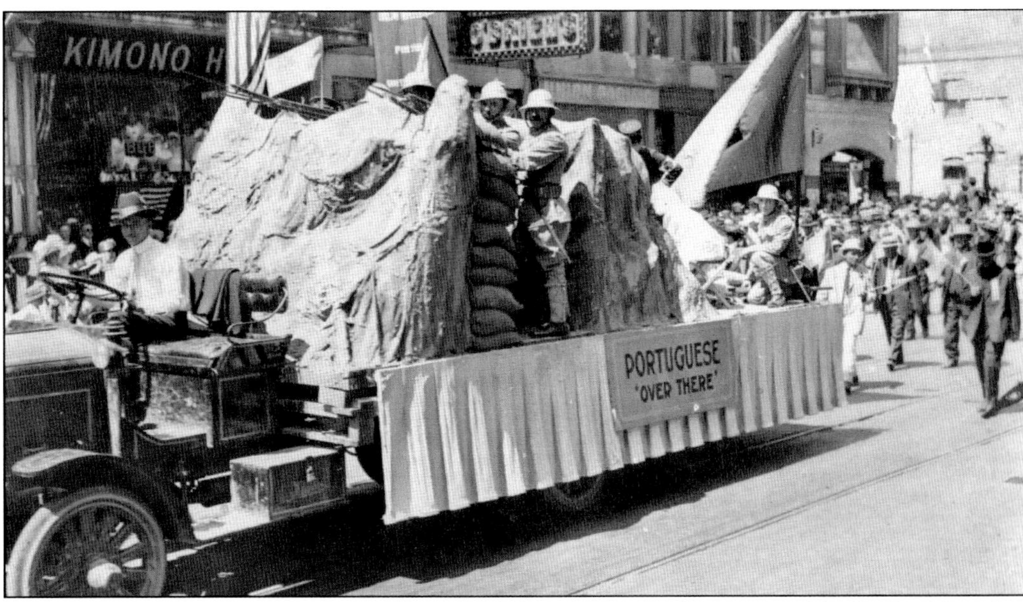

In 1916, the United States had not yet entered the Great War, but Portugal had. This Fourth of July float, built by Sacramento boatbuilders Manuel and Tony Nunes, honored Portuguese soldiers fighting in France. (Portuguese Historical and Cultural Society.)

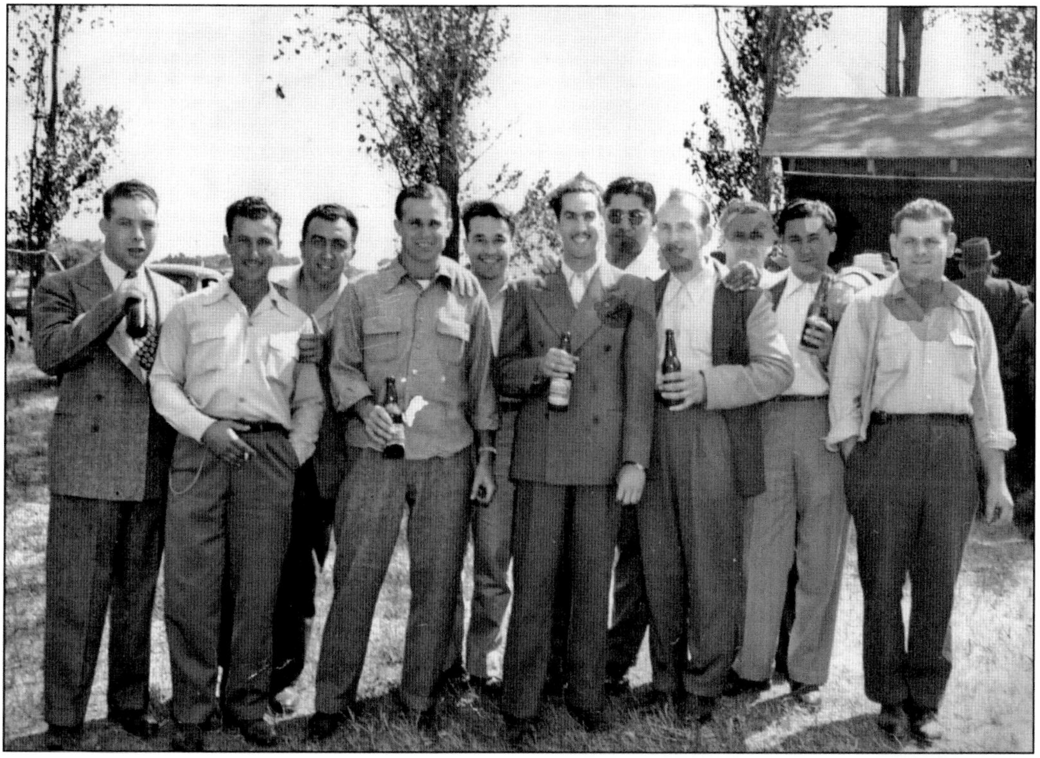

Sacramento's Pocket area also had a large Portuguese community, which held its own *festa* events. In 1946, this group of friends from Southside Park visited the Holy Ghost Festa on Pocket Road. Pictured are (left to right) Dan "Dirty Dan" Claudianos, Frank Crespo, Joe Souza, Frank Piva, Johnny "Cake Eater" Buscaglia, Armando "Streamline" Madera, Mose Cisneros, Al Balshor, Mario DiCristoforio, Joe Crespo, and Elrad "Alley Oop" Silvera. (Al Balshor collection.)

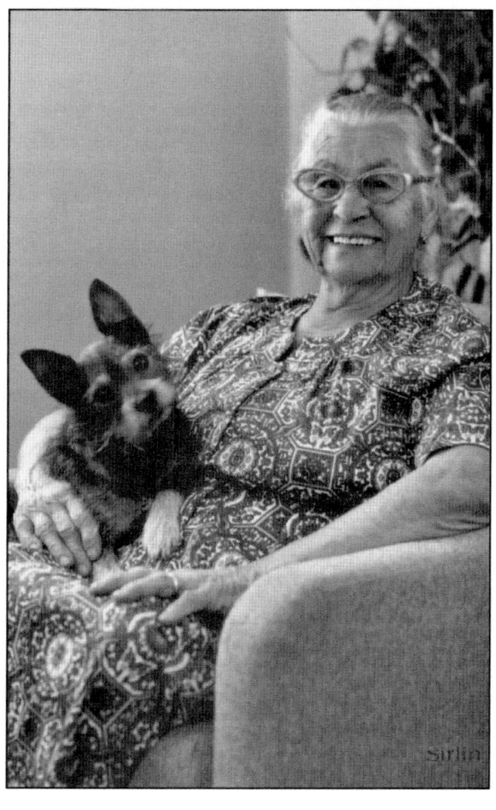

Graca Belchior and her husband, Arthur, left Portugal to work the sugarcane plantations in Hawaii in 1911. In 1915, they left Hawaii for Sacramento. In the United States, the name "Belchior" was recorded as "Balshor" at school registration. Arthur worked in various farms as a contract laborer and died in 1929. Graca, who was trained as a midwife, assisted with births throughout the neighborhood. She also worked at the California Packing Company cannery at Second and P Streets and picked fruit and vegetables, along with her children, in order to make ends meet after the death of her husband. She died December 14, 1974, at age 92. (Al Balshor collection.)

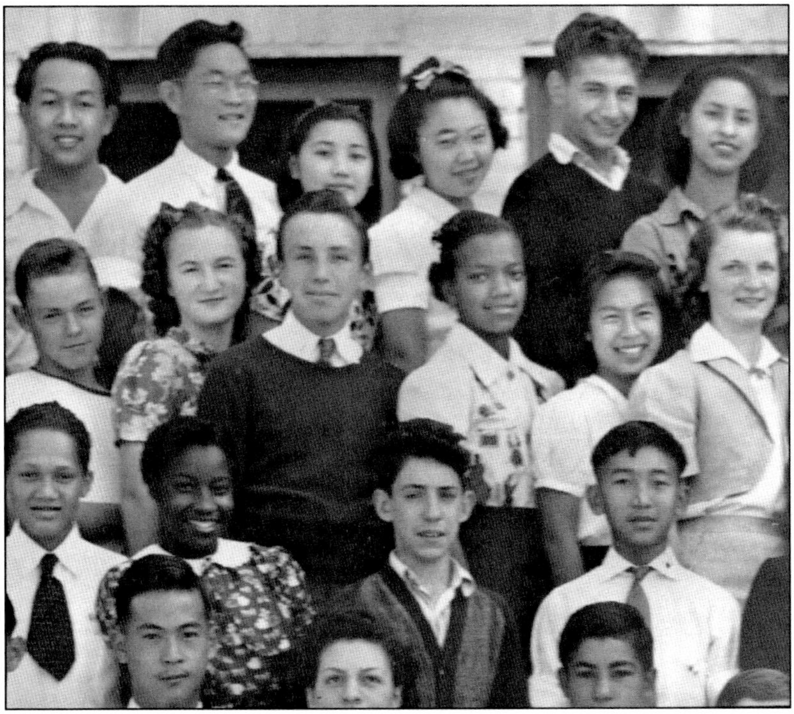

Graca Balshor's youngest son, Al, was born in his parents' home at 315 U Street in 1924. Originally she had planned to name him Antonio, after an older son who had died the year before, but Al's father had him baptized as Alberto Balshor. Al is third from the left in the second row in this Lincoln Junior High School class photograph. (Al Balshor collection.)

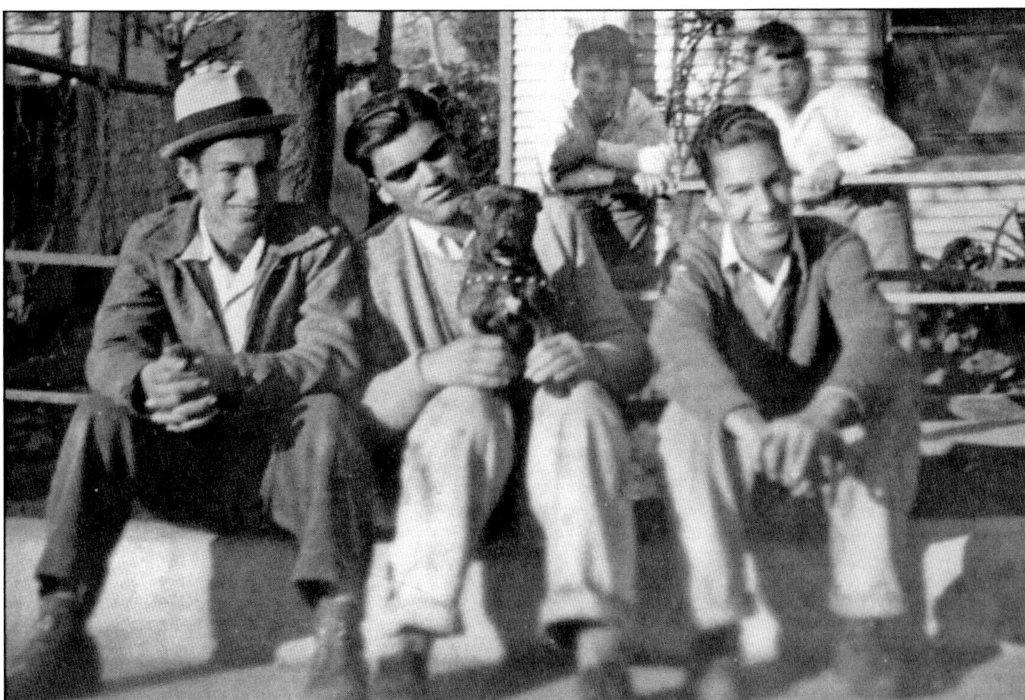

Al attended William Land Elementary School and Sacramento High School. He is in the background of this photograph, taken in front of 315 U Street, along with his friend Sam Brancato. In the foreground are (left to right) Frank Crespo, Joe Crespo, Herman Madera, and an unidentified puppy. (Al Balshor collection.)

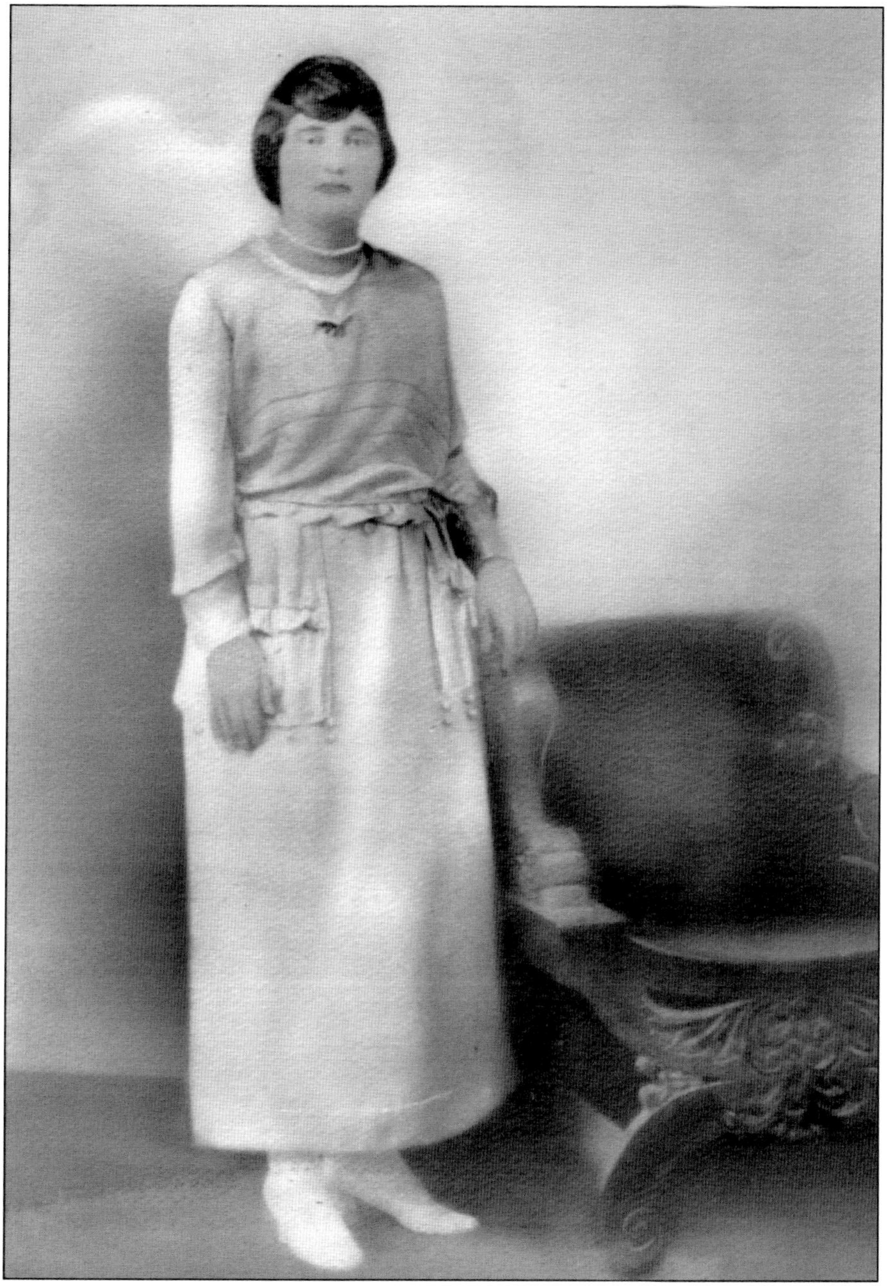

The Cape Verde Islands, off the coast of western Africa, were home to a unique culture. Colonized originally by Portuguese and African slaves, the islands were a provisioning station for Portuguese ships. In 1975, Cape Verde became its own independent nation. Cape Verdean culture is a fusion of African and Portuguese tradition and language. Many Cape Verdeans immigrated to Sacramento, including Emma de Veiga, born on the island of Fogo. She left Fogo to join her husband, Armand Monteiro, in the United States and later moved to Sacramento. Emma was a skilled seamstress and carpenter who built several additions to her home on T Street, including an apartment in the basement, to make room for her seven children. She died in 1980. (Georgina Montrond collection.)

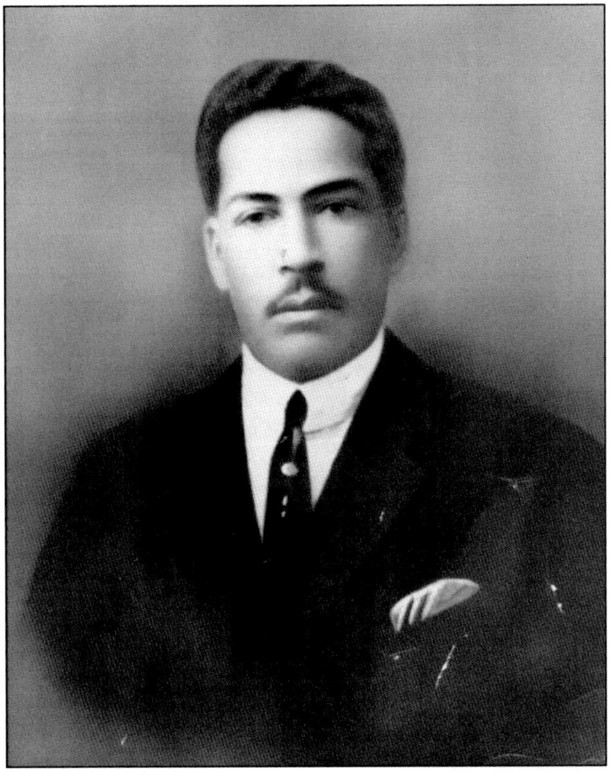

Armand Monteiro was born in Lisbon, Portugal. He immigrated to the United States before his wife, Emma, arriving in Massachusetts before moving to Sacramento. Armand found work in the foundry at the Southern Pacific shops, where he worked until he died in 1928 of blood poisoning. (Georgina Montrond collection.)

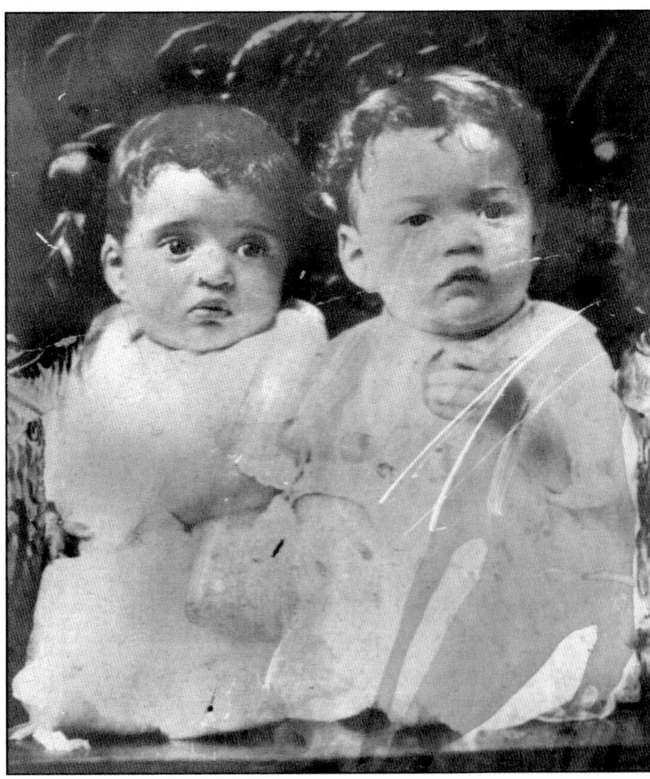

George and Georgina Monteiro, twin children of Armand and Emma, were born in 1926. They lived near Sixth and S Streets until a 1934 fire destroyed their home. Friends in Southside Park took them in, and the family relocated to Fourth and T Streets, where Georgina lives today. Georgina worked at the California Packing Company on Second and P, at the Blue Diamond almond plant, and for the State of California. (Georgina Montrond collection.)

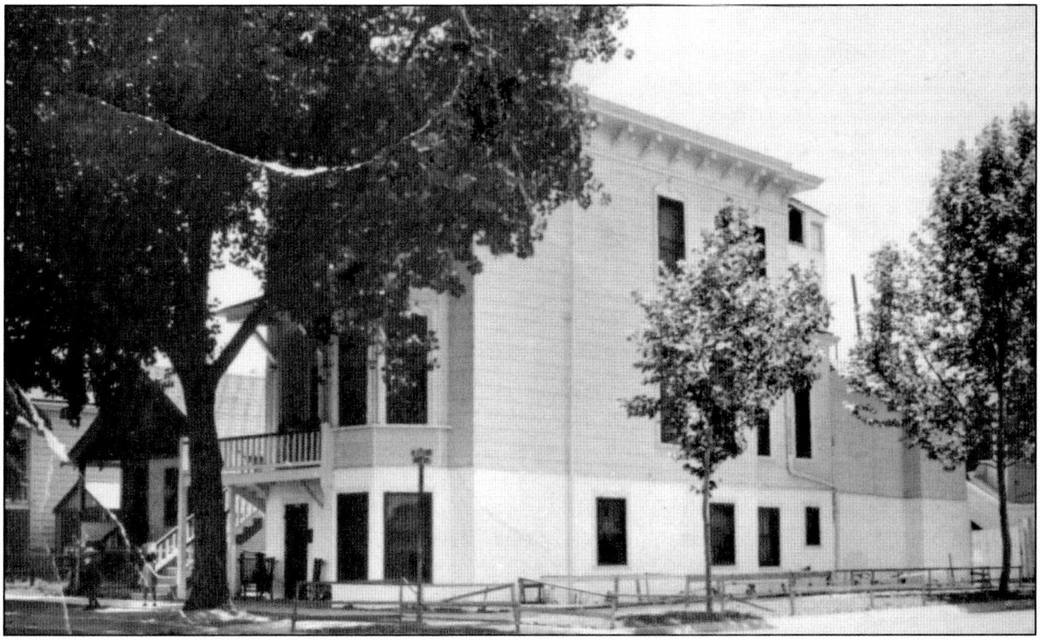

Mary Fernandes operated a boardinghouse on the corner of Fourth and S Streets, shown in this 1921 photograph. Many Cape Verdeans stayed here when they first came to the United States. Boardinghouses provided the first American home for many immigrant families who had no local friends or family to house them and were common in Sacramento's immigrant communities. (Portuguese Historical and Cultural Society.)

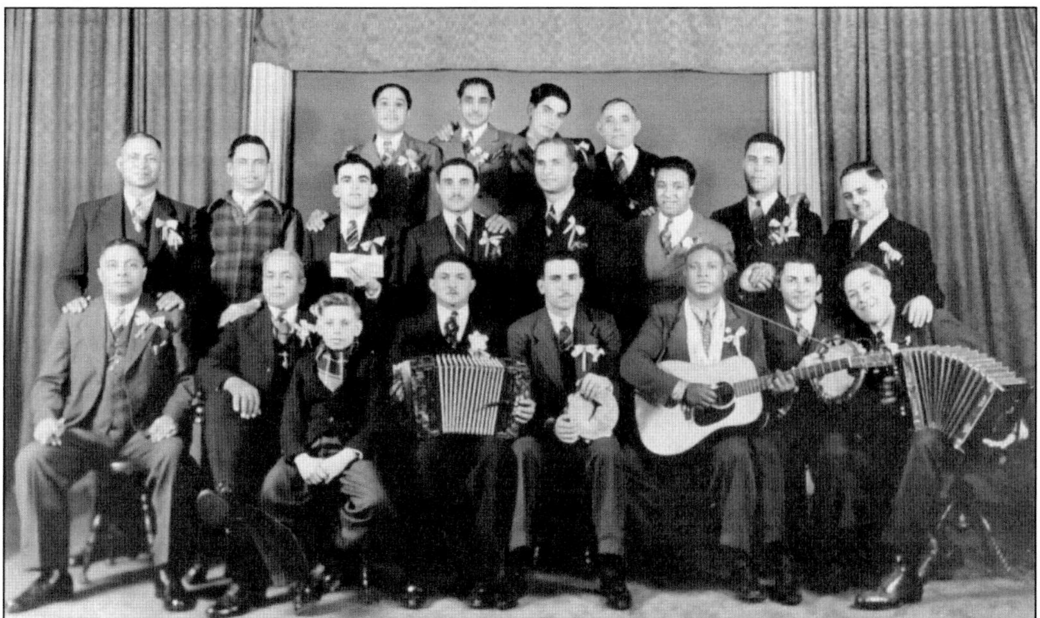

The Cape Verdean culture had its own traditions, its own language—*Criolou*, and its own music. The Cape Verdean New Year's Association held parties on New Year's Day, followed by a stroll through the neighborhood from door to door, wishing everyone a happy new year. (Portuguese Historical and Cultural Society.)

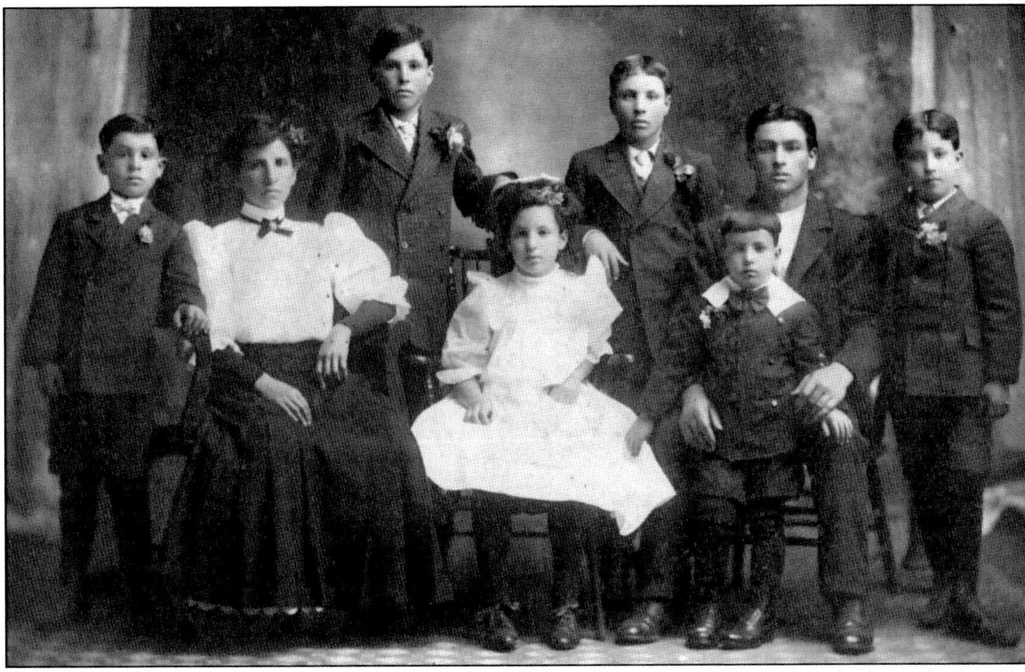

Manuel S. Vierra, the member of the Arizona Gang pictured on page 22, was born in Fial in the Azores. He grew up in Southside Park and raised a family. From left to right in this photograph are Marshall Vierra, Marie Vierra, Manuel J. Vierra, Mary Vierra, Joe Vierra, Frankie Vierra, Manuel Vierra Sr., and John Vierra. Mary was the mother of Colorado senator Ben Nighthorse Campbell. Manuel Jr. later opened a bar on Third Street in Southside Park. (Manuel Viera collection.)

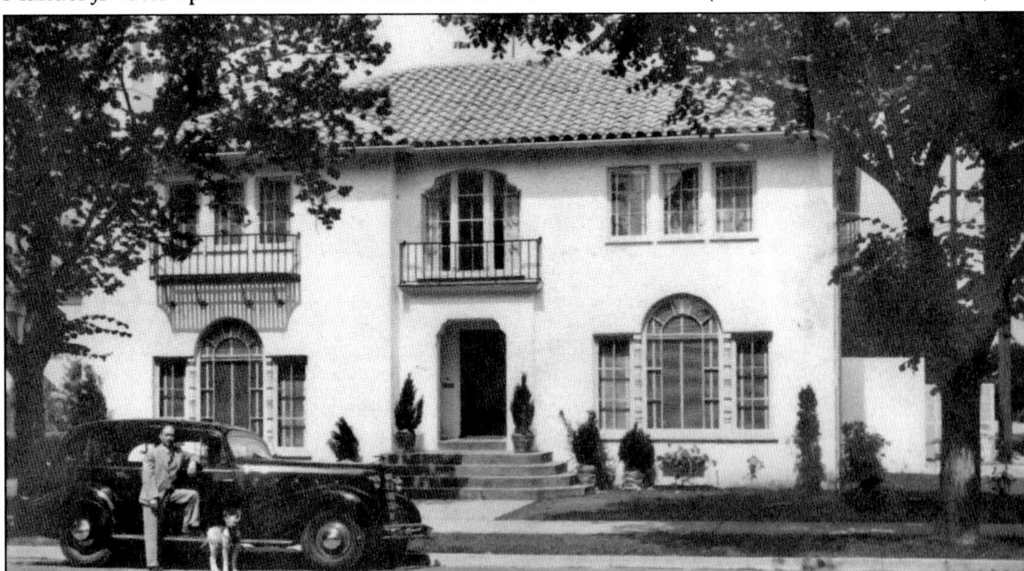

Sacramento's Chinese neighborhood was on the north end of downtown, between J and K Streets near the river, but Southside Park had its own Chinese population. One of the most successful Chinese businessmen in the city was W. Fong Yue. He emigrated from China in 1908 and in 1912 opened the Lincoln Market at 516 K Street. In 1938, he built this home at 2116 Sixth Street in Southside Park. (Inn at Parkside.)

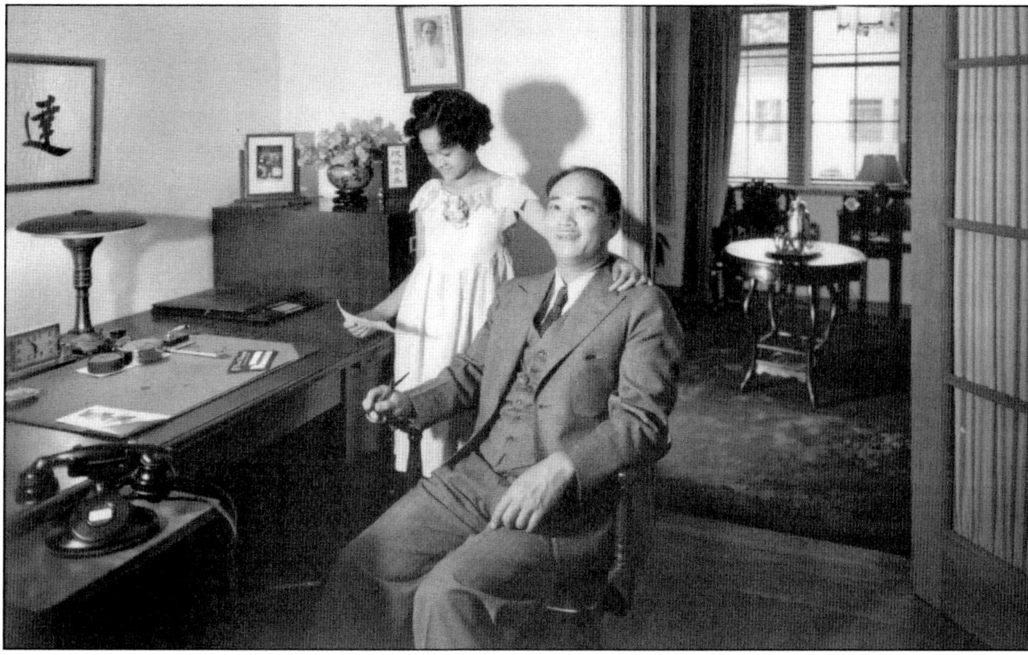

Fong's business interests made him quite wealthy, and he initially wished to build a mansion in East Sacramento or Land Park. Racial covenants on those neighborhoods prohibited him from buying property in those neighborhoods, so he had his home constructed in Southside Park, where there were no such restrictions. (Inn at Parkside.)

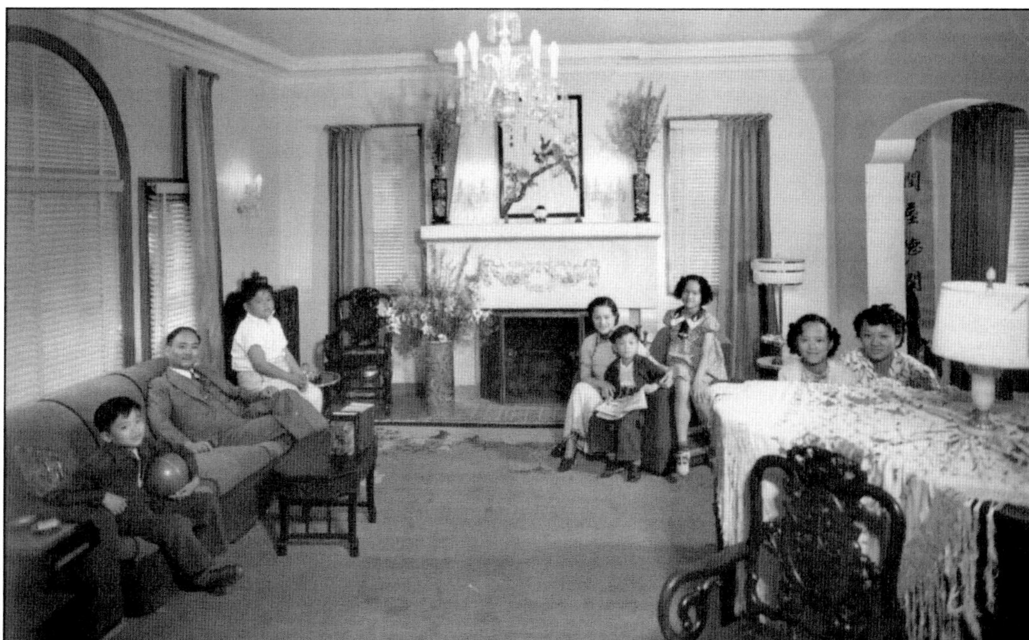

The mansion was home to Fong, his wife, Grace, and his six children, but it was also a meeting place for Chinese dignitaries, community organizations, and Chinese youth groups. W. Fong Yue died in 1978, greatly respected for his philanthropy and community spirit. Today his home is an elegant bed-and-breakfast resort and spa. (Inn at Parkside.)

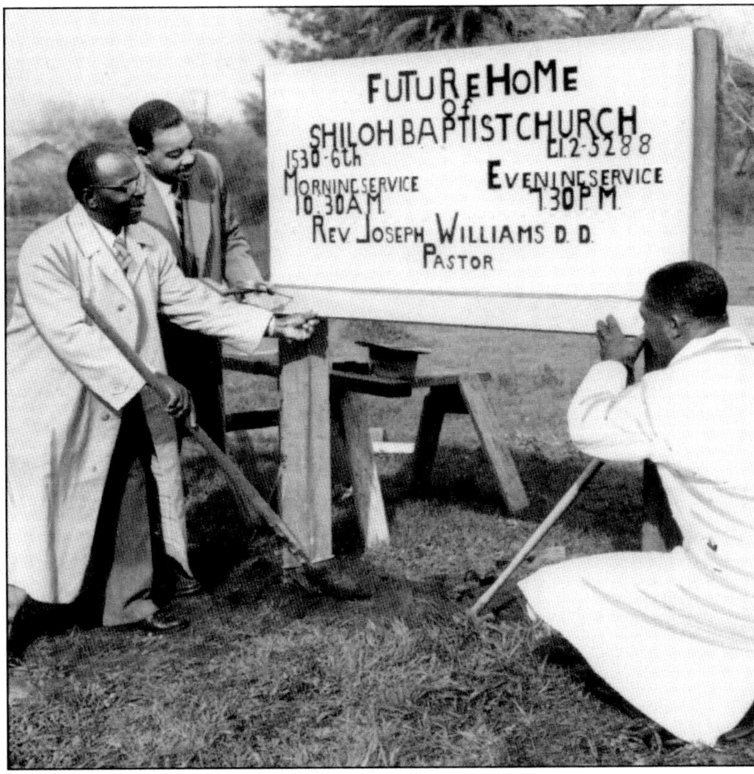

While there was not a particular African American neighborhood within Southside Park, they were present in the community, and their institutions were part of the neighborhood. Shiloh Baptist Church was founded in 1856. It moved several times before finding a home at Sixth and P Streets in 1905. In 1957, the church purchased property on Ninth Avenue and Thirty-sixth Street, and relocated there when Sixth and P was redeveloped. (Sacramento Archives and Museum Collection Center.)

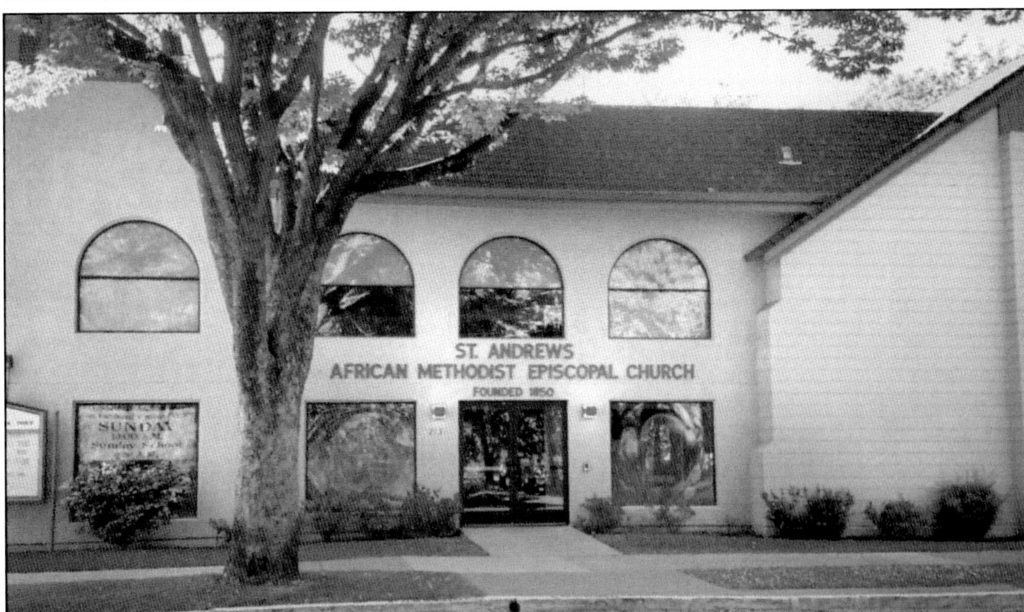

St. Andrew's African Methodist Episcopal Church of Sacramento, founded in 1850, was the first African American religious congregation on the Pacific coast. The original church was on Seventh Street between G and H Streets. In 1951, the church moved to its current location at Eighth and V Streets. The church was expanded in 1995 to include a new education building. The site of the original church is now a parking structure. (Author's collection.)

Sacramento's Japanese community was located roughly between Third and Sixth Streets and from K to P Streets. Sacramento's Japanese Buddhist Church, founded in 1899, is the second oldest Japanese Buddhist institution in the United States. After staying briefly at 1221 Third Street, it was moved to this structure at 418 O Street. In 1923, a fire swept through the church's dormitory, killing 10 students and damaging the building. (Japanese Buddhist Church.)

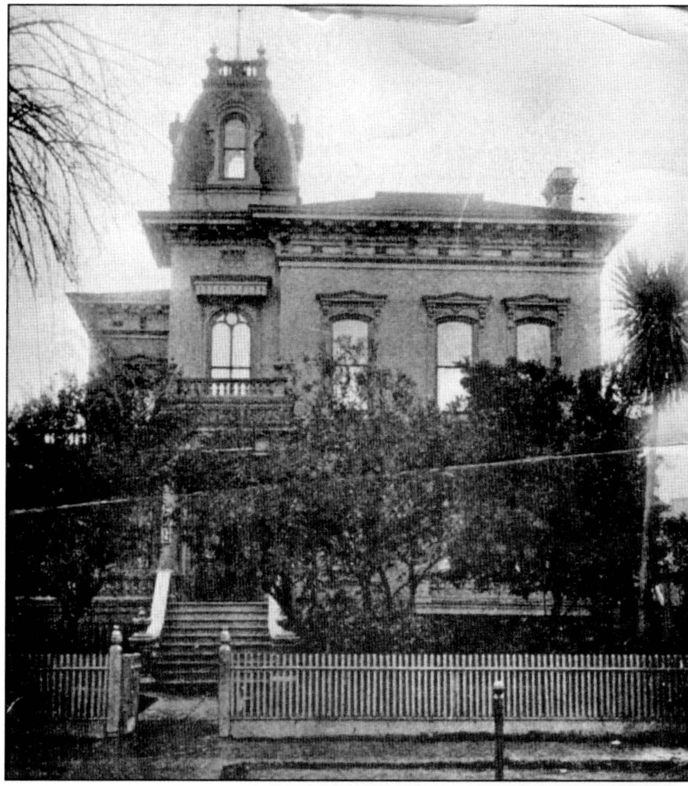

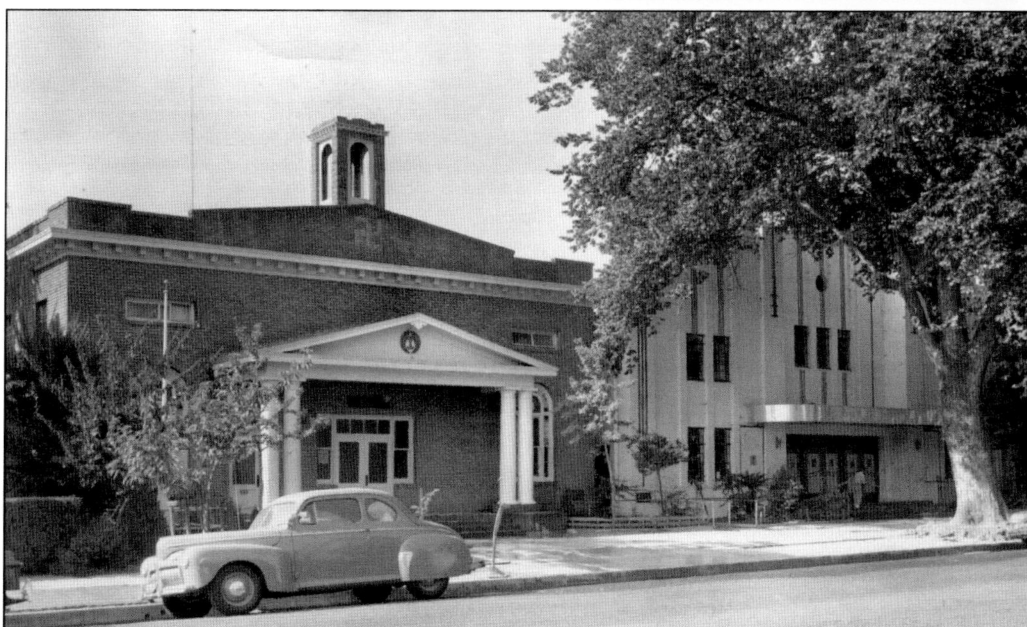

In May 1925, a new Japanese Buddhist church was completed to replace the fire-damaged original building. An auditorium, to the right, was completed in August 1937. The auditorium was used for events like the Obon Odori dance, as well as plays, sports, and other functions. (Japanese Buddhist Church.)

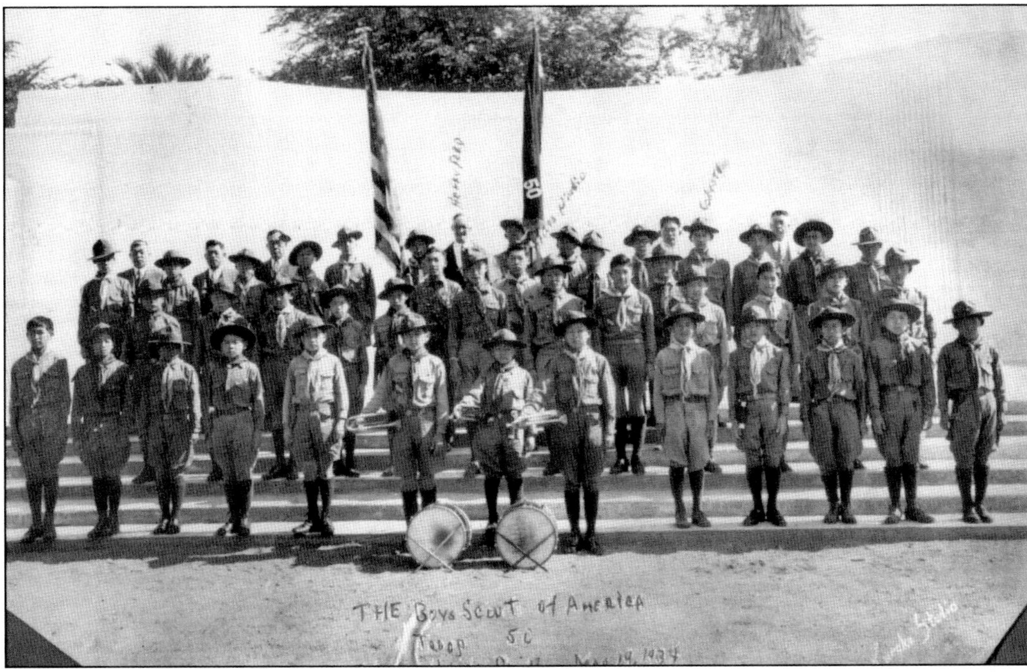

The Japanese Buddhist Church also sponsored community groups like Boy Scout Troop 50, whose members were originally all Japanese Americans. This photograph of Troop 50 was taken at the Callahan bandstand in Southside Park in May 1934. (Japanese Buddhist Church.)

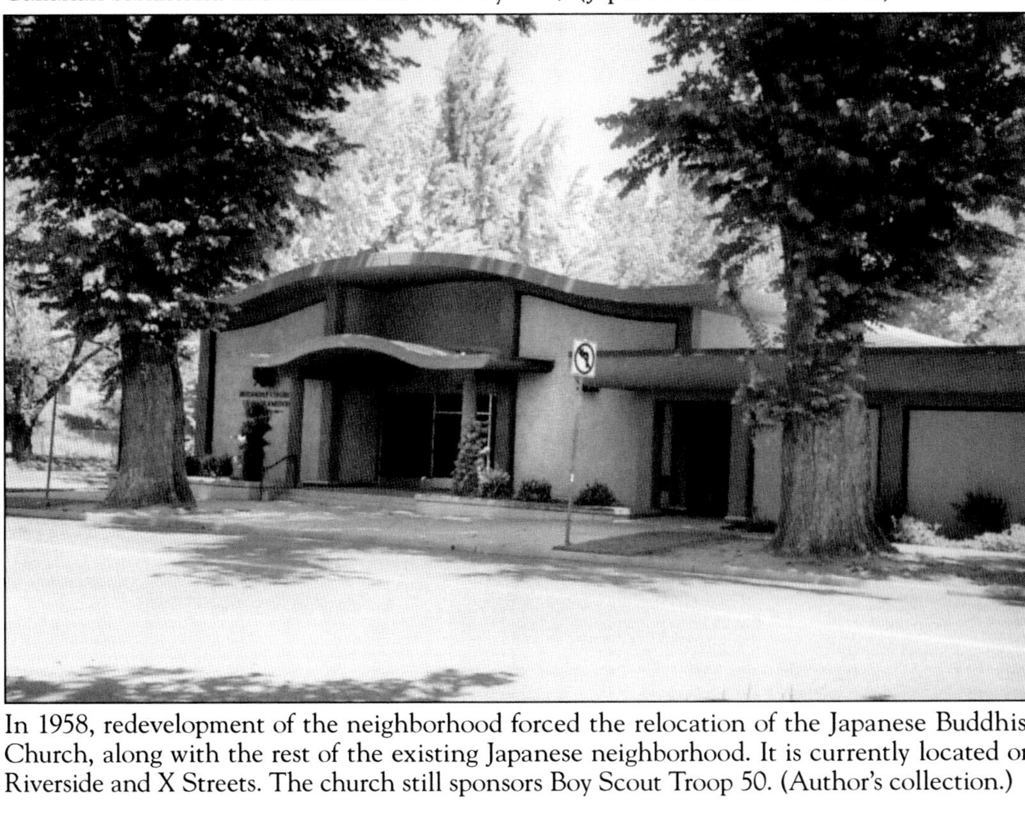

In 1958, redevelopment of the neighborhood forced the relocation of the Japanese Buddhist Church, along with the rest of the existing Japanese neighborhood. It is currently located on Riverside and X Streets. The church still sponsors Boy Scout Troop 50. (Author's collection.)

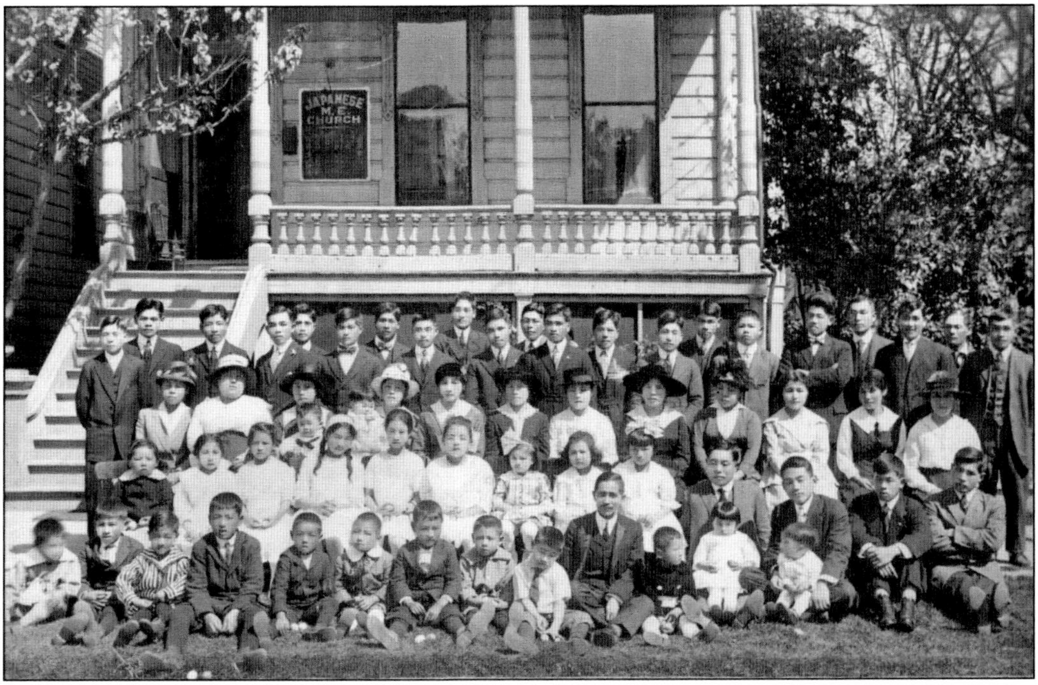

The first Japanese religious institution to open its doors in Sacramento was the Japanese Methodist Episcopal Church, founded in 1892. In 1918, this group photograph was taken on Easter Sunday at the church, located at 331 O Street. (Sacramento State Archives and Special Collections.)

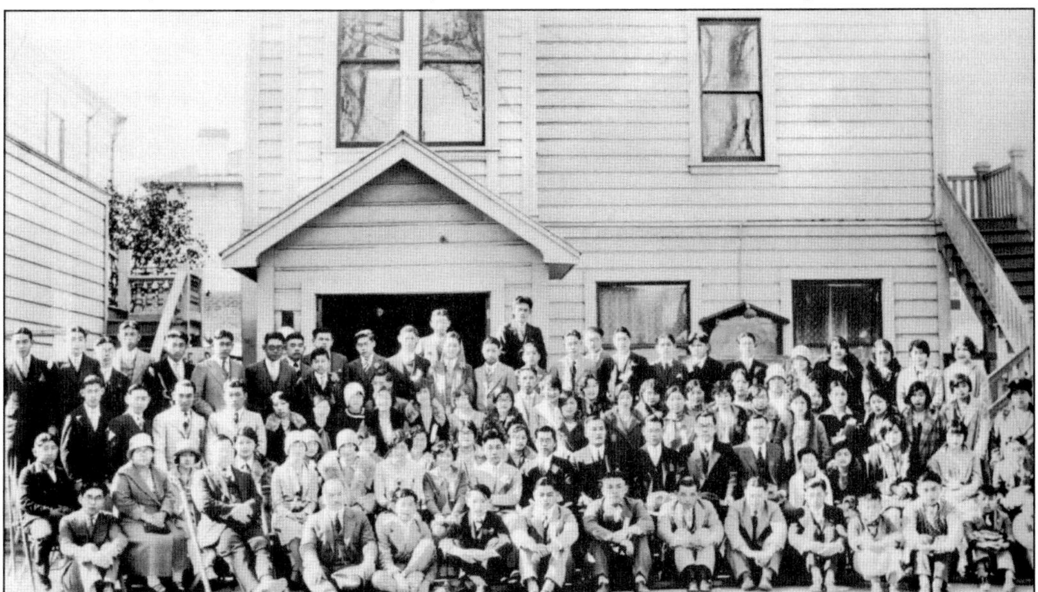

This gathering of the Sacramento Valley Young People's Christian Conference (YPCC) took place at the Japanese Baptist Church at Fifth and P Streets. YPCC gatherings brought together Nisei (second-generation Japanese, born in the United States) from around Northern California for social and religious activities. This church also sponsored a Boy Scout troop, Troop 41. (Sacramento State Archives and Special Collections.)

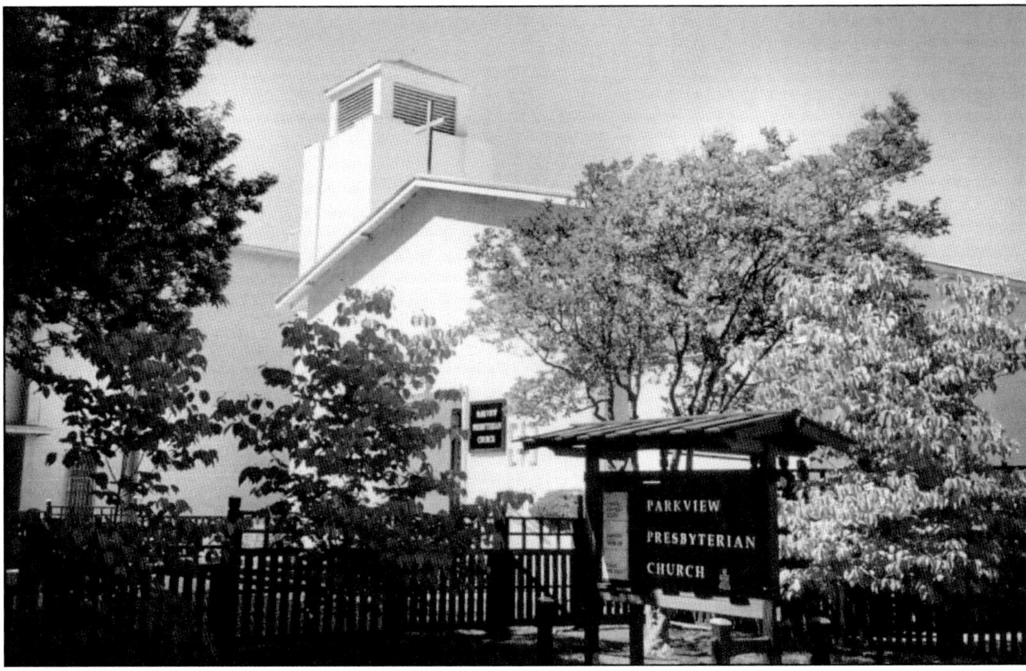

The Parkview Presbyterian Church is located at Eighth and T Streets. Founded as an offshoot of the Japanese Presbyterian Mission, the church opened its doors in 1940 and remains there today. Because it was located outside of the redevelopment zone, it was not forced to move like the churches and businesses in the heart of Japantown. (Author's collection.)

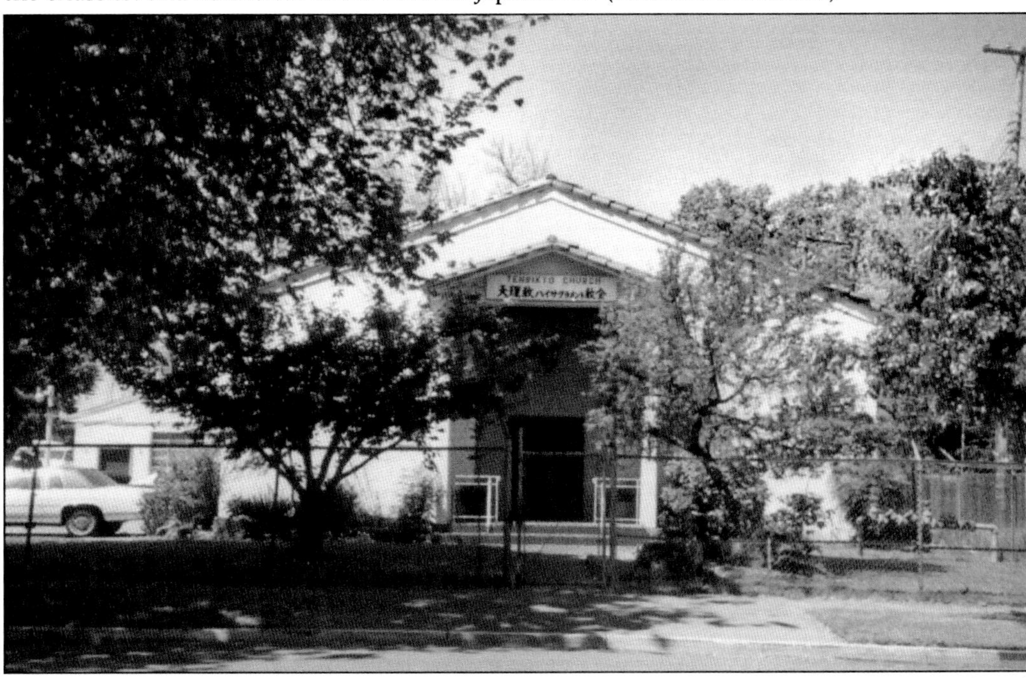

The Tenrikyo Church was founded by Foundress Miki Nakayama. Sacramento's Tenrikyo Church opened in 1933 and was originally located on Second and N Streets. It was relocated to Sixth and W Streets, across the street from Southside Park. (Author's collection.)

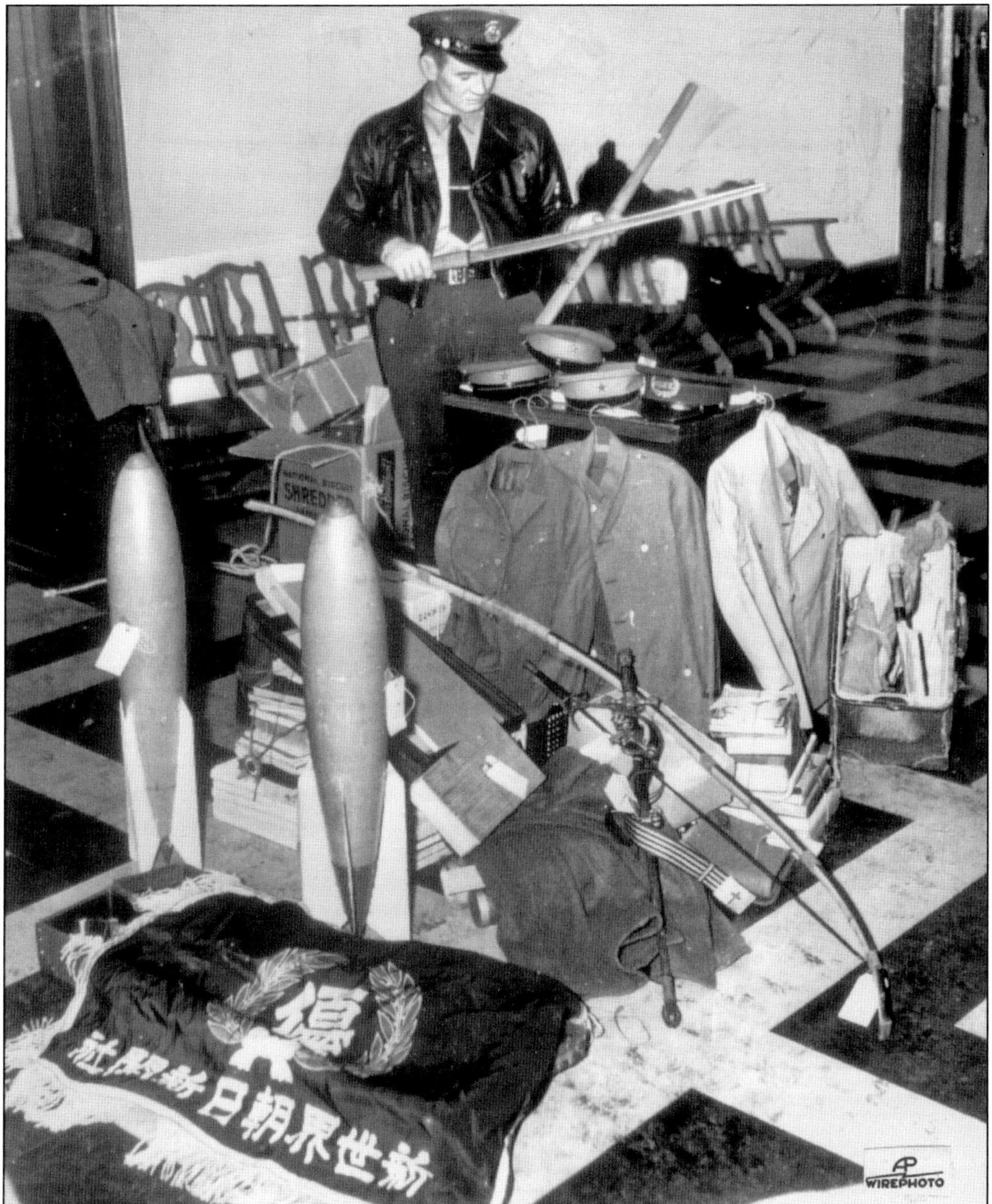

The attack on Pearl Harbor began a dark period for Japanese Americans. The FBI and police conducted raids on persons considered suspect. One such raid in Sacramento, on February 16, 1942, resulted in the seizure of this collection of items, including old Japanese army uniforms, ceremonial swords, empty bomb casings, and a wrestling banner. On February 19, 1942, Pres. Franklin D. Roosevelt signed Executive Order 9066, which set the stage for the internment of "enemy aliens" and "non-aliens" (citizens). By May that year, Sacramento's Japantown was emptied. Its residents, like others on the West Coast, were shipped to isolated camps in remote parts of the western United States. Most of Sacramento's Japanese population was interned at Tule Lake, California. (USC Archives.)

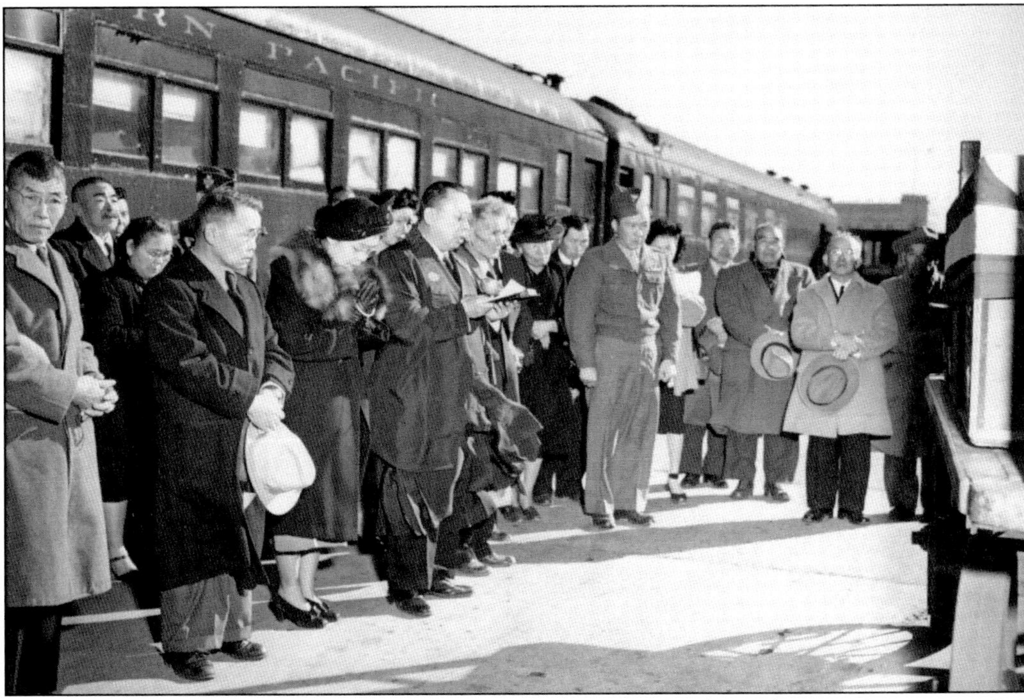

Many Nisei men joined the army during World War II and fought with great distinction. Cpl. Tadashi Takeuchi of Sacramento was killed in action in France in October 1944. In this photograph, his body has arrived at the Sacramento train station for burial. (Sacramento State Archives and Special Collections.)

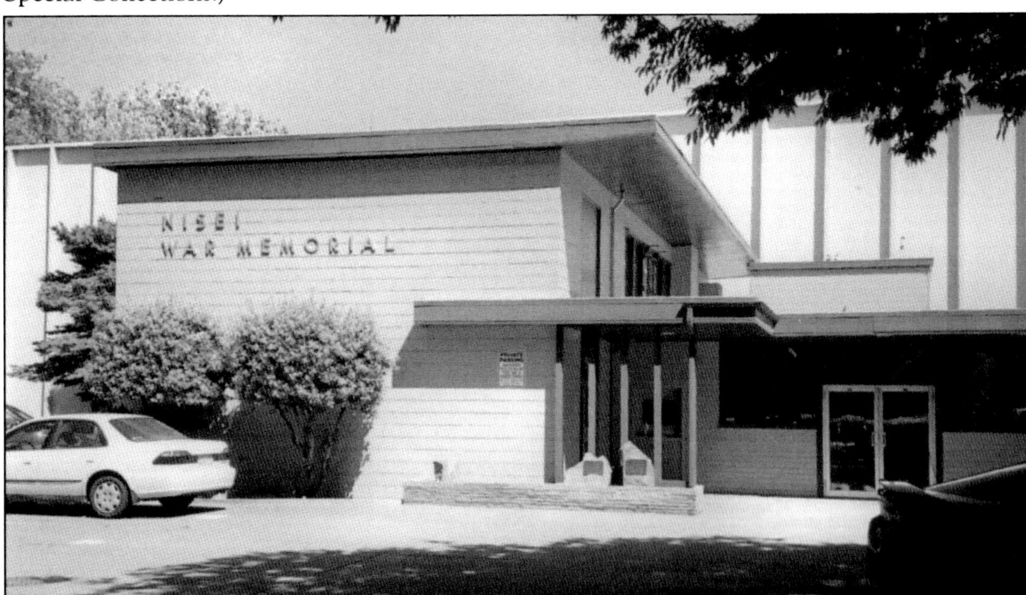

The Nisei War Memorial on Fourth and O Streets was dedicated on December 11, 1955. Although it was constructed comparatively recently, this building is the only remaining structure of Sacramento's Japantown. The names of Sacramento Japanese who died in action during the Second World War are listed on a plaque near the building's entrance. (Author's collection.)

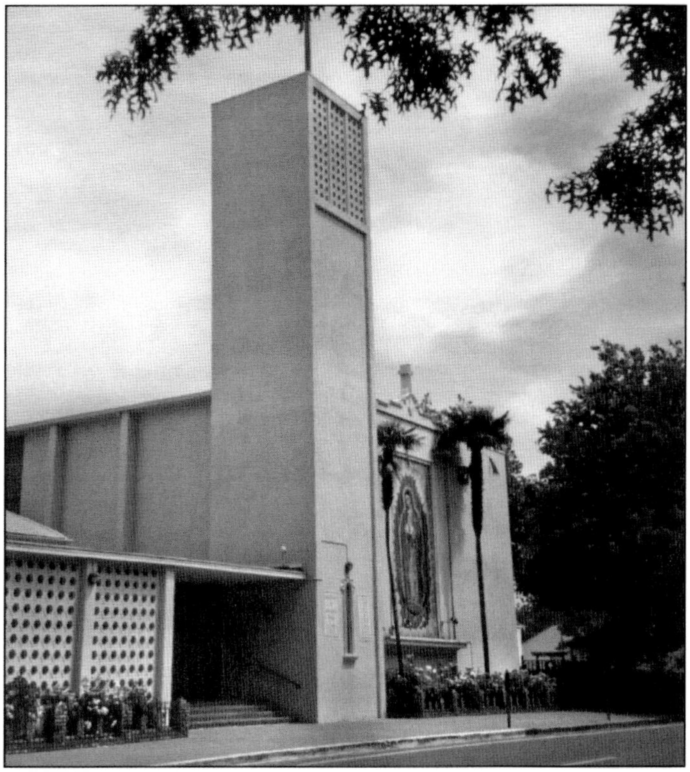

Our Lady of Guadalupe Church, on T Street between Seventh and Eighth Streets, served the Latino residents of Southside Park. Its original location was at Third and O Streets. While California was once part of Mexico, many Mexicans immigrated to Sacramento, and many found homes in Southside Park. Before the founding of Our Lady of Guadalupe, Spanish-speaking residents went to the Cathedral of the Blessed Sacrament on K Street or to St. Mary's on Seventh and T, whose parishioners were mostly Italians. (Author's collection.)

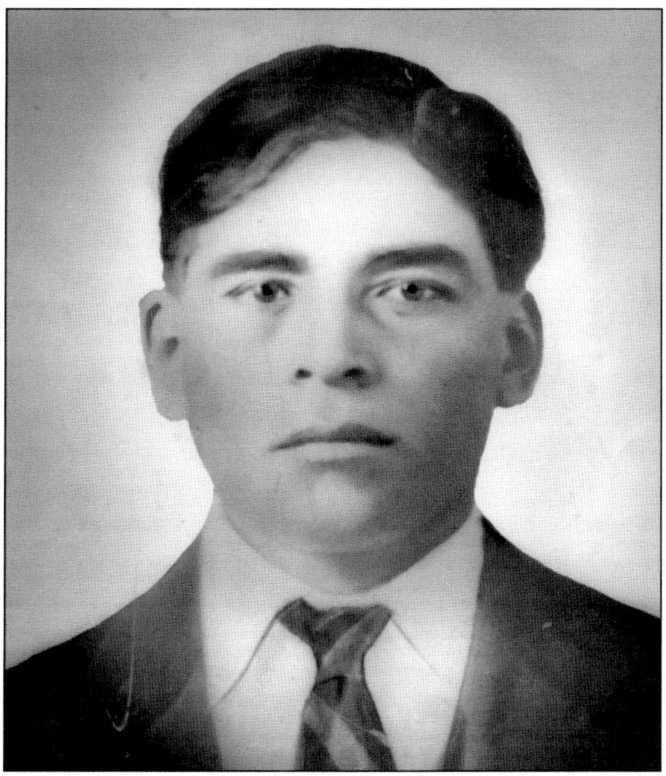

Pablo Lopez was born in Mexico and came to the United States in 1900. His first job was in Quincy, California, before coming to Sacramento. He worked at Sacramento Rice Company on Front Street. He was so dedicated to his work that he tried to return to work two days after a heart attack and nearly came to blows with his boss, who wanted him to recuperate for longer. (Antonio Lopez collection.)

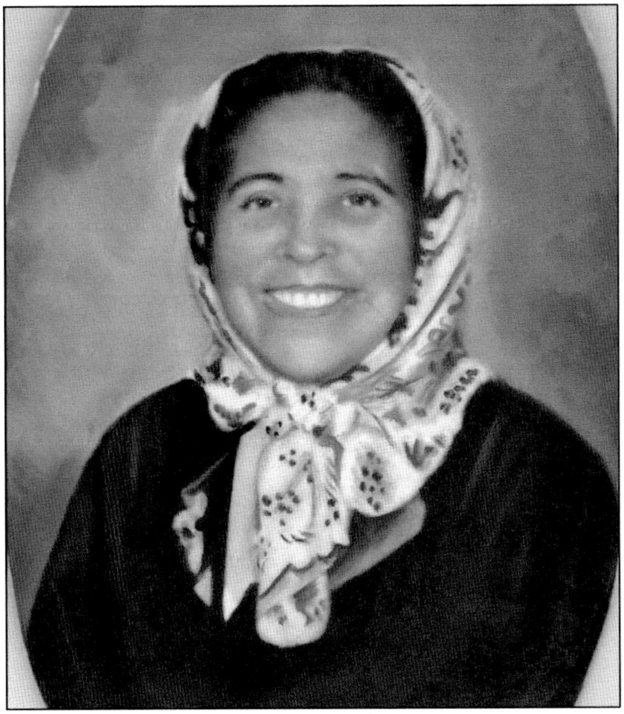

Concepcion De Lopez raised 10 children in their family home on S Street. Pablo and Concepcion worked picking fruit and saved money to buy the house for $5,000 in 1942. Tony, their son, says she made homemade tortillas every day and believed that if someone came to her door wanting food, they should be fed, no matter what. (Antonio Lopez collection.)

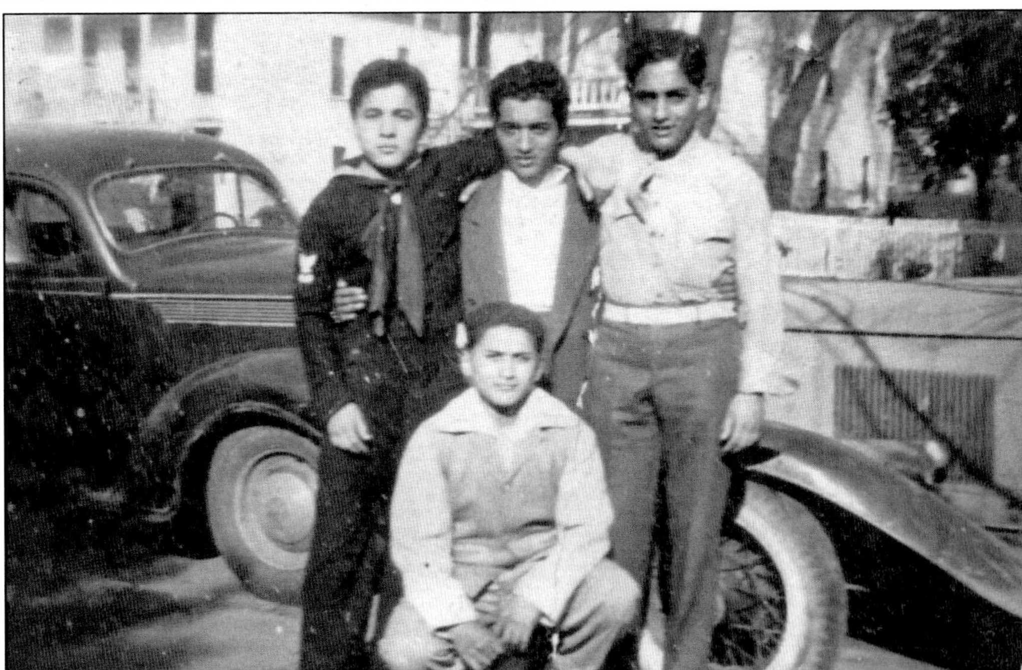

Four of the Lopez children, in front of their house on S Street, are, from left to right, (kneeling) Antonio; (standing) Jose, John, and Pablo. Antonio "Tony" Lopez still lives in the house where he was raised and helped organize opposition to prostitution in Southside Park. "This is the best neighborhood in town!" says Tony, "If I won the lottery, I wouldn't move from this place." (Antonio Lopez collection.)

Tony Lopez poses with his friend George Montero (left) in front of the bandstand at Southside Park. Tony's only complaint about the neighborhood was that there was no swimming pool until 1953. Nearby Riverside Baths was restricted to whites only. They could visit McKinley Park's pool, but it was a long streetcar ride away. Nonwhites were allowed there, but, according to Tony, "They gave you dirty looks." (Antonio Lopez collection.)

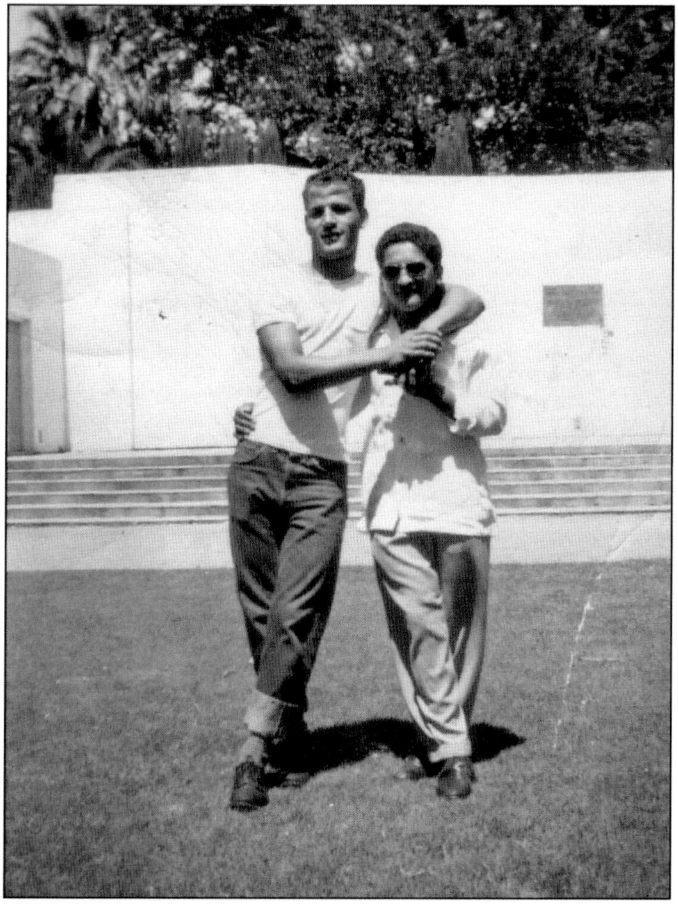

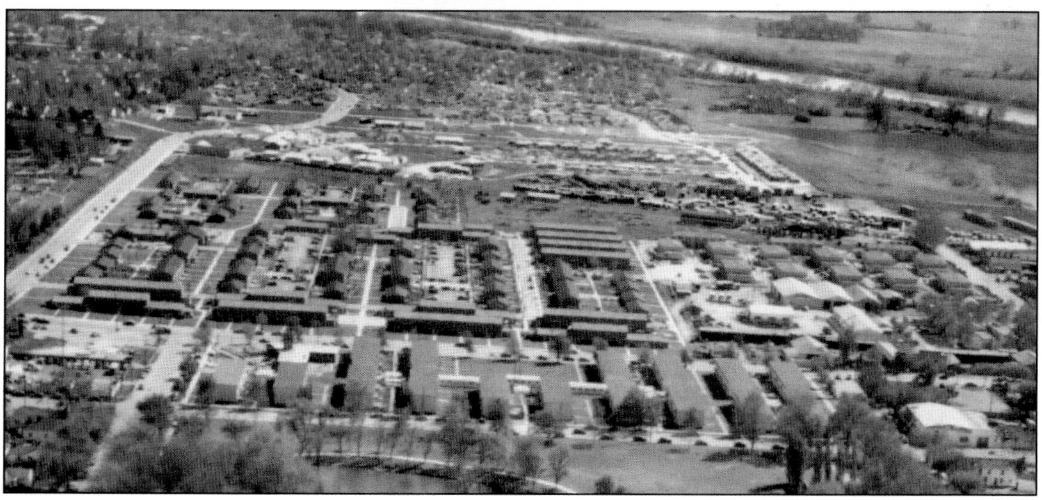

South of Broadway were the New Helvetia and Seavey Circle housing projects. This photograph was taken shortly after World War II, when homes for veterans were desperately needed. The baseball fields south of the park on X Street were displaced to make way for temporary barracks transported from army bases in Vallejo, which were known as Callahan Homes. (Sacramento Archives and Museum Collection Center.)

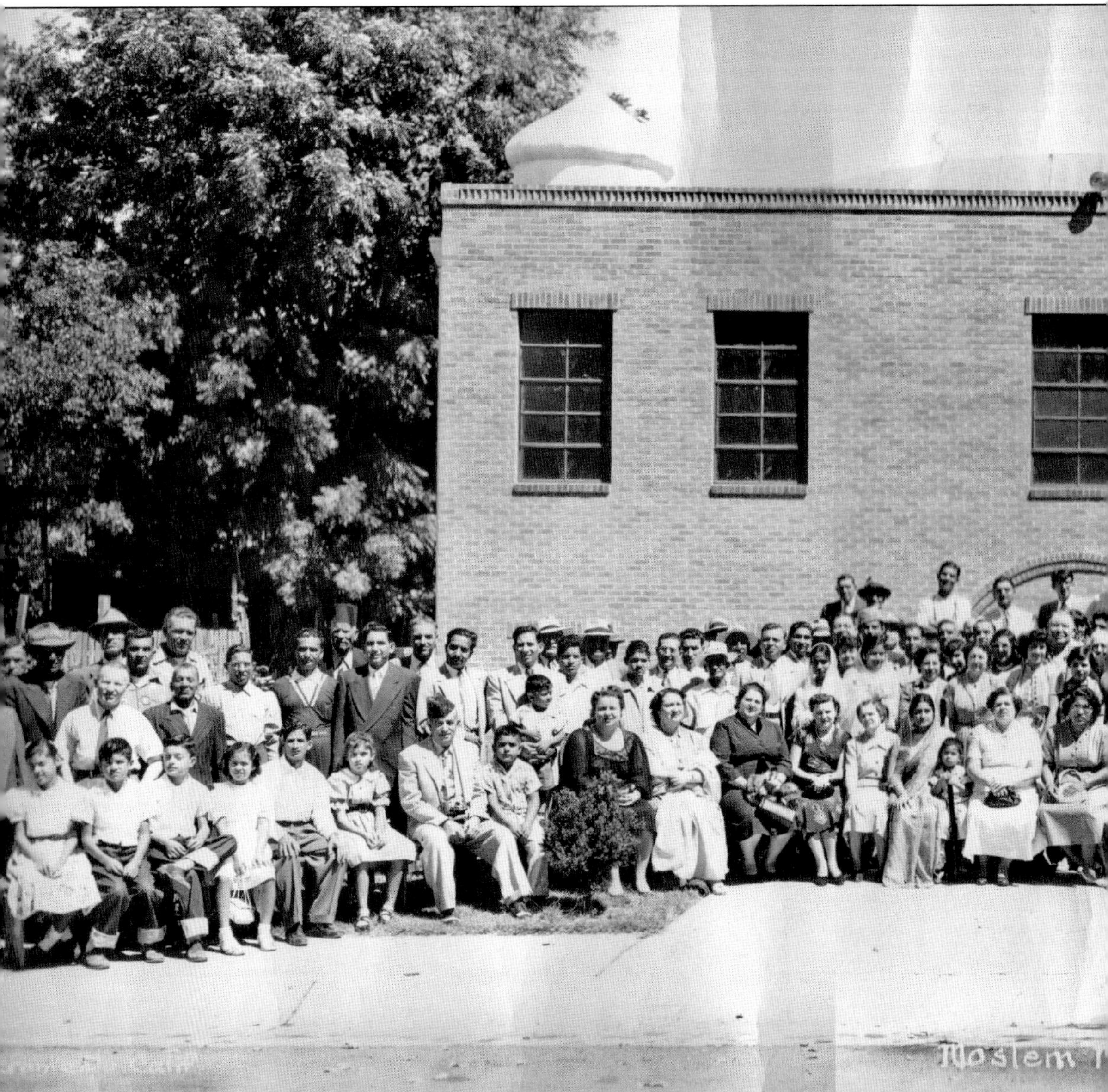

Many of Sacramento's early Moslem population came from the region of India that is now the nation of Pakistan. Some came as farmers, and others worked on the railroad. Indian citizens had British passports and were not subject to the racial exclusion laws that affected other Asians like Chinese and Japanese. Saddullah Khan, an immigrant from India, was a successful hotel and motel owner who came to Sacramento in the 1940s. He sold all his properties and used

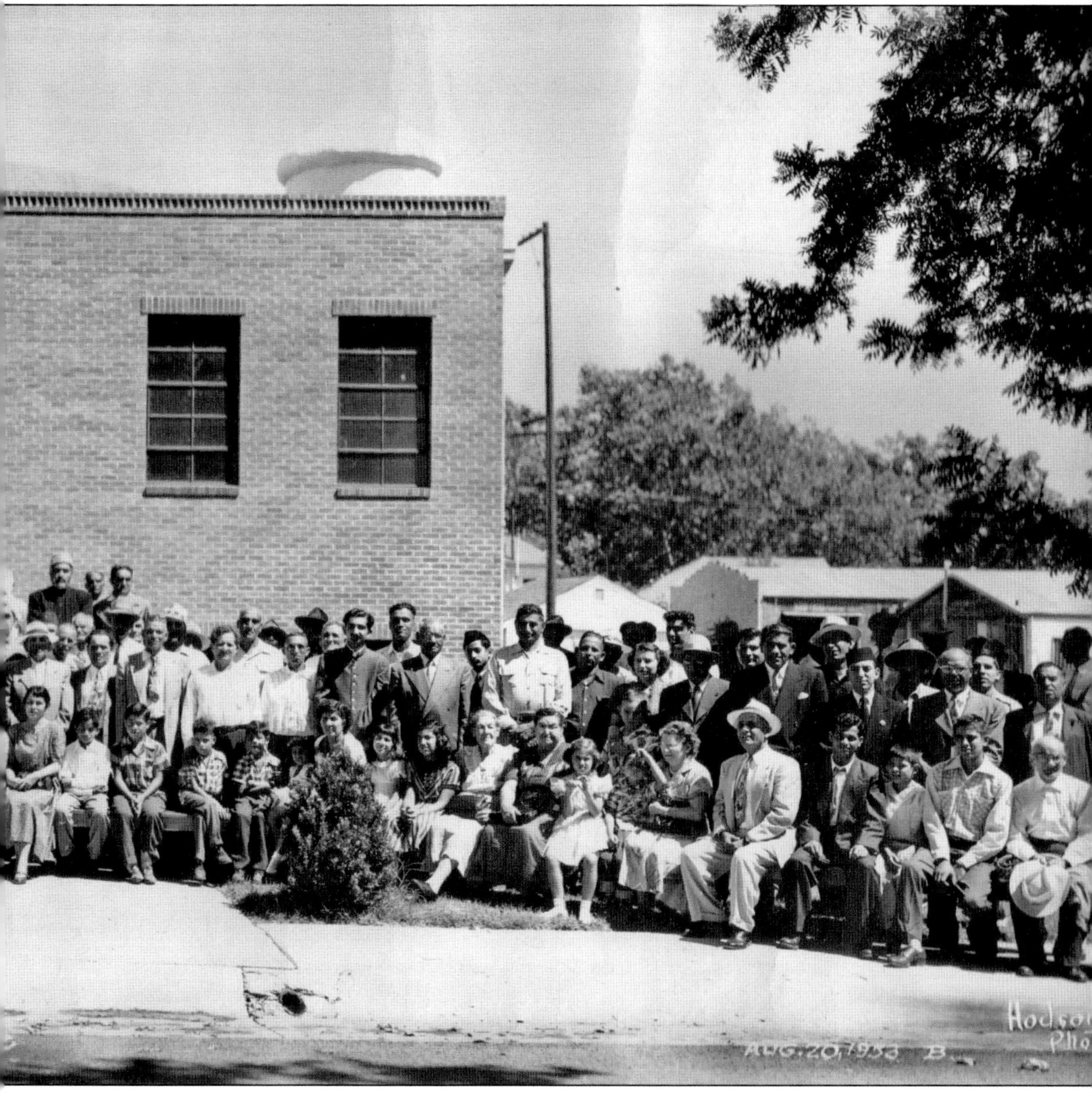

his money, as well as private donations, to build a mosque on V Street between Fourth and Fifth Streets. It was the only mosque in the region, attracting worshippers from throughout the Sacramento Valley, and is the oldest mosque in the western United States. The mosque provides services including education and health programs for Sacramento's Moslem community. (Ibrahim Hamdani collection.)

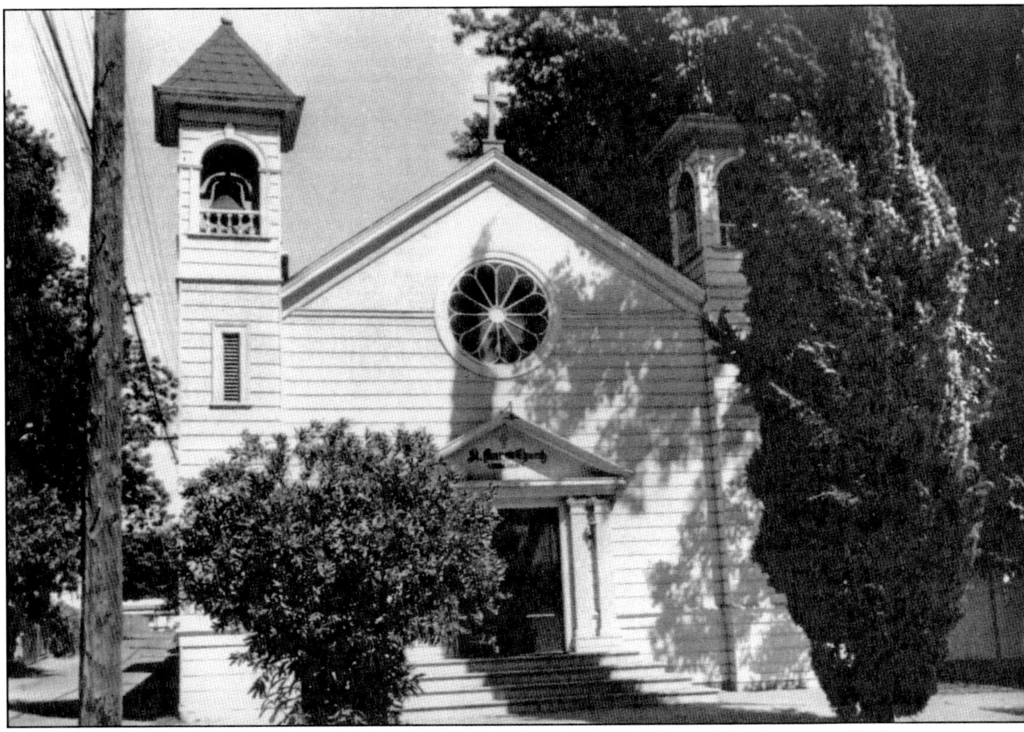

Southside Park's Italian community was spread out along S and T Streets all the way out to Nineteenth Street, but most attended church at St. Mary's Church. Originally located at Eighth and N Streets, the church was moved to the corner of Seventh and T Streets in 1915. Fr. Silvio Masante, a priest at St. Mary's, had a weekly radio program on KROY. He served in the U.S. Army as a chaplain during World War II. (Italian Cultural Society.)

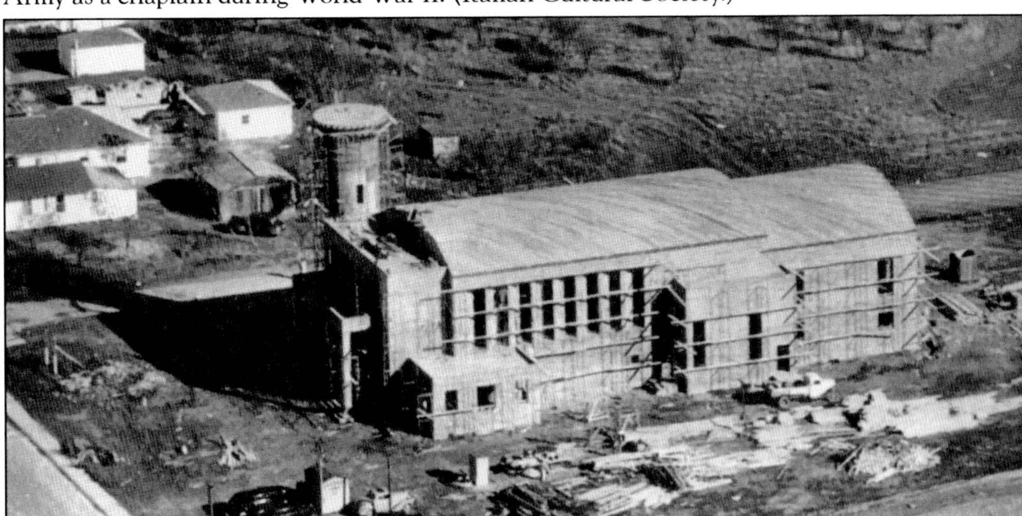

St. Mary's was a small church, and as early as the 1930s, many felt it should expand or relocate. The local Catholic diocese felt that there were enough churches in the central city, so the new location for St. Mary's was selected at Fifty-eighth and M Streets. This photograph shows the new church under construction. Once the church was completed, many parishioners moved to East Sacramento. (Italian Cultural Society.)

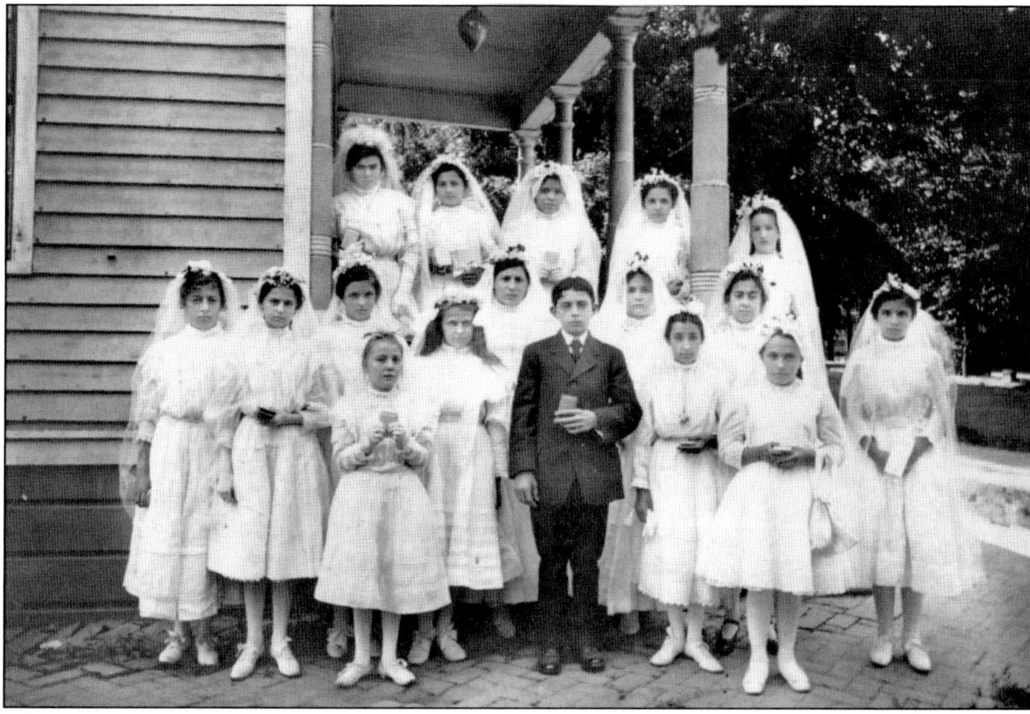

The original St. Mary's location was near Eighth and N Streets. This First Communion photograph was taken in 1909, six years before the move, outside the rectory. (Italian Cultural Society.)

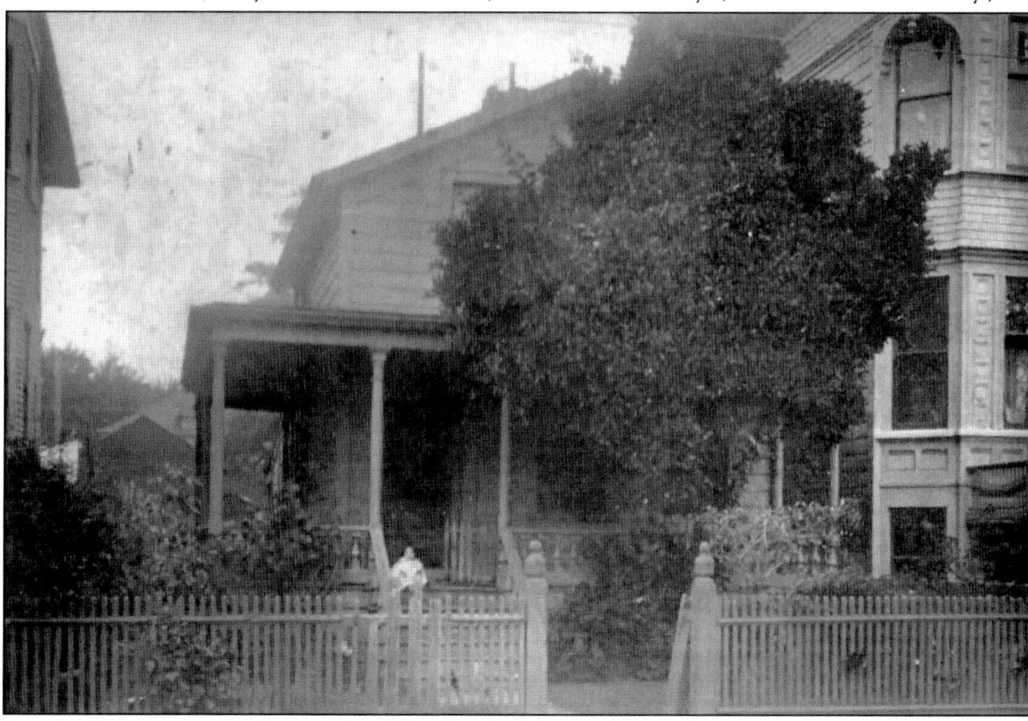

Rosalia Leoni sits on the porch of the house where she was born, at 1415 P Street. (Italian Cultural Society.)

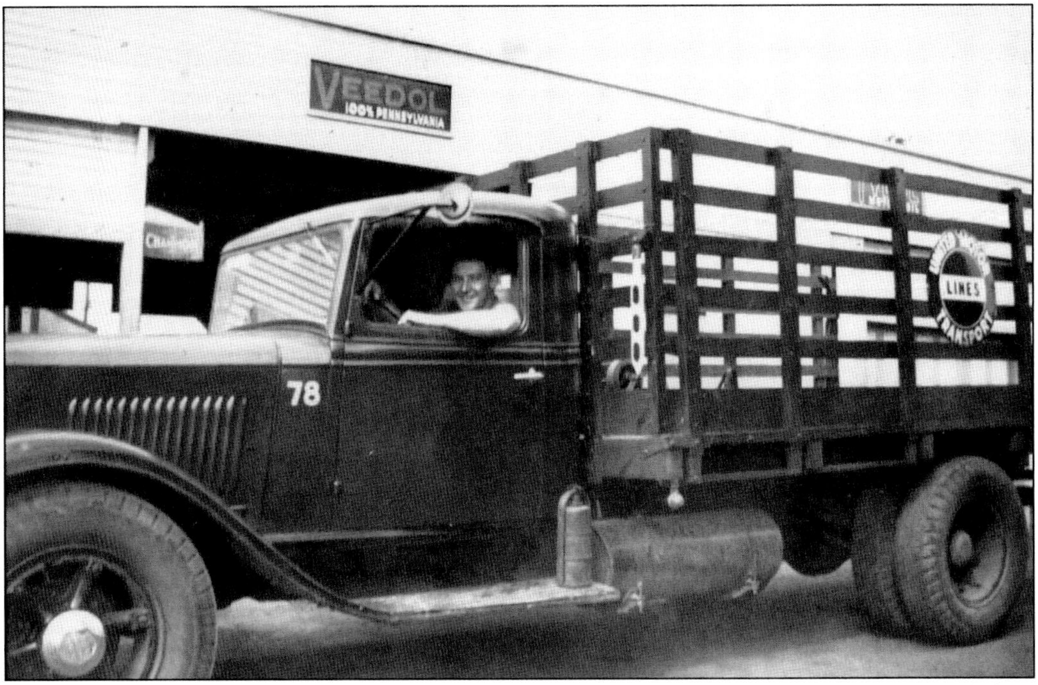

Ettore "Ed" Mores was born in Broderick, across the river in Yolo County, in 1915. His father, Angelo, immigrated to the United States from northern Italy, and his mother was born in the Italian-speaking portion of Switzerland. For much of his life, he drove trucks for a living. Here Ed is pictured in the truck he drove for United Motor Transport Lines. (Ed Mores collection.)

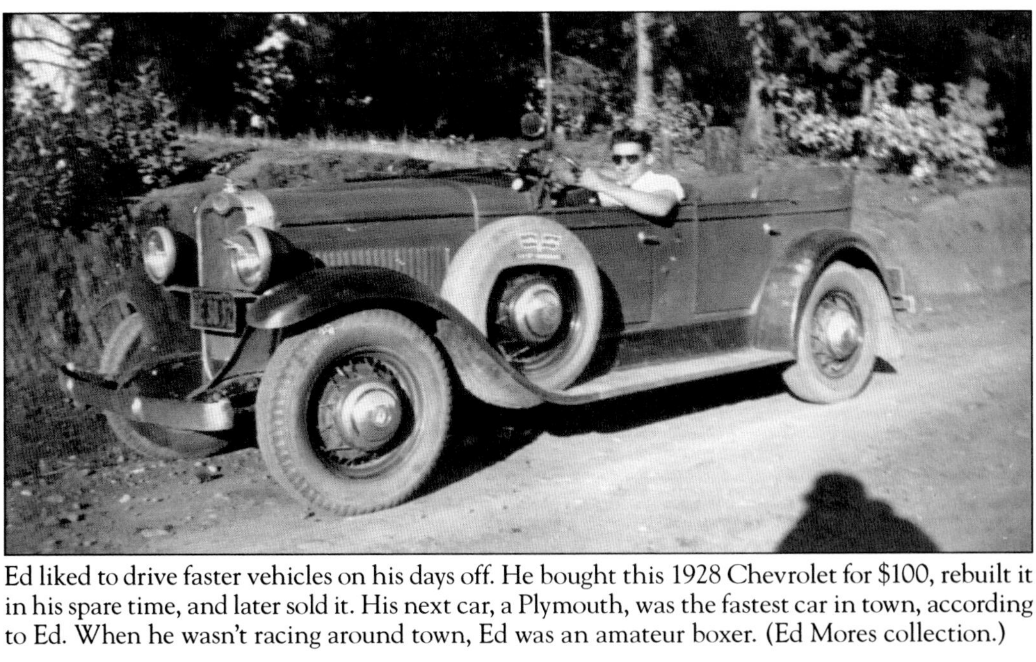

Ed liked to drive faster vehicles on his days off. He bought this 1928 Chevrolet for $100, rebuilt it in his spare time, and later sold it. His next car, a Plymouth, was the fastest car in town, according to Ed. When he wasn't racing around town, Ed was an amateur boxer. (Ed Mores collection.)

Four

Southside Park at Work

Southside was surrounded by industry. To the north, the Southern Pacific shops and yards belched fire and smoke. To the west, a row of warehouses hugged the river, serving riverboat traffic. To the south, an assortment of canneries, mills, and distribution centers hugged the city limits. At its heart, two sets of railroad tracks ran through the neighborhood.

Southern Pacific (formerly Central Pacific) was the dominant railroad in California for many decades, and Sacramento was its industrial heart on the West Coast. They operated the shops on the north end of town and maintained the original railroad route across the Sierra. The R Street line was essential to serving industries along that route.

Western Pacific, the last transcontinental railroad, ran their main line through Sacramento between Nineteenth and Twentieth Street. They also served the industrial corridor, which ran along Whitney Avenue between Q and R Streets.

Sacramento Northern, an electric railroad, operated a belt line that ran around the edge of Sacramento's original city limits. Beginning at the M Street Bridge, the tracks ran down Front Street and turned east on X Street. This line was shared with Central California Traction, an electric railroad that ran from Stockton to Sacramento. At the corner of X and Alhambra, the Sacramento Northern line turned north up Alhambra Boulevard to C Street, while Central California Traction went south through Oak Park. Both lines carried freight. Sacramento Northern also operated a passenger route through downtown Sacramento, but the city did not want freight cars operating through the middle of downtown.

It was almost a truism in Southside that everyone worked for either the Southern Pacific or at a cannery. While these were the largest employers, there were many other industries in Sacramento. Icehouses, bakeries, dairy distributors, general merchandise warehouses, and grain mills were found throughout the city. Local breweries and wineries quenched Sacramentans' thirst. Truck terminals picked up produce from remote farms, performed local deliveries, and eventually took over much of the railroads' freight service. And for every job, there was a Southsider who needed work.

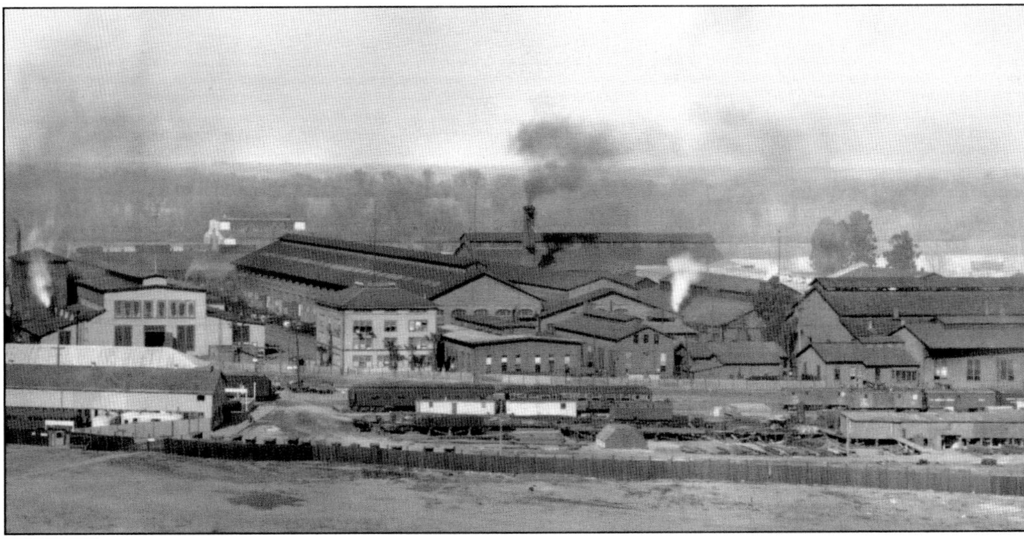

The Southern Pacific locomotive works was a massive complex that produced everything from entire locomotives to electroplated silverware and interior woodwork. On the left are the boiler shop and erecting hall. Between them is the transfer table, where locomotives could be shuttled between the shops' bays. Behind these buildings, the roundhouse is visible. To the right are the planing mill, blacksmith shop, hammer shop, and other specialty shops. (Western Railway Museum Archive.)

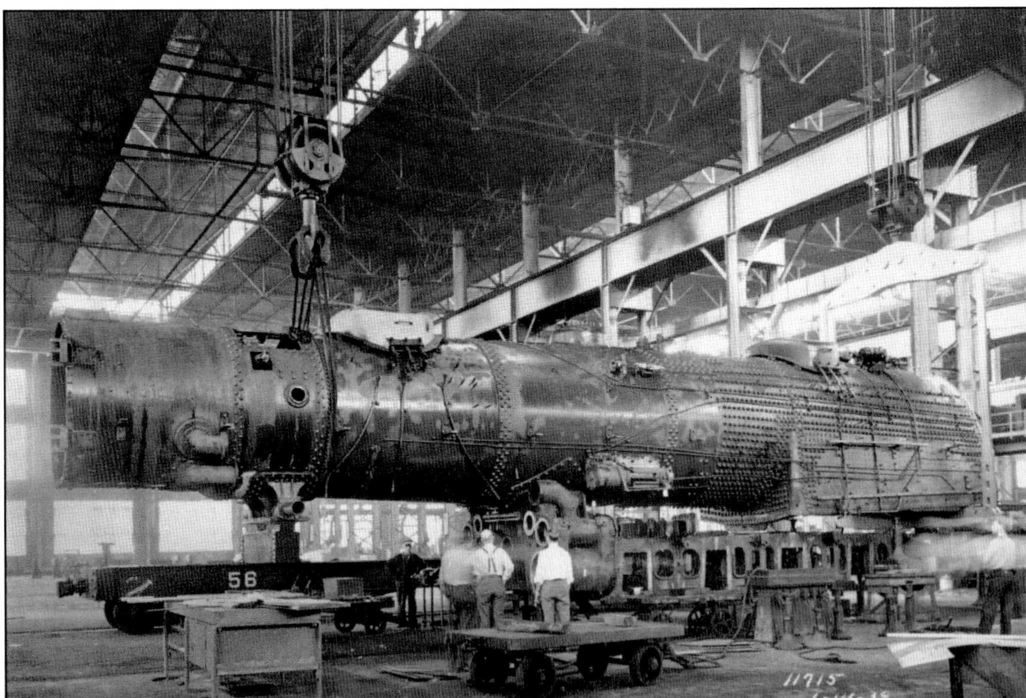

In the boiler shop, boilermakers used heavy equipment like banding rolls, shears, and riveting machines to construct and repair boilers, tenders, smokestacks, and tanks. The shops grew over time, constructing and rebuilding new structures as the railroad expanded and technology changed. (Western Railway Museum Archive.)

The erecting shop was the nucleus of the shops, where the products of other shops' manufacturing processes were assembled into steam locomotives. The Sacramento Locomotive Works was the only shop west of the Rocky Mountains where full-sized locomotives were built from the ground up. (Western Railway Museum Archive.)

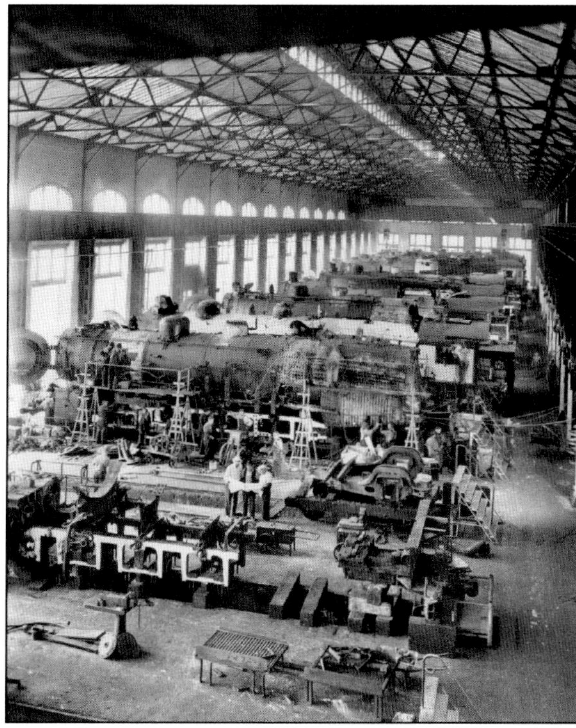

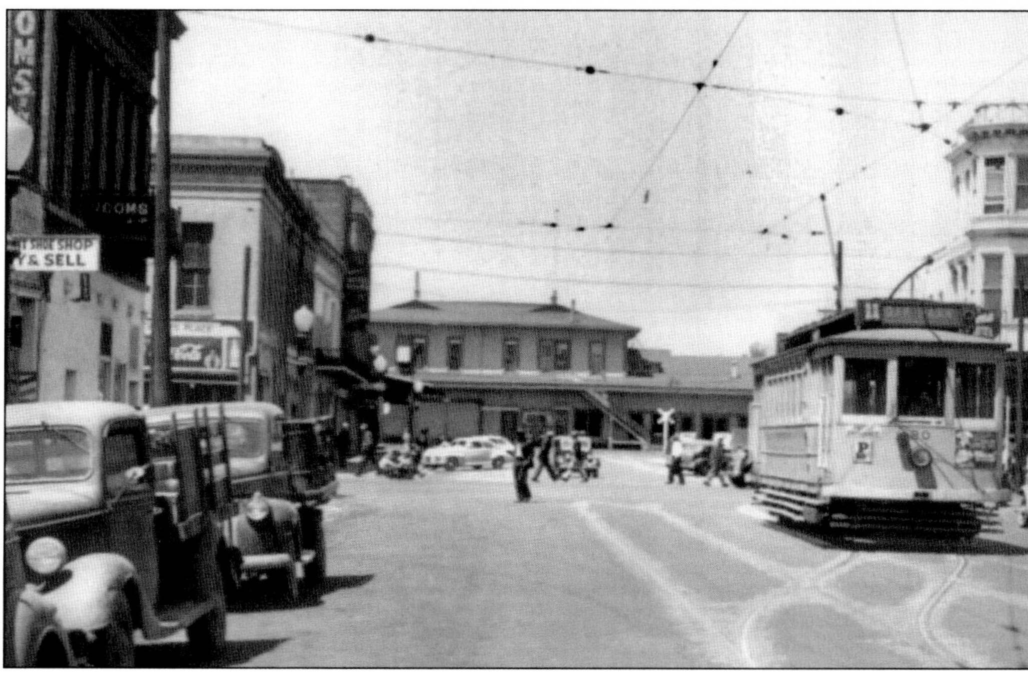

In addition to the manual labor of the shops, the Southern Pacific needed an endless flow of paperwork to keep its complex operation running smoothly. Manny J. Viera Jr., grandson of Manuel S. Vierra of the Arizona Gang, worked in the freight office (visible in the background). His father and grandfather worked in the hammer shop, but young Manny was good with numbers and worked as a waybill clerk. (Western Railway Museum Archive.)

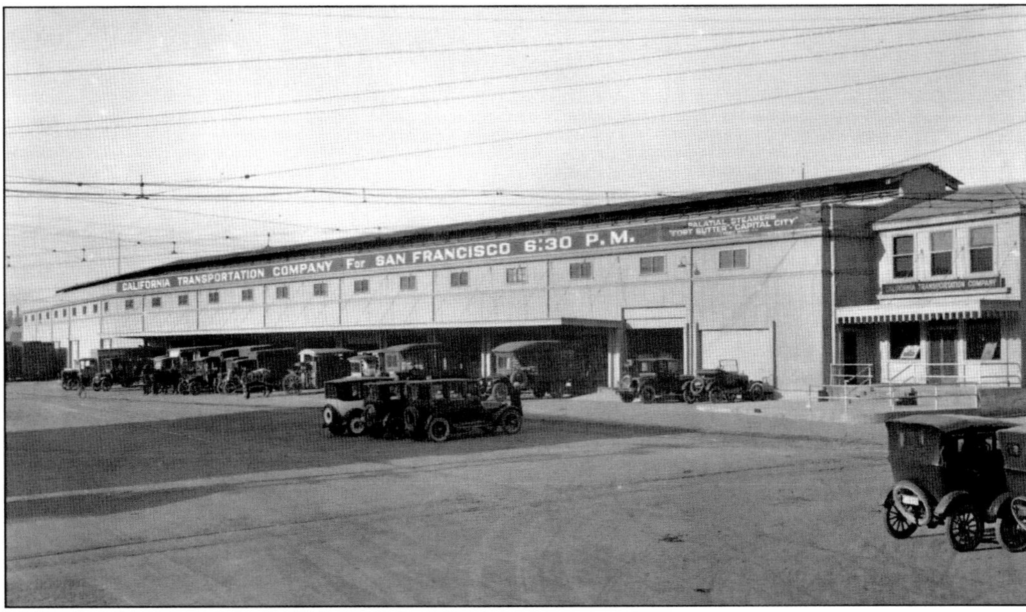

The California Transportation Company warehouses along Front Street transferred freight between railroads, riverboats, and trucks. Southern Pacific and Sacramento Northern locomotives shuffled freight cars here, just south of M Street. Switching moves along Front Street often blocked the M Street bridge. Because that bridge was the main highway out of town to the west, switching often resulted in traffic snarls. (Western Railway Museum Archive.)

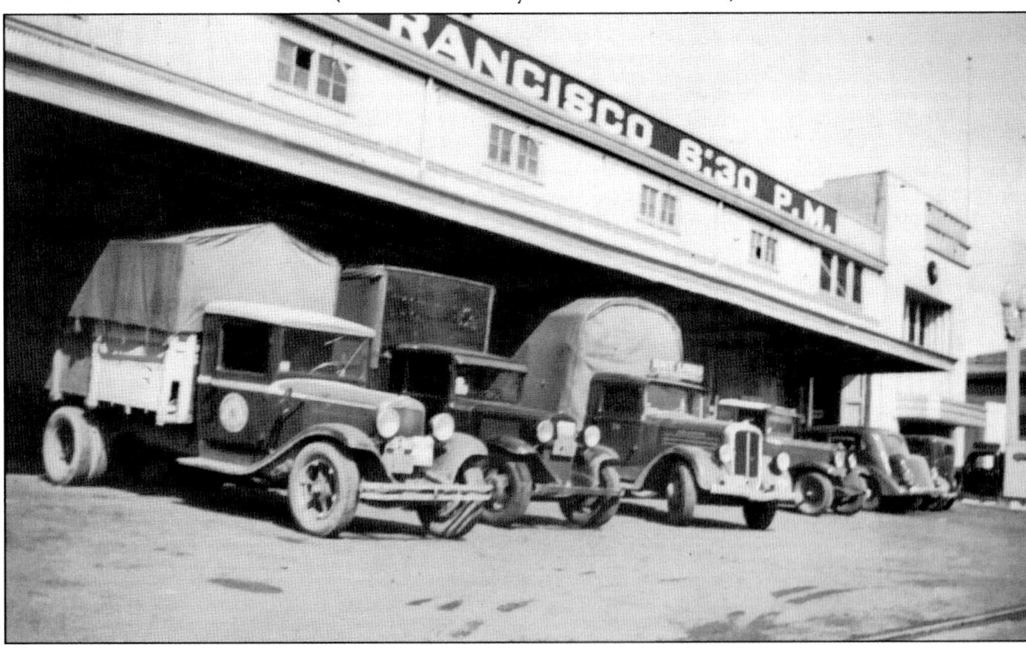

Trucking firms like United Motor Transport scheduled their produce runs to arrive at the riverside in time to meet boats heading downstream to markets in San Francisco. Ed Mores drove his produce truck to regional farms in Rocklin, Roseville, Auburn, and Newcastle. He had to be back at the river depot by 6:00 p.m. to meet the riverboat that shipped the produce to the Bay Area, which left at 6:30 every day. (Ed Mores collection.)

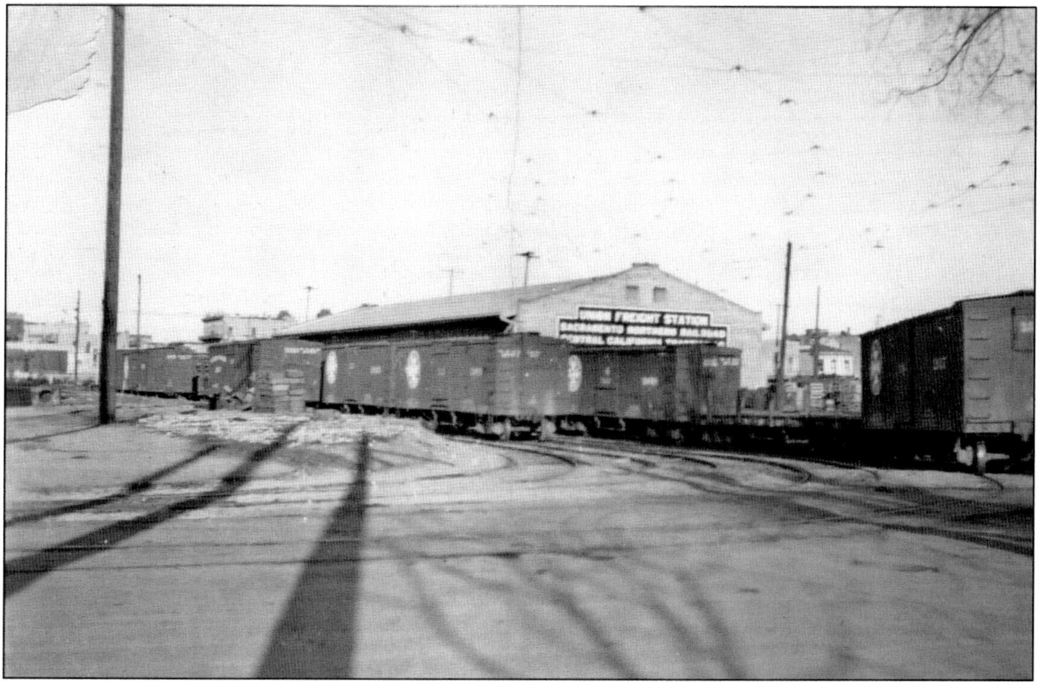

Sacramento Northern (SN) and Central California Traction shared a freight depot and office on Second and N Streets, at the southern end of their industrial belt line. Sacramento was the middle of the SN system, which ran from Oakland to Chico through the central valley. SN was an electric railroad, and the wires delivering power for trains are visible above the yard tracks in this photograph. (Western Railway Museum Archive.)

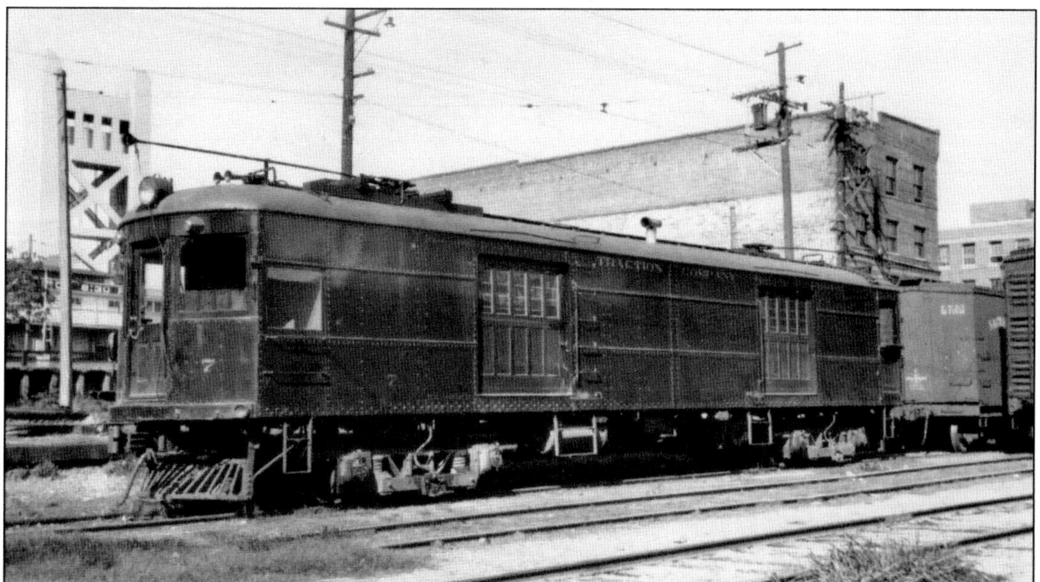

Central California Traction (CCT) was also an electric railroad, and it ran from Sacramento to Stockton. This electric freight motor could pull railroad cars, but its interior could also be used to haul freight. In the background, part of the Tower Bridge, built in 1935, is visible. Trains ran over the Tower Bridge on their way south to Oakland. (Western Railway Museum Archive.)

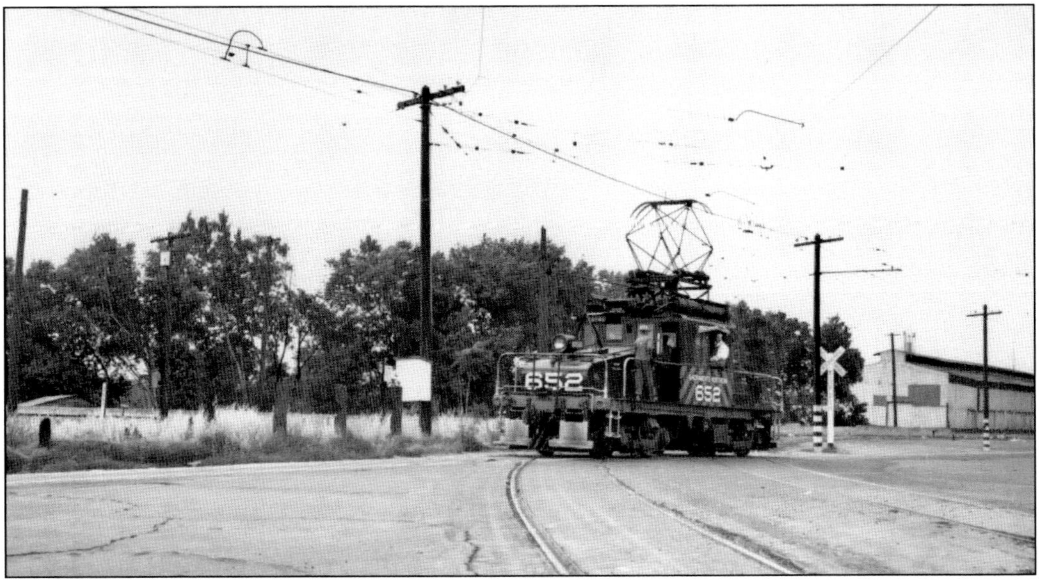

A maze of track was found at Front and R Streets. Sacramento Northern ran straight down Front Street. Both Western Pacific and Southern Pacific turned east here, to serve industries on R Street. Southern Pacific's Walnut Grove branch ran in the background, following the river into the delta. A Sacramento Northern freight motor runs through the middle of this scene. (Western Railway Museum Archive.)

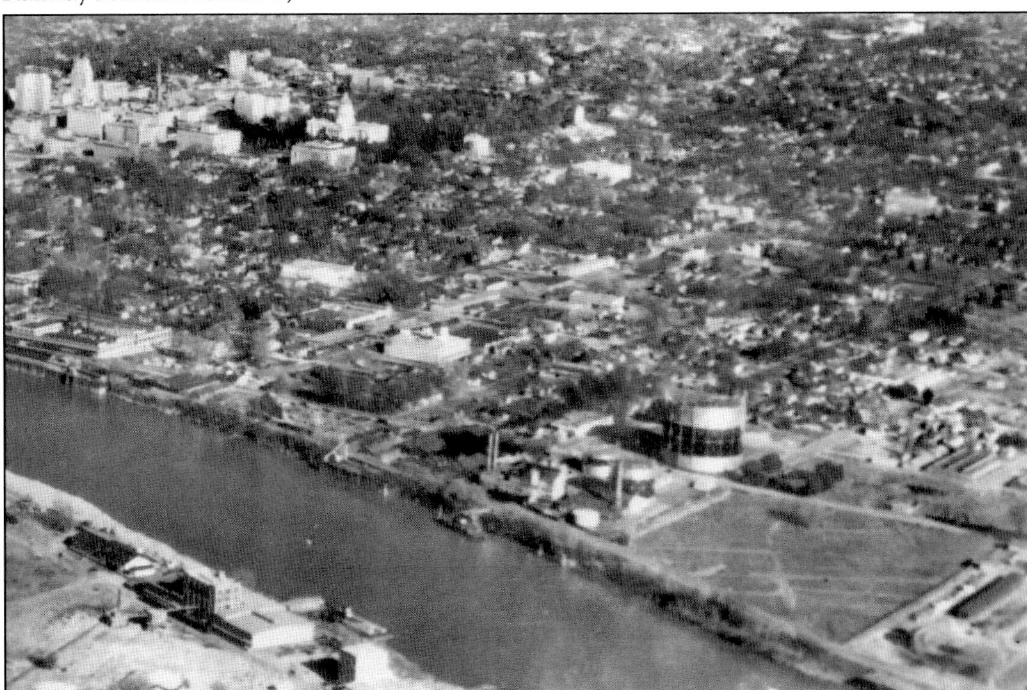

This aerial photograph shows much of Southside Park's industrial district along Front and R Streets. The Del Monte cannery, far left, was the workplace of many Southsiders. To the right of the cannery is the Lincoln School. The tanks on the lower right are the Pacific Gas and Electric gas plant on Front Street. (USC Archives.)

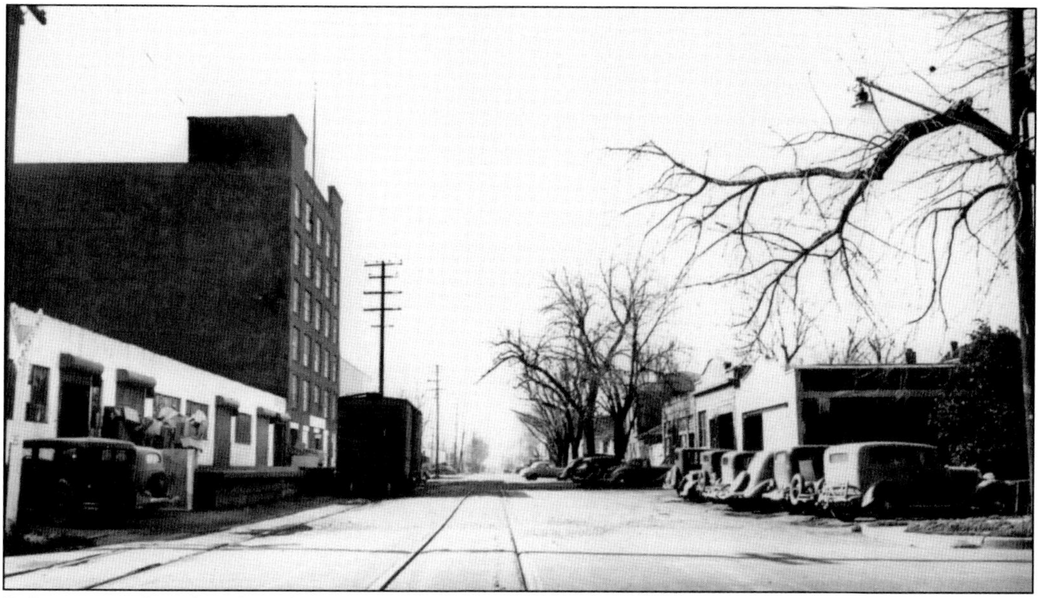

R Street was lined with industries all the way through the center of town, with frequent railroad spurs and loading docks. At the corner of Eleventh and R, industrial buildings of various sizes are visible. On the left is a large warehouse originally built to store automobiles. On the right is an electrical components distributor. Once R Street was paved, trucks competed with railroads for freight traffic and rights-of-way. (Sacramento Archives and Museum Collection Center.)

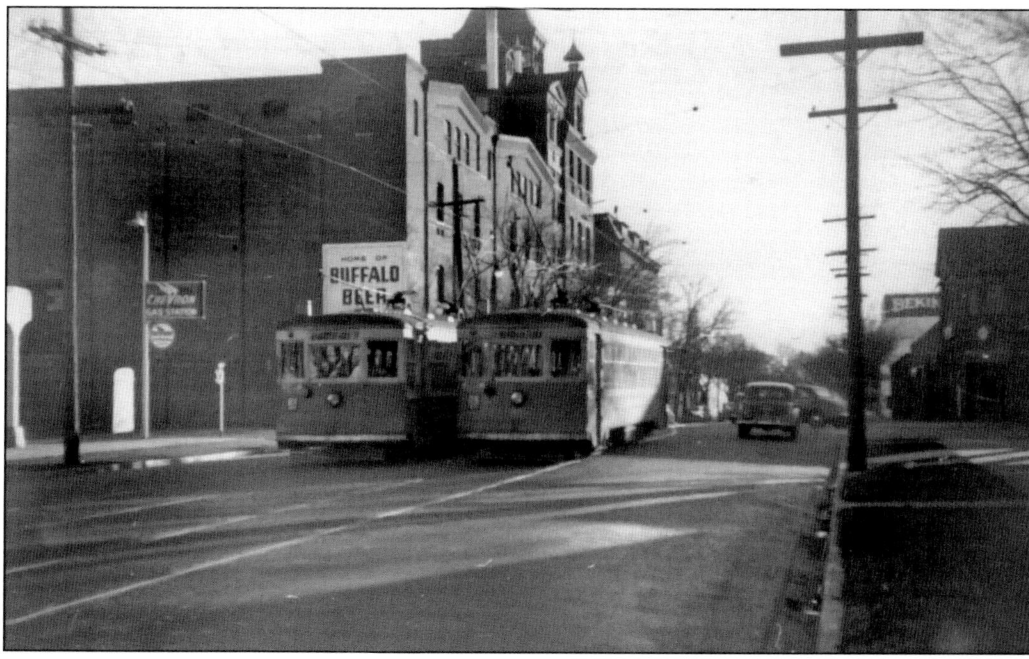

The Buffalo Brewery, established in 1890, was a two-block complex located between Twenty-first and Twenty-third Streets along R Street. They produced the popular Buffalo, Gilt Edge, and Ruhstaller beers and were served by three railroad spurs on R Street. As this photograph shows, they were also conveniently close to the Twenty-first Street streetcar line. (Western Railway Museum Archive.)

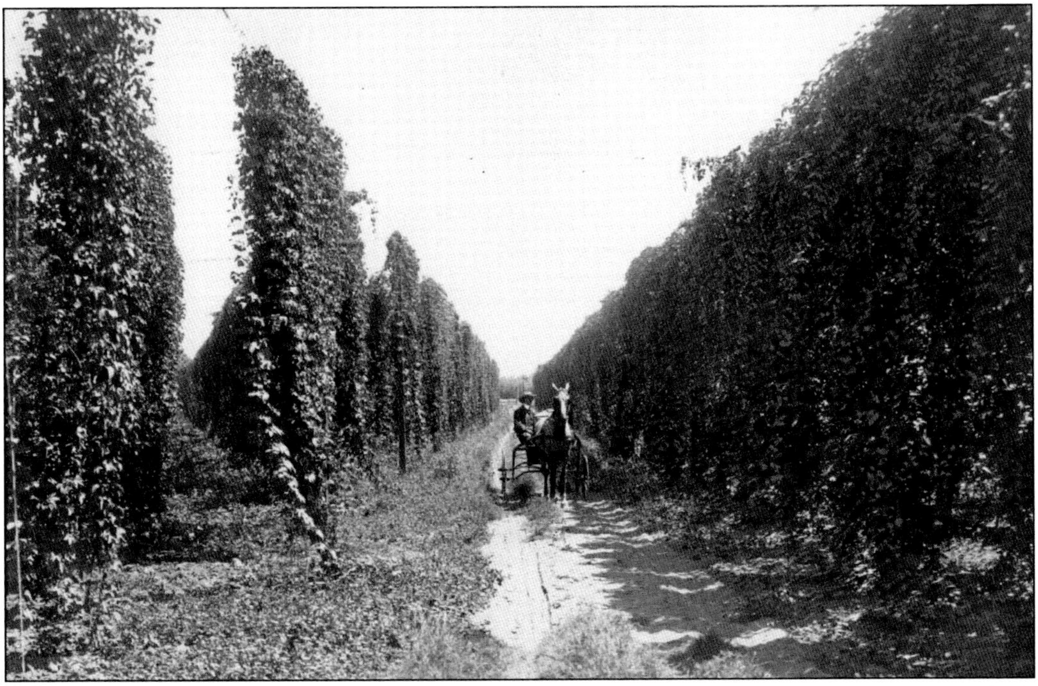

The many hops fields south of Sacramento were a testament to the city's thirst for beer, understandable given Sacramento's hot summer climate. Until the construction of neighborhoods like Riverside and Land Park, south of Southside was mostly hops fields. Hops were shipped in by rail along R Street, as were the grapes used in Sacramento's wineries. (USC Archives.)

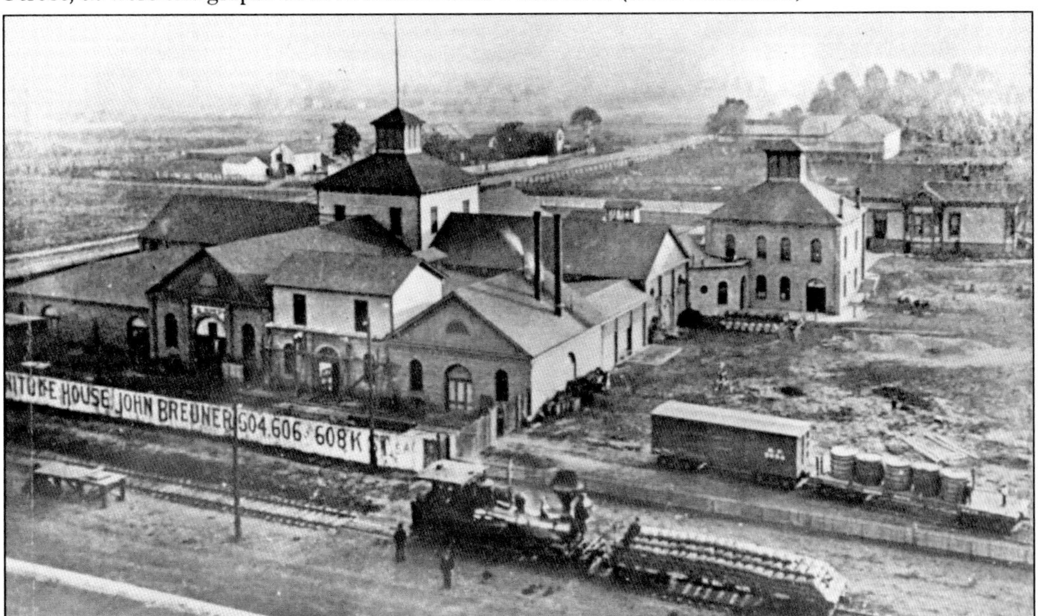

The California Winery was located on R Street between Twenty-first and Twenty-second Streets. The winery was owned by Manuel Nevis of Pico, an island of the Azores, who had also established two other wineries, the Eagle Winery at Eighteenth and P Streets and the Pioneer Winery at Twentieth and R Streets. (Portuguese Cultural and Historical Society.)

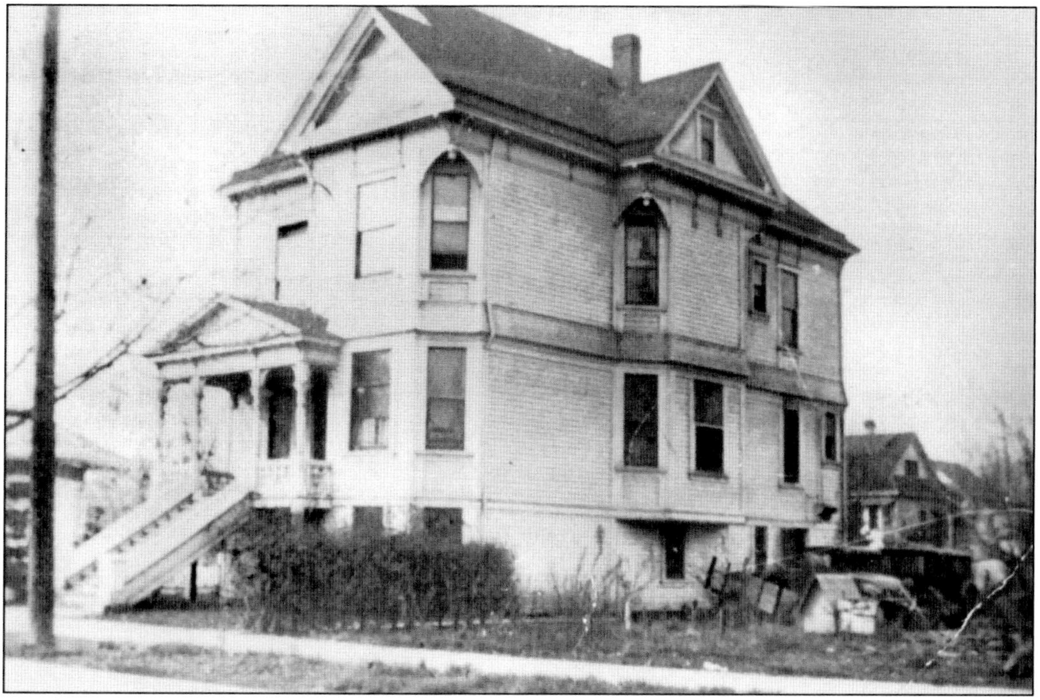

In addition to being a successful vintner, Manuel Nevis was also a master carpenter. He built his family's home at 1822 Twenty-first Street. The solid oak staircase was hand-carved with bunches of grapes around its newel posts. Manuel Nevis was found dead at his winery on September 20, 1907, overcome by fumes in a wine vat. (Portuguese Cultural and Historical Society.)

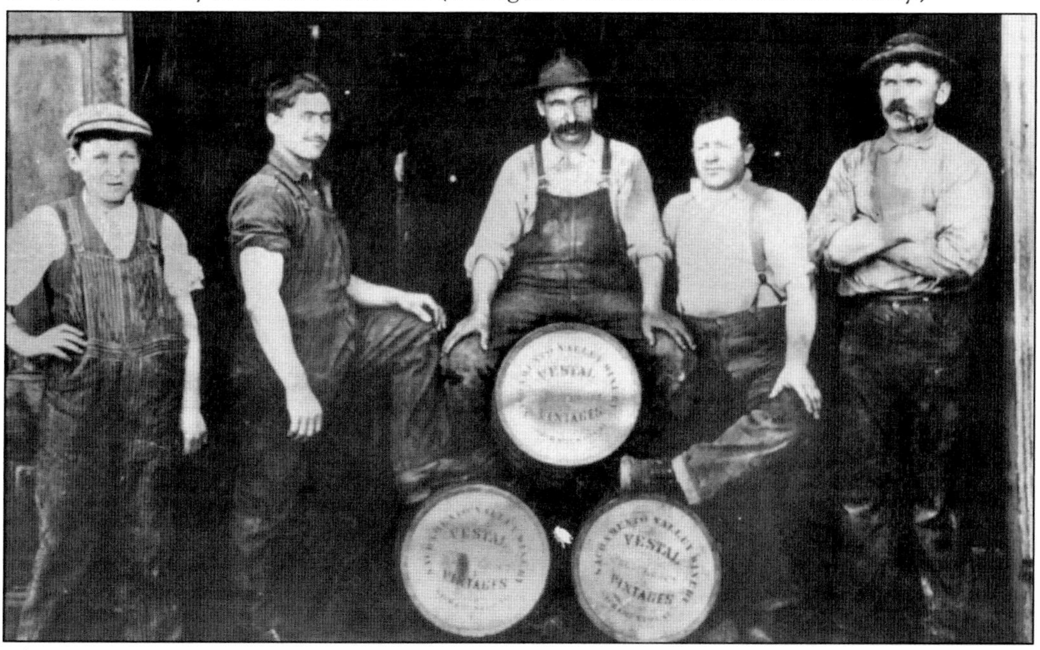

The Pioneer Winery was reopened as the Sacramento Valley Winery in 1911 under new ownership and operated until 1918. They produced wine under the name Vestal Vintages. Winemaker Vittorio Colombiani is second from the left in this photograph. (Italian Cultural Society.)

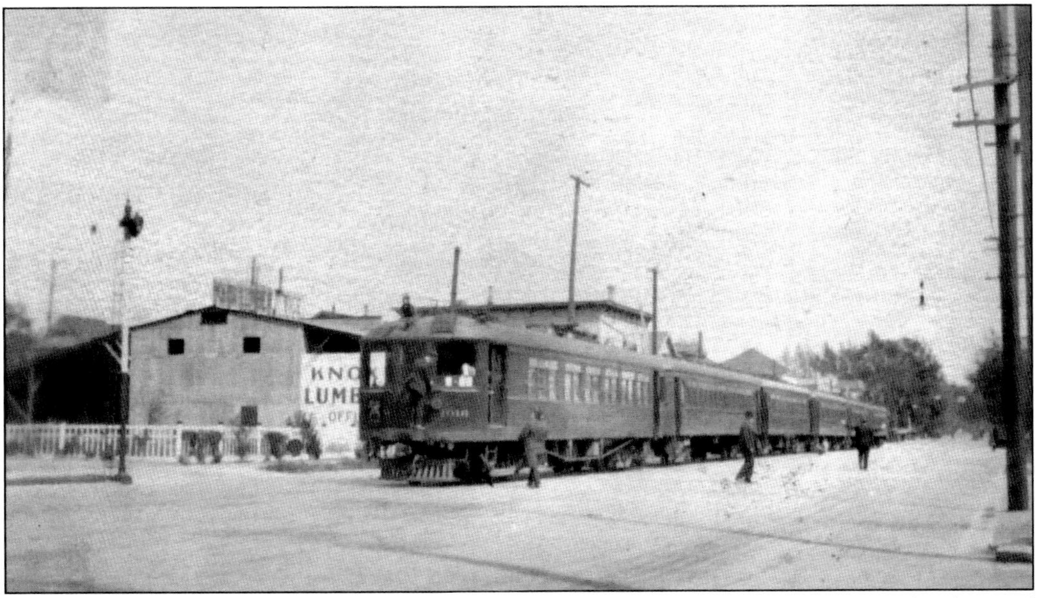

Several lumberyards were located on the southern end of Front Street. The Knox lumberyard occupied most of the block between Front and Second and S and T Streets. The passenger train in the foreground is unusual because normally Front Street was not used for passenger service. (Western Railway Museum Archive.)

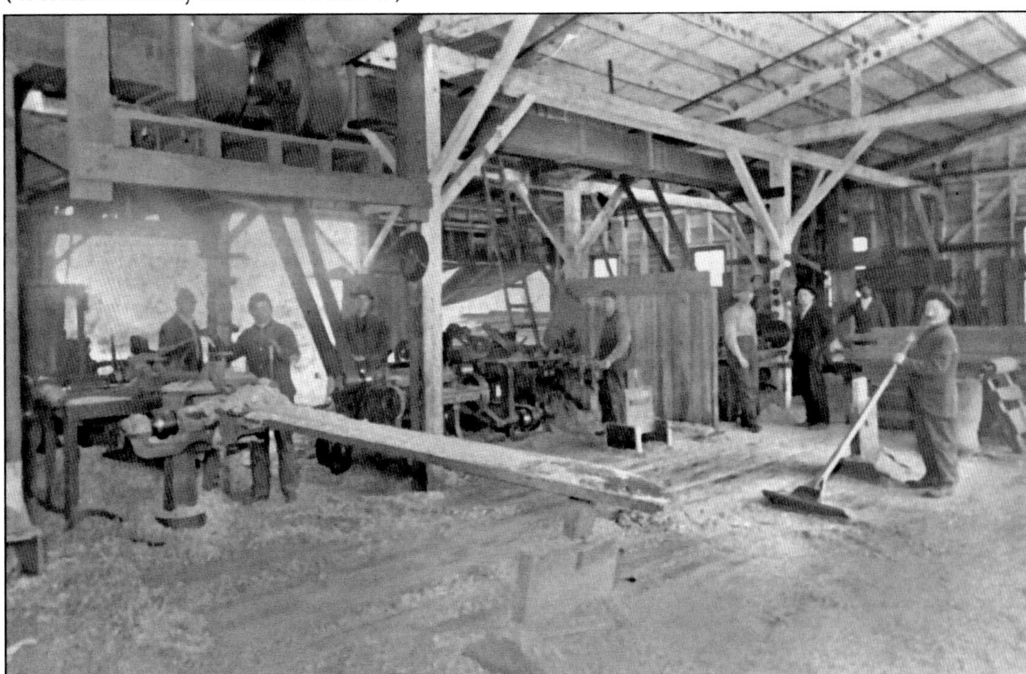

The Friend and Terry Lumber Company was located on a large lot on Front and V Streets. The power equipment in this photograph is belt-driven. All were attached to an overhead shaft connected to a steam power plant that drove all the tools at once. A grocery warehouse was later built on this site, and the Towe Auto Museum currently occupies the warehouse. (Portuguese Cultural and Historical Society.)

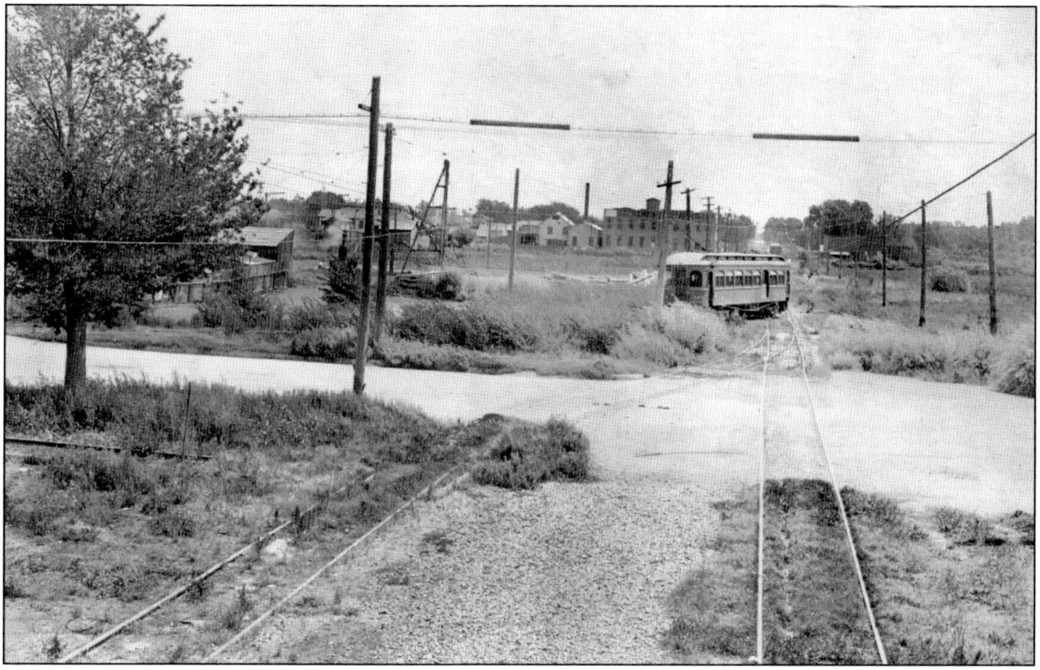

The SN belt line turned east at X Street, just north of the Y Street levee, which is visible to the right in this photograph. The interurban car on the tracks, again an oddity because of its location on the freight line, is probably an inspection car. The Sacramento Soap Company factory is visible in the background. (Western Railway Museum Archive.)

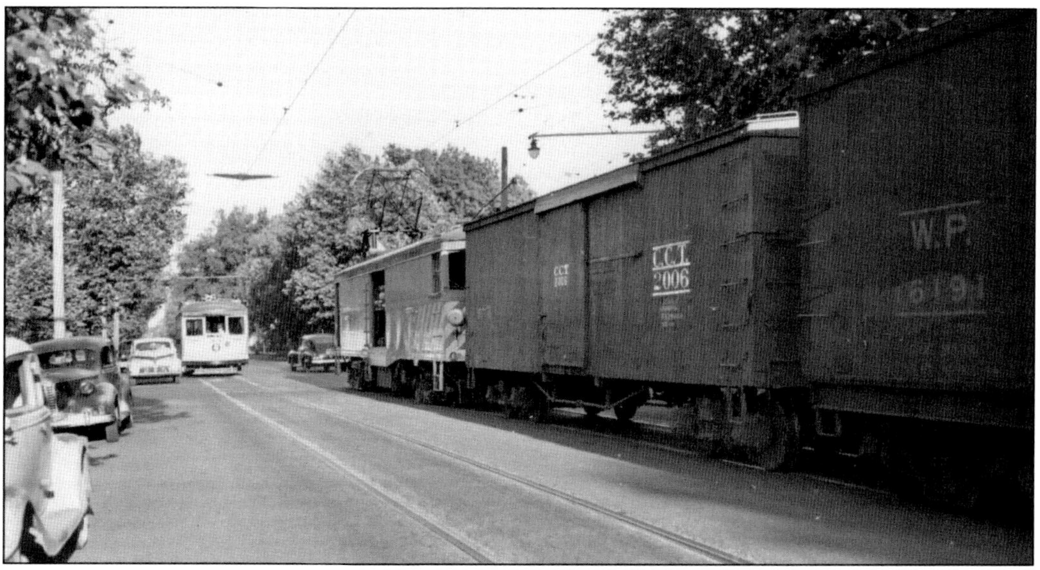

East of Eighth Street, the belt line joined Central California Traction's streetcar and interurban line. The line was double-tracked to allow trains to pass each other and avoid blocking the way of the streetcars. Here a CCT box motor passes a streetcar bound for downtown Sacramento. Motorists on X Street had to be careful to avoid freight trains that ran down the middle of the street. (Western Railway Museum Archive.)

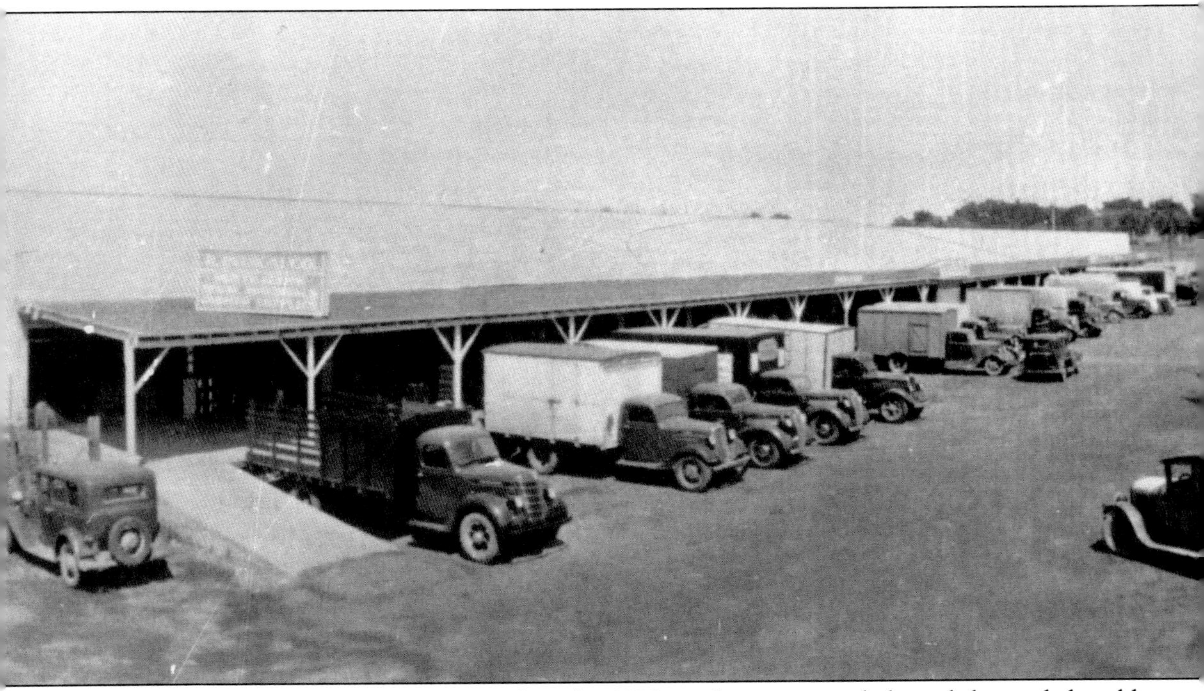

After the Y Street levee was removed in the 1920s, industry expanded south beyond the old city limits. The Sacramento Produce Market was organized in 1933 by almost 600 local farmers, mostly Japanese, Italian, and Chinese. Located on a large lot south of Broadway on Fifth Street, the Produce Market allowed farmers to sell directly from their trucks but eventually became a distribution and resale terminal. On the right side is the Market Club, founded by the Tomeida

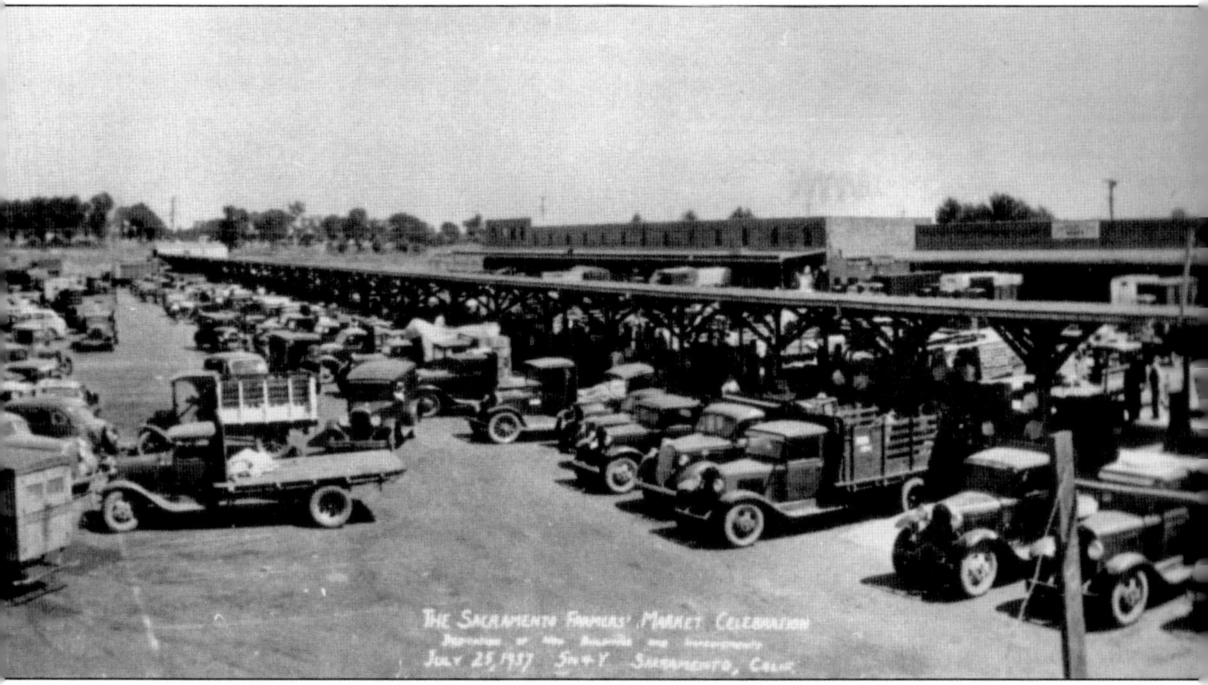

family. The Market Club provided an on-site restaurant for breakfast and lunch during the day and a bar and gambling hall in the evenings. Some of the shippers here include companies like Chick's Produce (owned by the Cecchettini family), Hoi Sum Egg, G&S Produce, and Pompei Produce. (G&S Produce.)

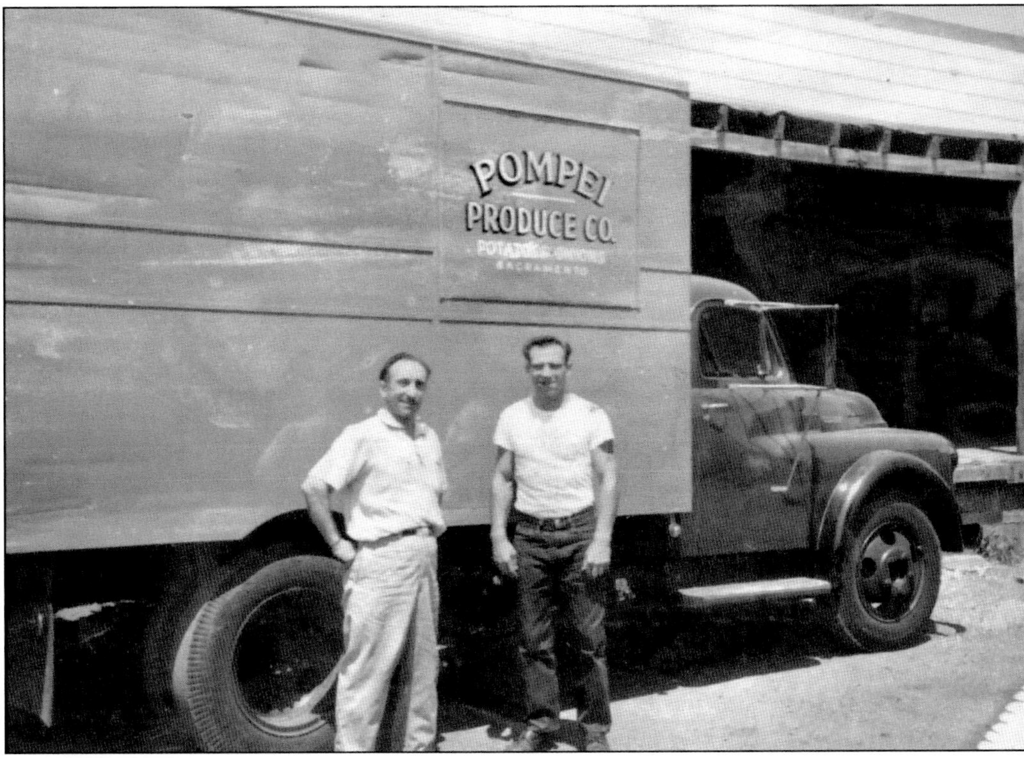

The Pompei family started their produce business in the market in 1955. Here Romeo Pompei Sr. (left) and Fred Pompei pose in front of the company delivery truck. Pompei specializes in onions and potatoes. (Pompei family collection.)

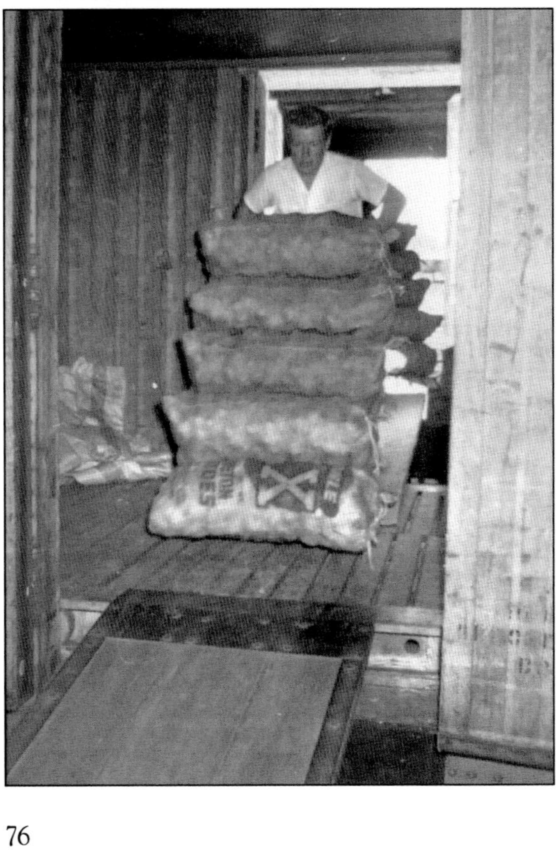

In addition to trucks, the Produce Market was also served by rail. Here Bill Pompei rolls five sacks of potatoes from refrigerated railroad cars into the warehouse. Note that there are two cars spotted next to each other on adjacent spurs, with boards used to transfer goods to the nearer car, then onto the warehouse loading dock. (Pompei family collection.)

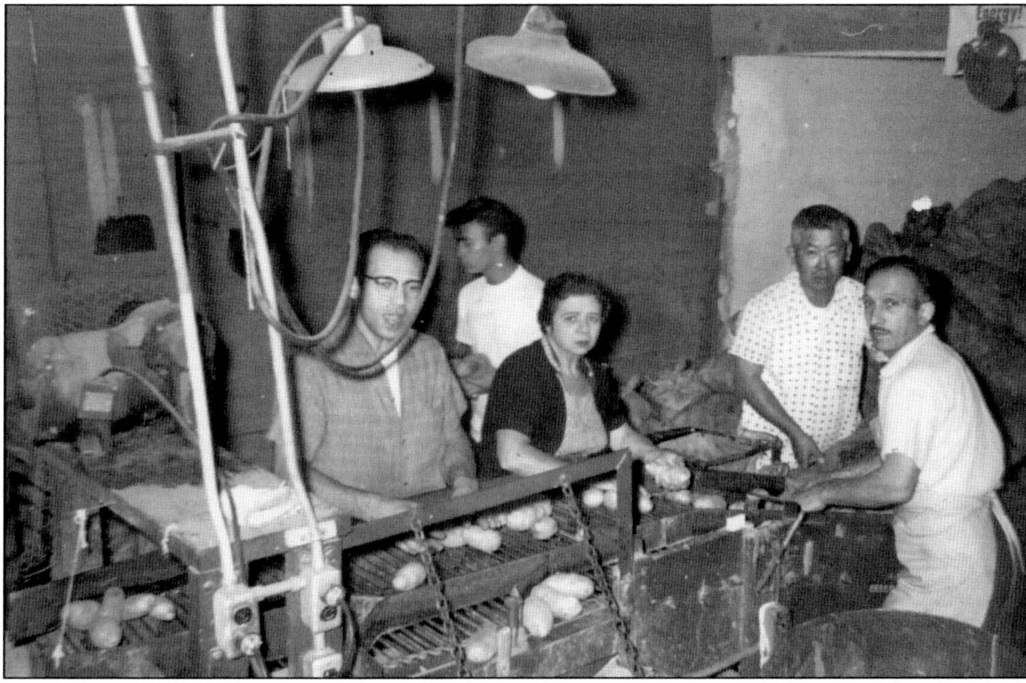

Pompei Produce is a family business, and often several generations work side by side. Here, from left to right, Fred Pompei, Sonny Pompei, Lara Pompei, "Pop" Otani, and Romeo Pompei Sr. sort potatoes. (Pompei family collection.)

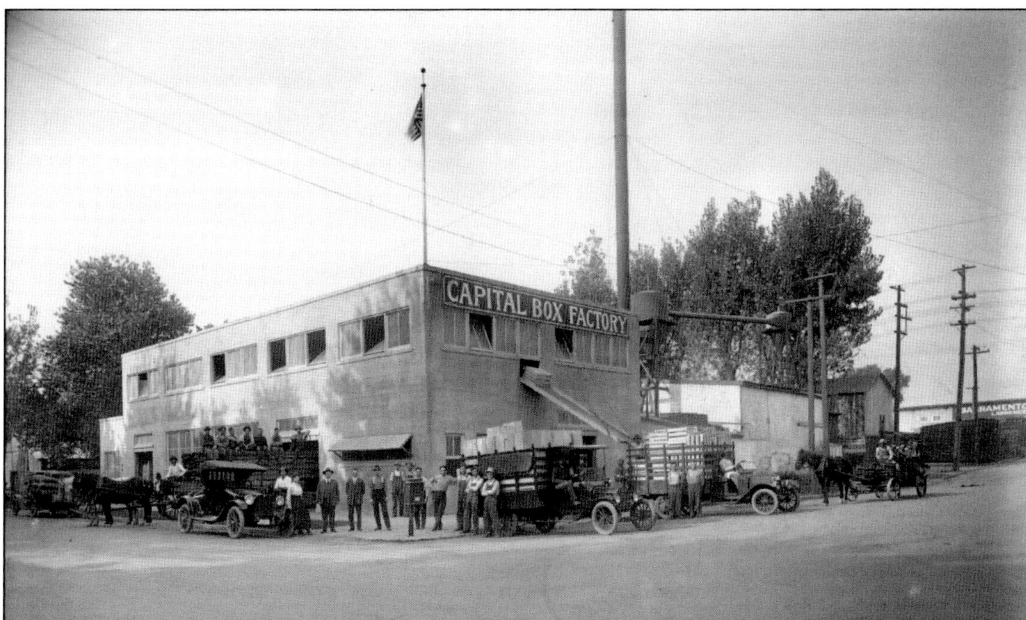

The Capital Box Factory on Second and Q Streets, like the earlier Pioneer Box Factory, specialized in making packing boxes for other businesses. Neighborhood kids would often scour alleys for scrap lumber, which could be sold to companies like Capital Box Factory. "If it's wood, it's good!" was the motto of Gene Plecas, who grew up in Southside. (California State Library.)

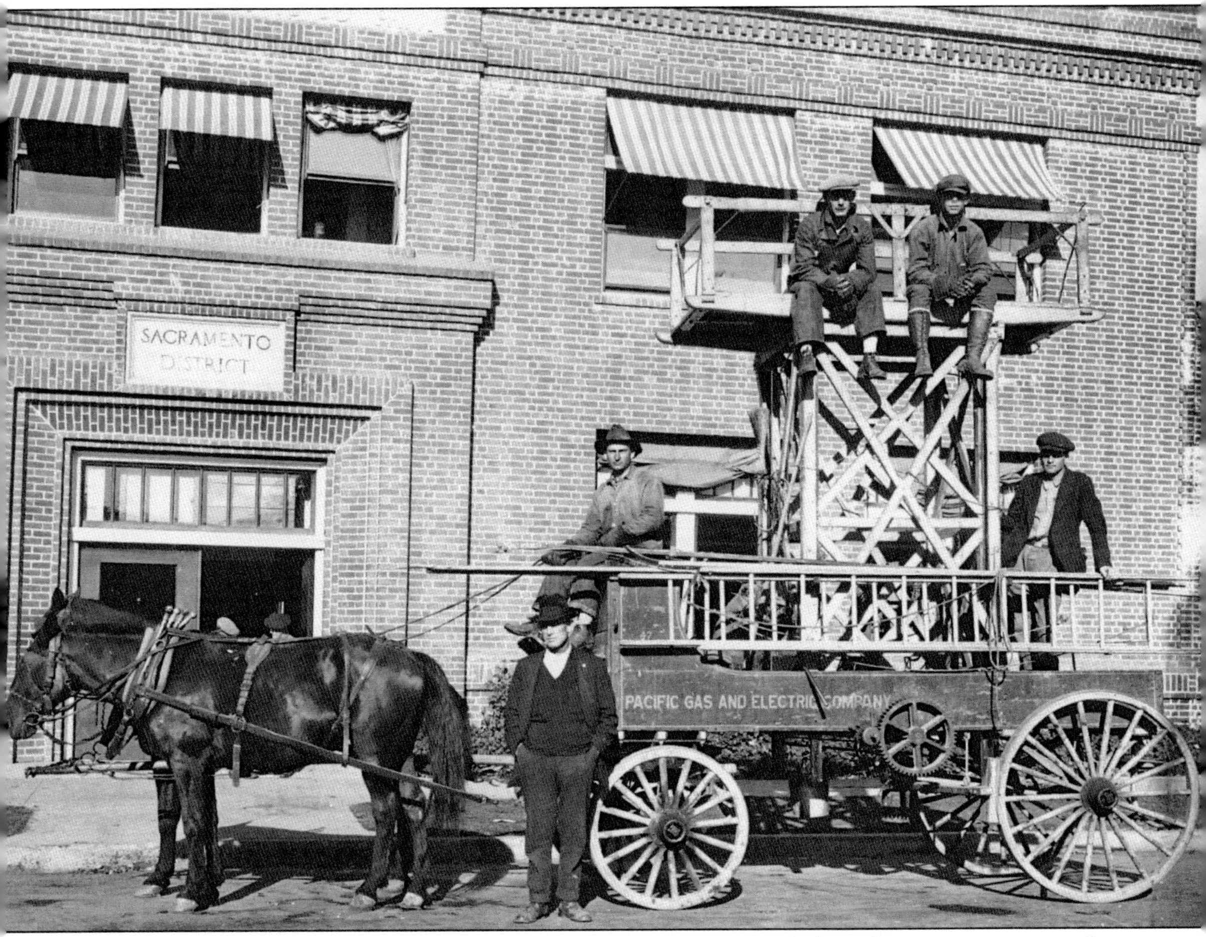

Pacific Gas and Electric had many facilities in Sacramento, including the extensive gasworks at Front and T Streets and a smaller facility at Eighth and S Streets. This horse-drawn line car was used to work on overhead power lines. (California State Library.)

Five

A Shop on Every Corner

Corner stores were everywhere in Southside Park. For a neighborhood with minimal public transportation and where few people owned automobiles, neighborhood stores were a necessity. Family-owned corner stores also provided employment for immigrant families, and many families lived in residential floors above the stores where they worked.

Corner grocery stores often catered to the ethnic communities where they were located. In addition to carrying products familiar to immigrant groups, the owners of a corner grocery were more likely to speak the language of immigrants in the same neighborhood. The corner store served a social function as well, as one might encounter anyone who lived in the neighborhood at the store. Specialty stores provided goods and services ranging from haircuts to mortuary services. Neighborhood bars served as social gathering places in the evenings, and bars that served food were often lunchtime destinations for working people.

For those who had to travel beyond the neighborhood's boundaries, Southside Park had several streetcar lines. Working people, always mindful of money, often chose to walk rather than ride, but streetcars gave them the ability to quickly get around town at a reasonable price.

As automobiles grew more commonplace in Southside Park, businesses to service them were needed, including automobile repair shops and gas stations. Like other Southside Park businesses, these were often family-run shops.

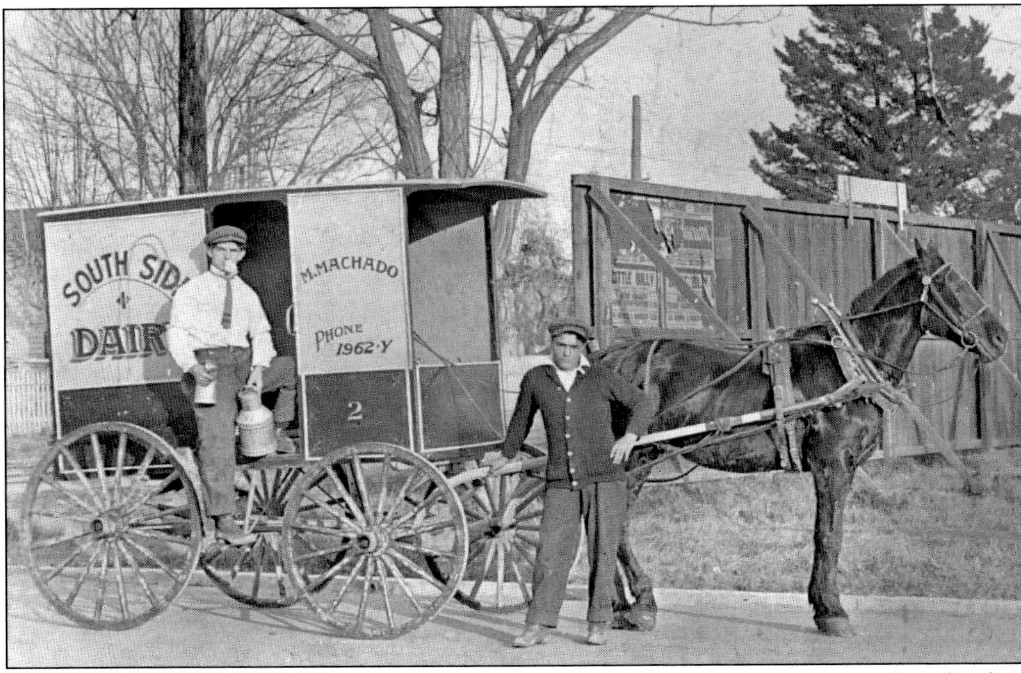

Manuel Machado was born on the island of Pico in the Azores in 1887. He purchased a dairy business on C Street and delivered milk throughout Southside in horse-drawn carts. Machado's Southside Dairy also employed Manuel Fonts Jr. (left) and Laurindo Silva (right). (Portuguese Cultural and Historical Society.)

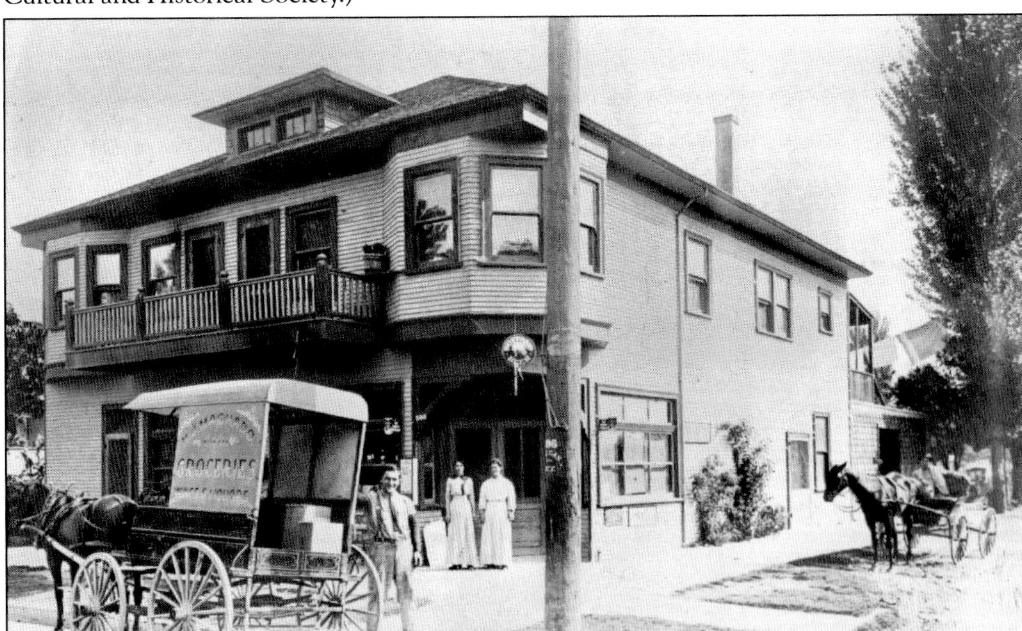

After marrying Elsie Garcia in 1913, Manuel purchased this store at 500 T Street. They later relocated the store, moving to 601 T Street in 1926. There was a bar in back of the relocated store that had earlier been a bicycle and automobile repair shop. (Portuguese Cultural and Historical Society.)

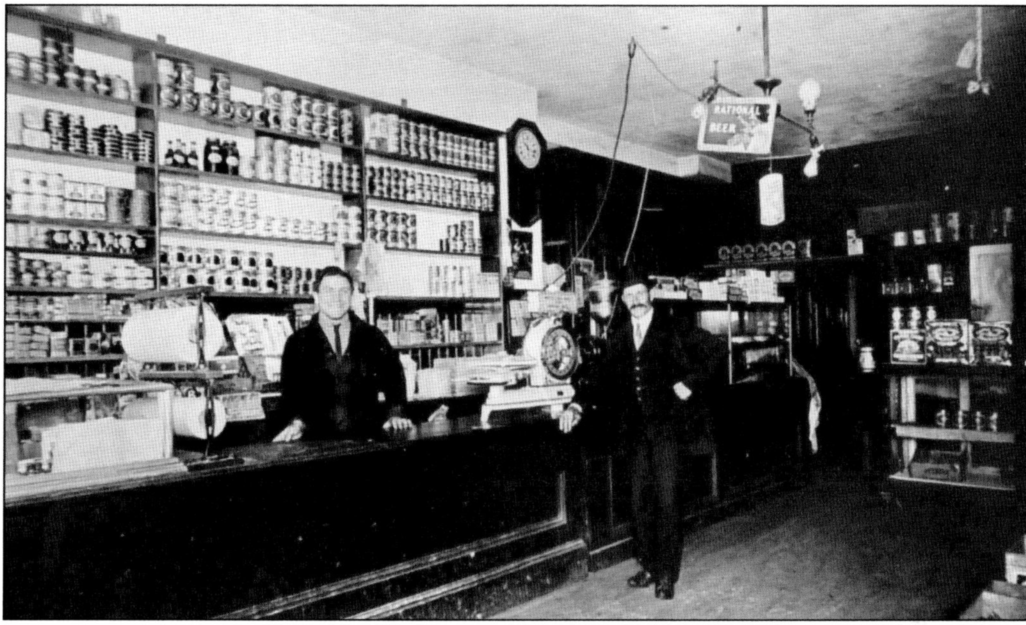

Machado's grocery store carried specialty items like linguica, dry codfish, and wine. For a while, the back room was the Southside Improvement Club's meeting room. The store at 601 T Street is still in use as a grocery store, although under different ownership. (Portuguese Cultural and Historical Society.)

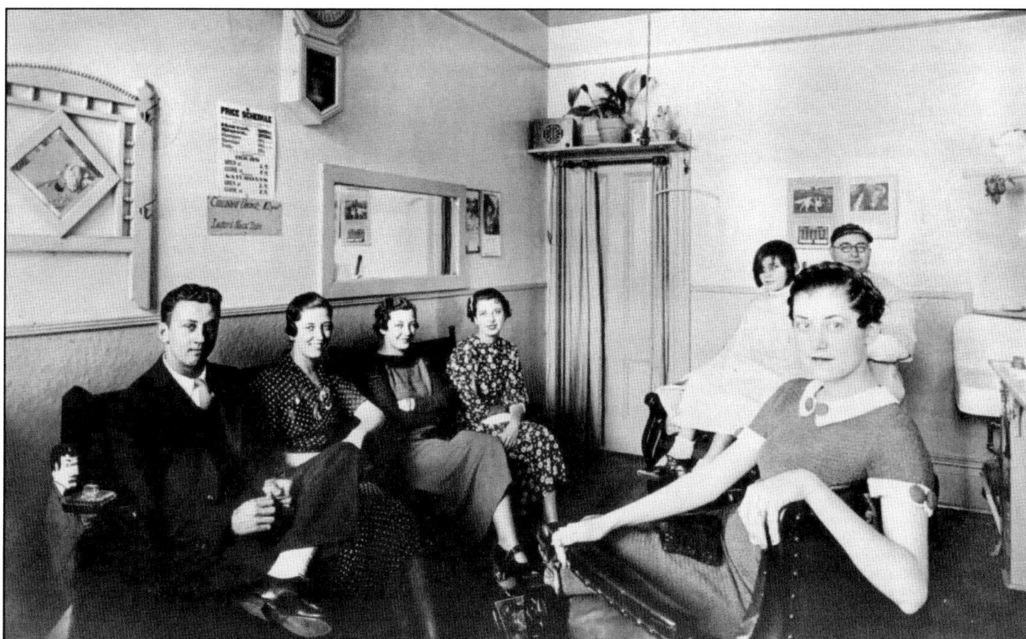

The A. F. Rose barbershop was located at 1624 Eleventh Street and was considered the most popular barbershop in town. It was rare to see women in a barbershop. Typically only men patronized them and women went to separate beauty parlors, but three of these women lived in the apartments upstairs. The barber, Tony Rose, is seated in back in this c. 1935 photograph. (Portuguese Cultural and Historical Society.)

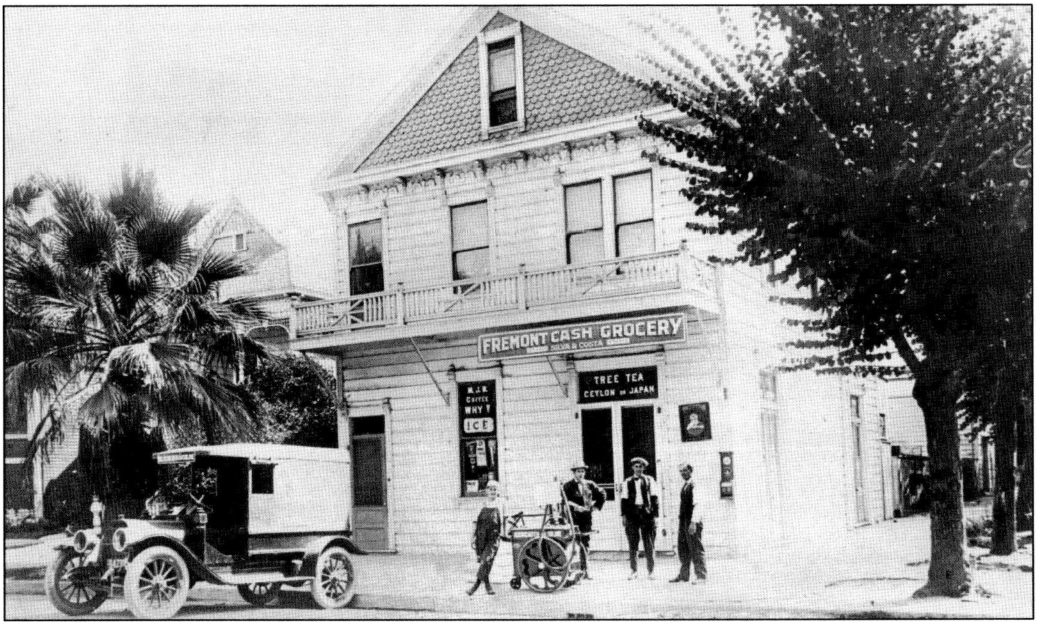

Manuel Enos came to the United States in 1872 and became a hops grower in Yolo County. He moved to Sacramento and started this grocery business at 1500 Q Street in 1894. He became involved in local politics, was very active in the Portuguese community, and helped found St. Elizabeth's Church. He was killed by a motorist in San Francisco in 1927. (Portuguese Cultural and Historical Society.)

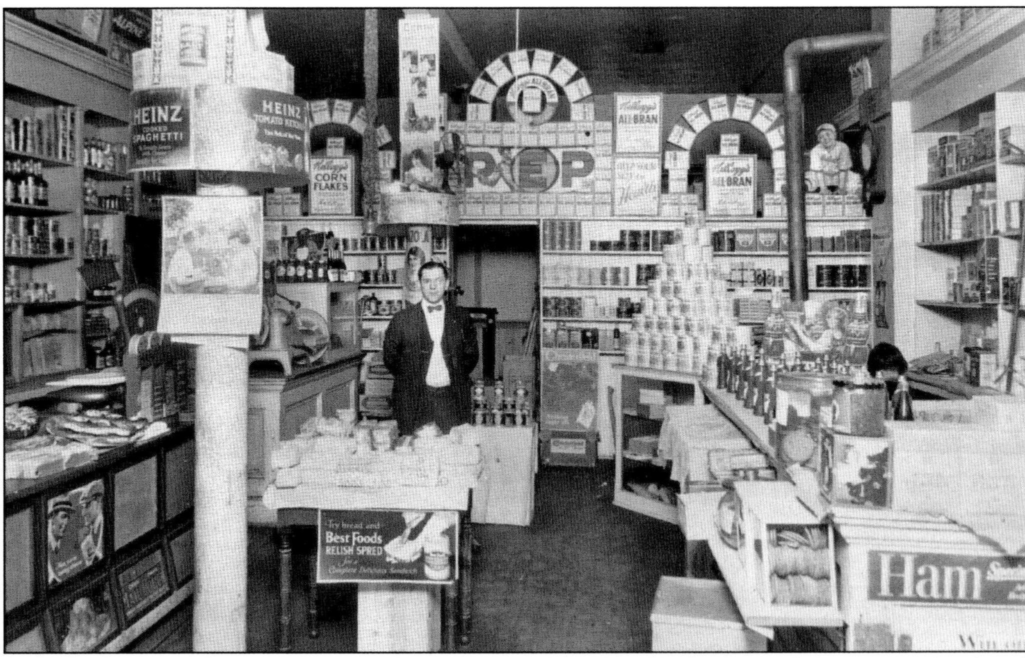

Manuel Enos' son Alfred took over the store at 1500 Q Street and was also very involved with civic affairs. He was president of the Southside Improvement Club in 1939 and helped organize Roaring Camp in Southside Park. The building was recently restored after a fire and currently houses a coffee shop. (Portuguese Cultural and Historical Society.)

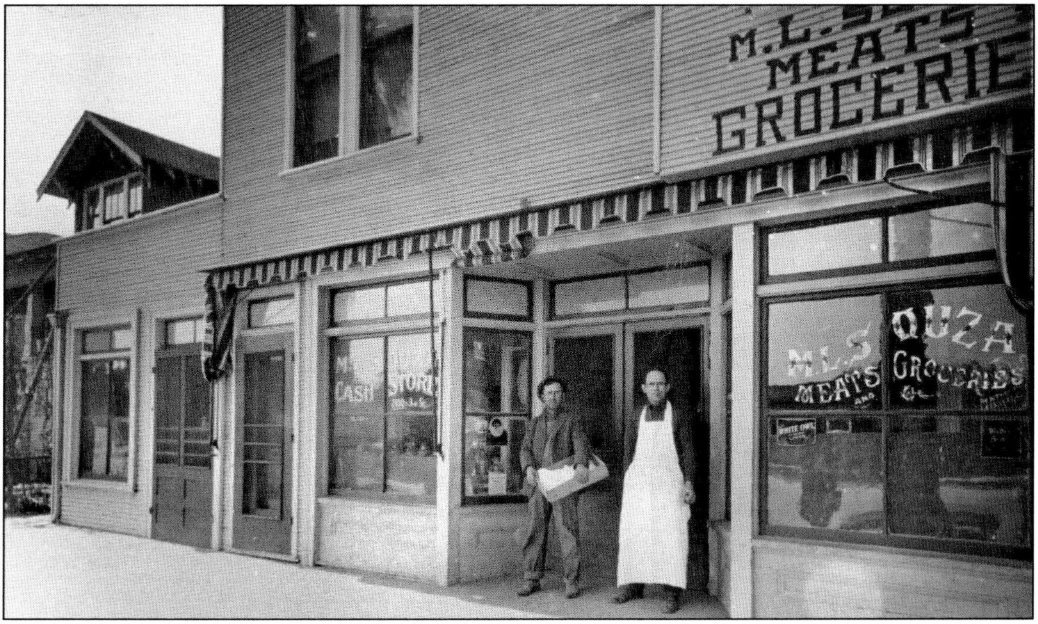

Manuel Leal Souza had a varied career after leaving the island of Pico, working as a farmhand, fisherman, and railroad worker. In 1915, he opened a grocery business on Third and U Streets. He relocated across the street to the southwestern corner in 1920, where the store remained until his death in 1932. Joaquim "Milhomes" Silva, selling cheese, and butcher Frank Terra, are standing in front of Souza's store. (Portuguese Cultural and Historical Society.)

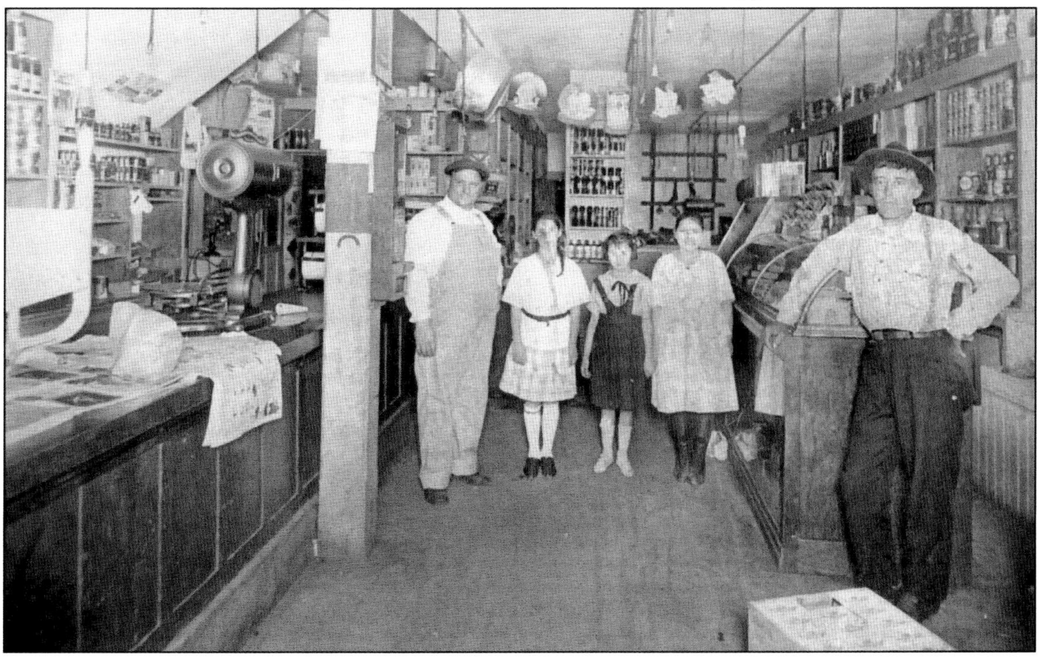

Inside the M. L. Souza Cash Store are, from left to right, Manuel Leal Souza, Anna Souza, Dora Bettencourt, Gloria Souza, and Manuel Machado. Manuel Souza took a wagon out at 3:00 every morning to collect fresh produce and meats for his store. The store also included a barbershop, operated by a man known as "São Miguel." (Portuguese Cultural and Historical Society.)

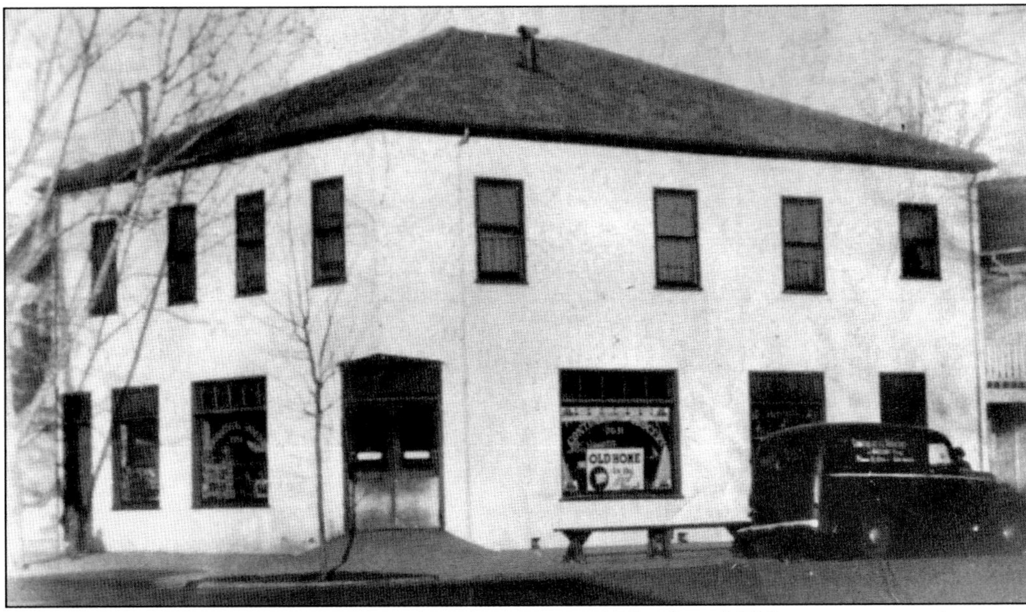

The Continental Grocery Store stood at the corner of Third and U Streets, across the street from Souza's store. It was established in 1912 by John Morais, who owned the store until 1929, when he relocated his grocery business to Walnut Grove. The "Continental" name indicated that the Morais family was from the mainland of Portugal, on the European continent. (Portuguese Cultural and Historical Society.)

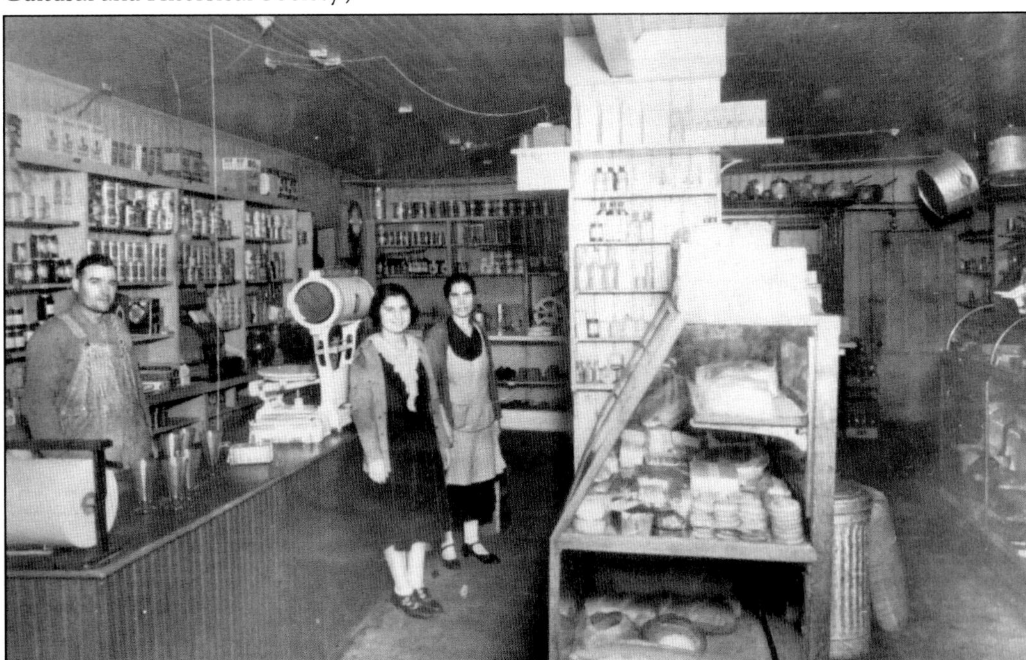

John Madeira bought the store in 1929 and renamed it with his family name. His family lived in the apartments above the store. In this 1930 photograph, John is on the left, his daughter Diolinda is in the middle, and his wife, Lucinda, is on the right. (Portuguese Cultural and Historical Society.)

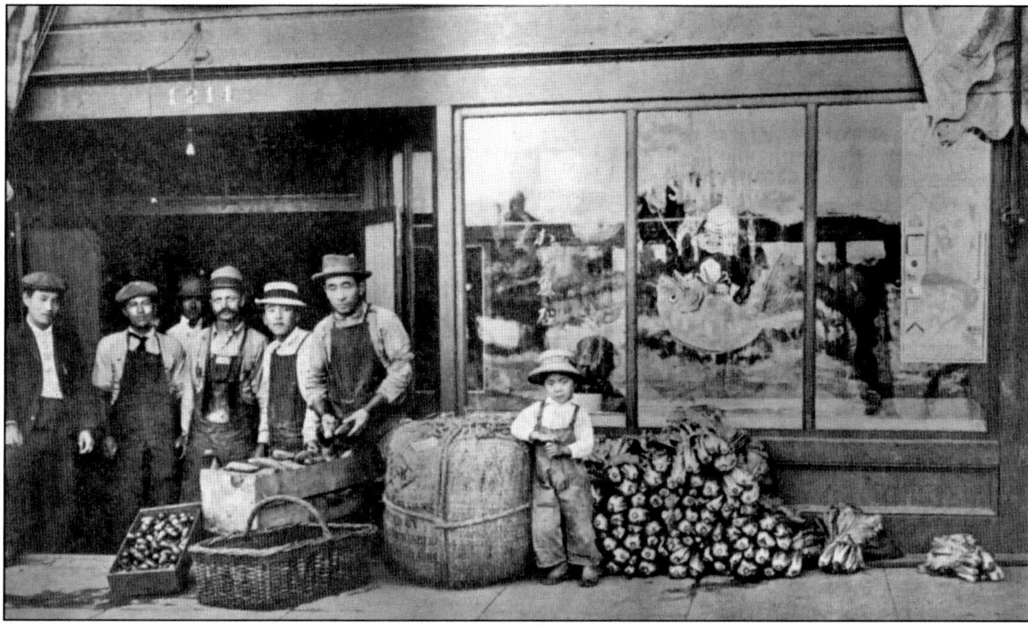

Japantown featured many retail shops, boardinghouses, and services catering to the needs of the Japanese community. The Mikado Fish Market was located at 1214 Third Street. The store was opened in 1910 by Ryukichi Fujita and Kanjiro Miyasaki. (Sacramento Archives and Museum Collections Center.)

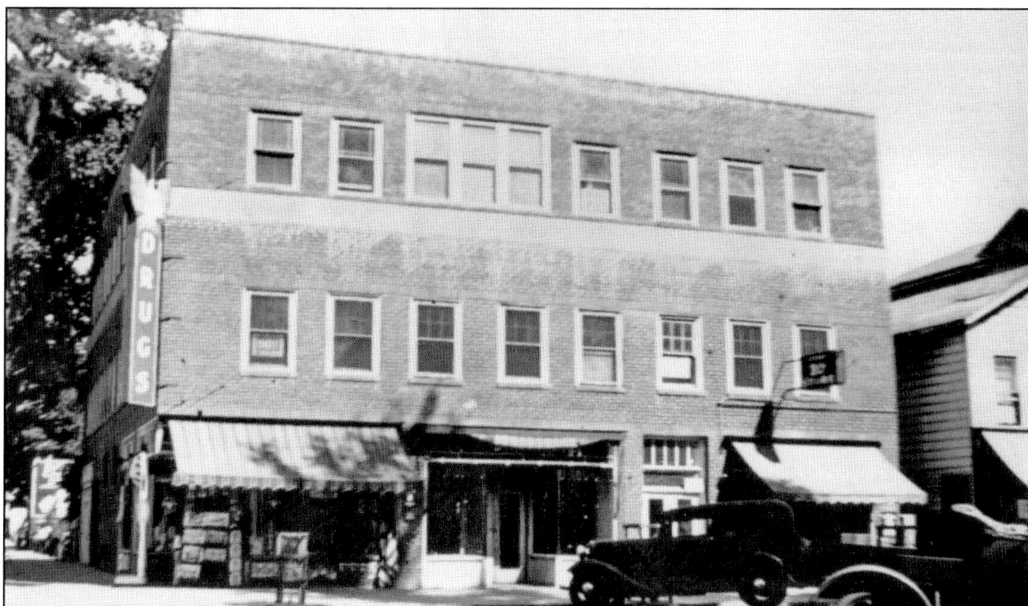

The Agnes Hospital was founded by druggist Tsunesaburo Miyakawa in 1922. Dissatisfied with the way Japanese were treated by Caucasian hospitals, he expanded his Eagle Drugstore into a full-service hospital at 1405 Fourth Street. The hospital featured modern medical equipment, private rooms, and interpreters. The hospital closed because of unpaid patient bills during the Great Depression, and the building later became the Grand Hotel. (Sacramento State Archives and Special Collections.)

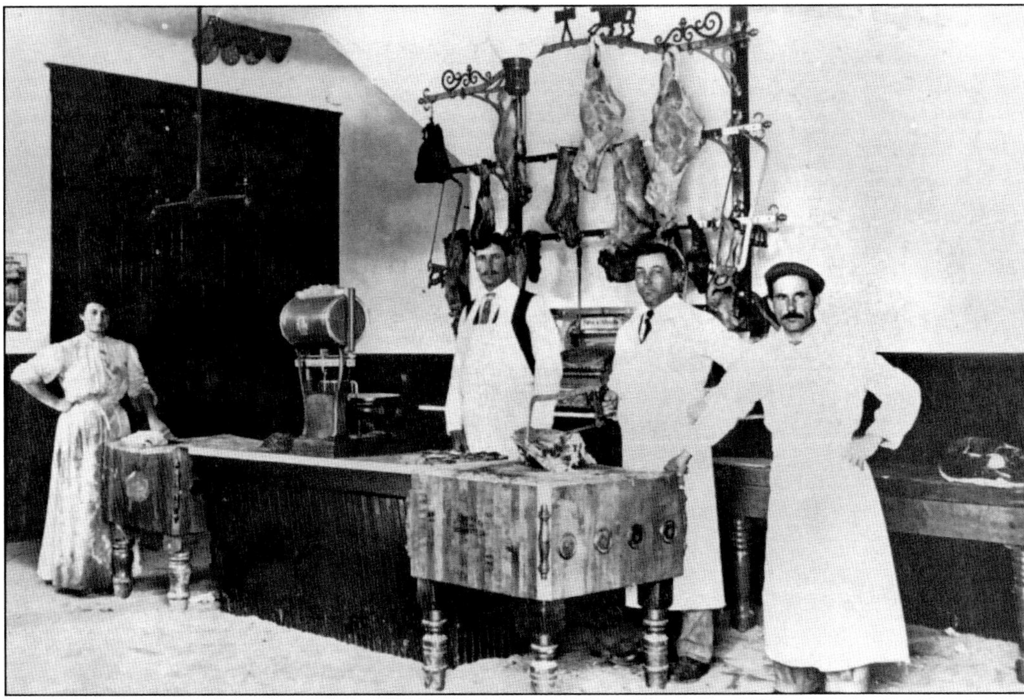

The Belvedere Meat Market was located at 330 S Street and was owned by Manuel Almeida and Tony Silva. They opened for business in 1907. The building still stands in 2007 and is currently occupied by Vallejo's Restaurant. (Portuguese Cultural and Historical Society.)

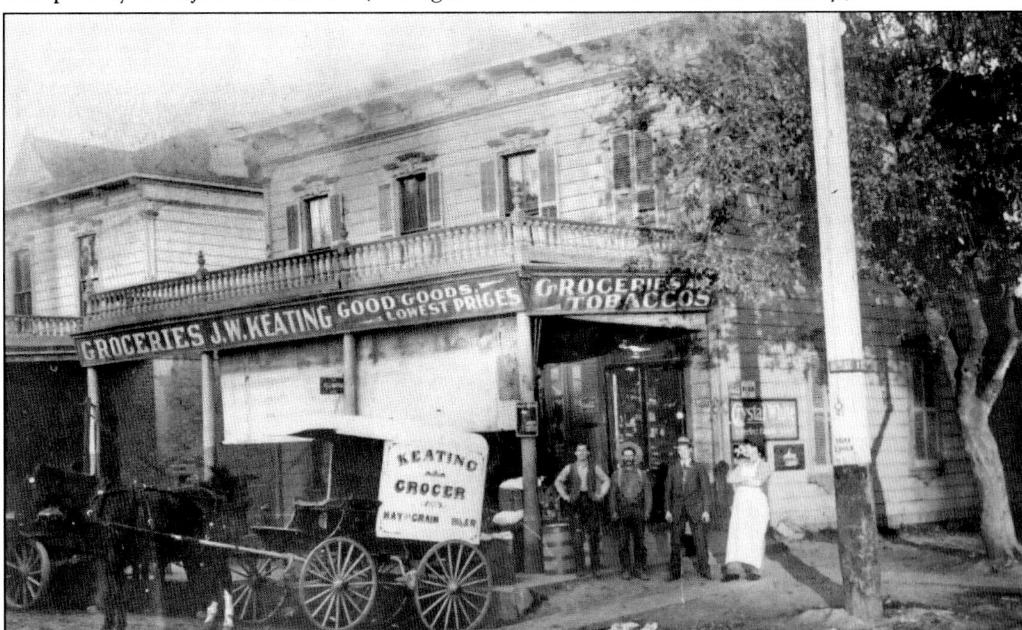

This photograph of J. W. Keating Groceries, located at the corner of Eleventh and R Streets, was taken in 1911. The man in the large hat is Joe F. "Milomes" Silva, who owned a farm in the Pocket area. When Silva came into town, he always stopped by Keating's store to pick up a few groceries and a can of Prince Albert tobacco. (Portuguese Cultural and Historical Society.)

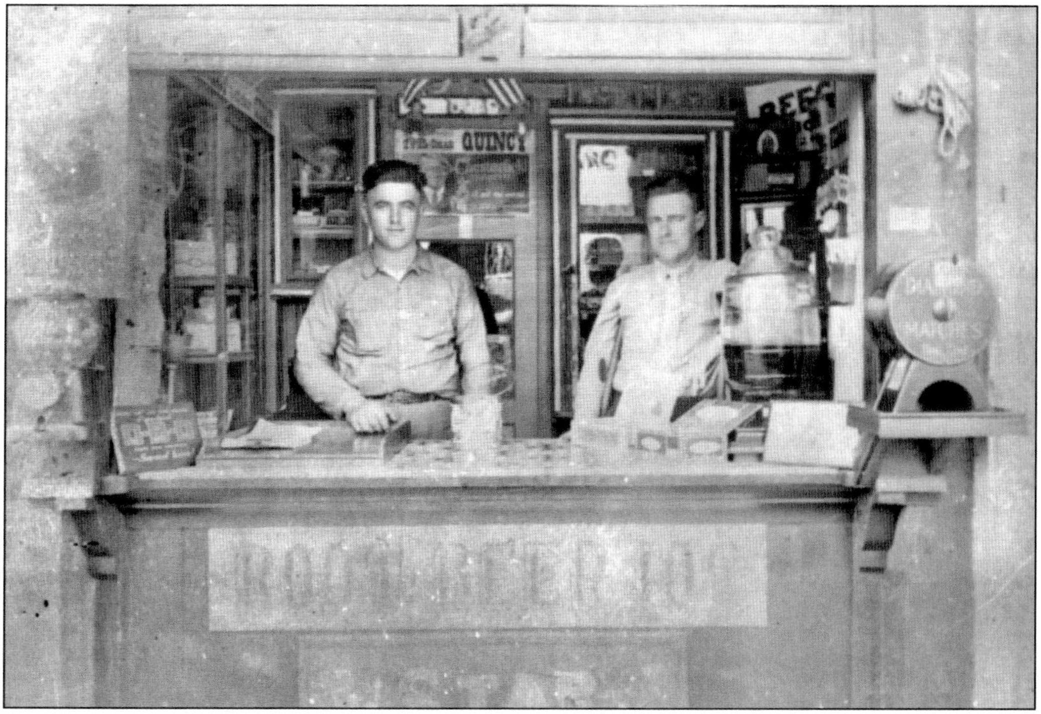

La Rosa, an Italian restaurant located at 813 L Street, opened its doors in 1927. In this 1931 photograph, owner Settino "Sam" D'allesandro and an employee man the tobacco stand in front of the restaurant. It's not known which man is D'allesandro. (Italian Cultural Society.)

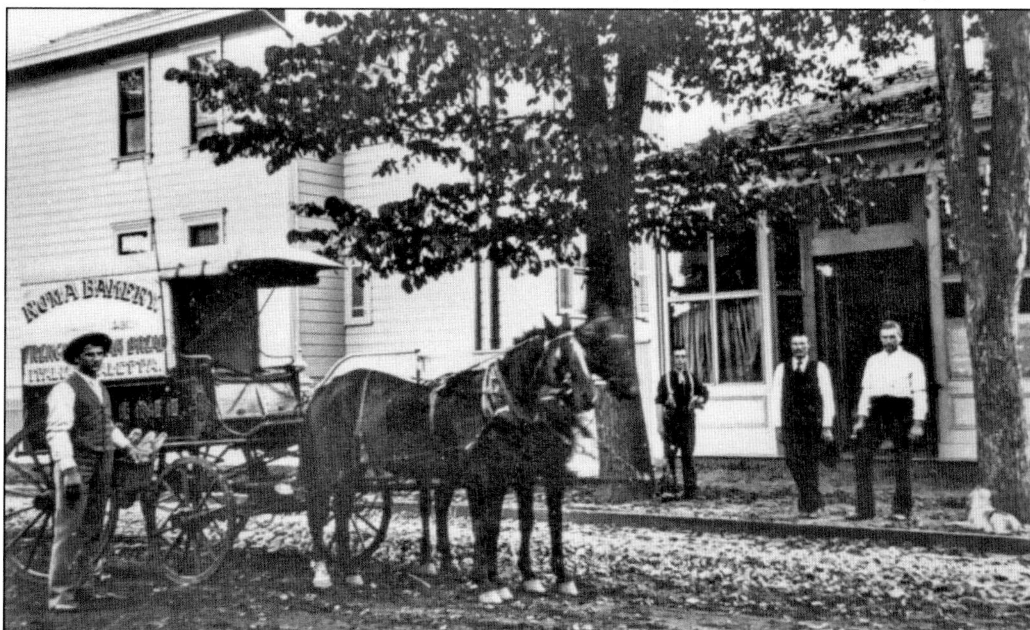

Roma Bakery was located near Third and J Streets, and their delivery cart was a familiar sight in Southside. Roma delivered bread to businesses as far away as Broderick. (Italian Cultural Society.)

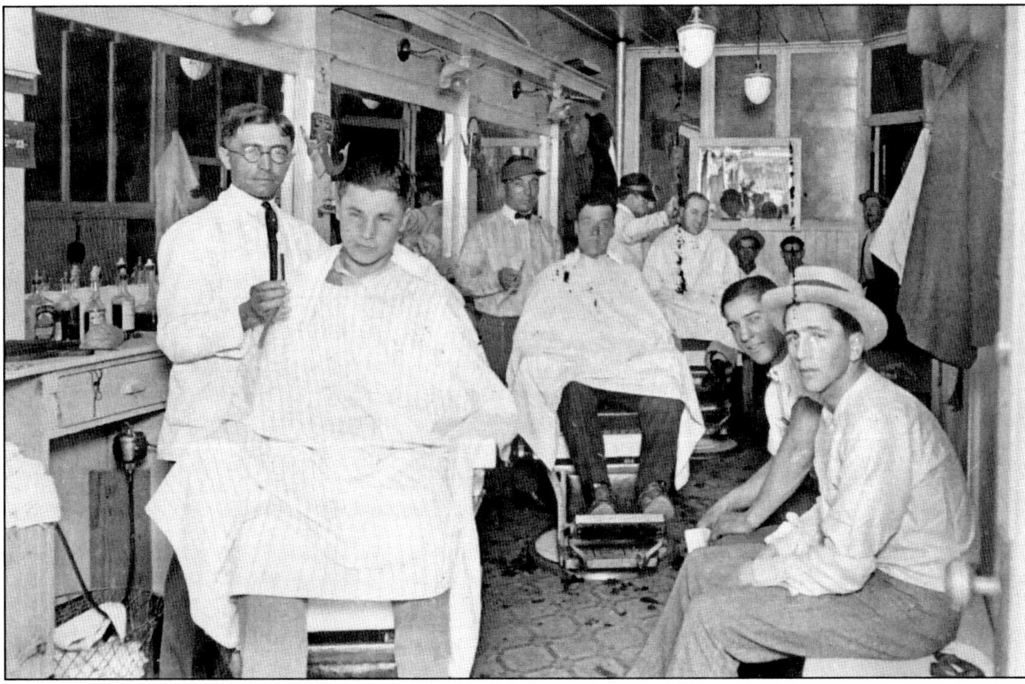

This photograph of Joe Silva's Barbershop at 1024 Fourth Street was taken in 1924. For many men, a weekly trip to their favorite barbershop, followed by a trip to their favorite bar, was a regular routine. Frequently these establishments were right next door to each other; this barbershop was one door down from the White Front Café. (Portuguese Historical and Cultural Society.)

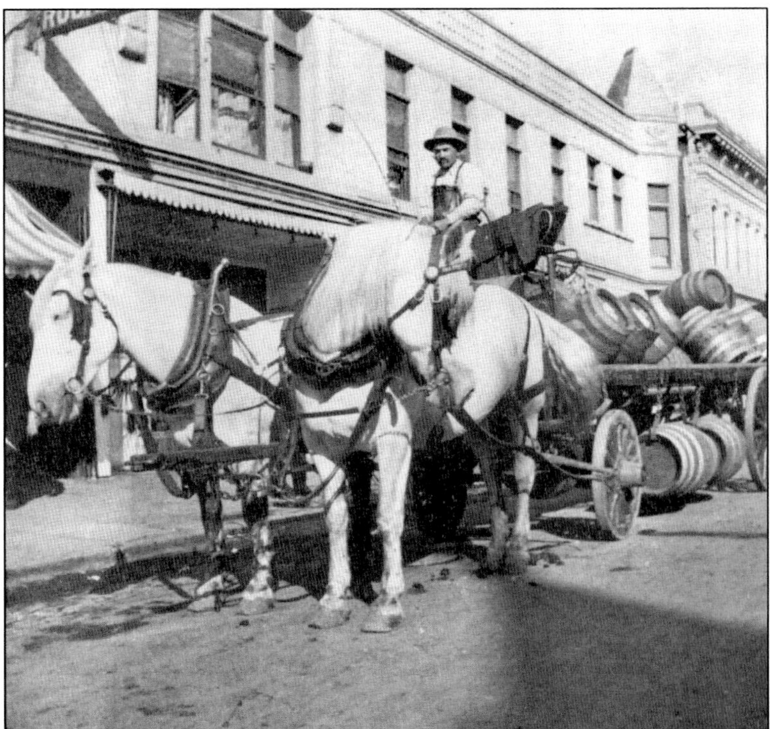

Sacramento's wineries and breweries provided beverages for its many bars. Reportedly, even Prohibition did little to limit alcohol consumption in Sacramento, although the breweries and wineries had a rough time, focusing on soft drinks, near beer, and sacramental wine until the Volstead Act was repealed. This beer cart is in front of the White Front Café, located at 1022 Fourth Street, in 1914. (Portuguese Cultural and Historical Society.)

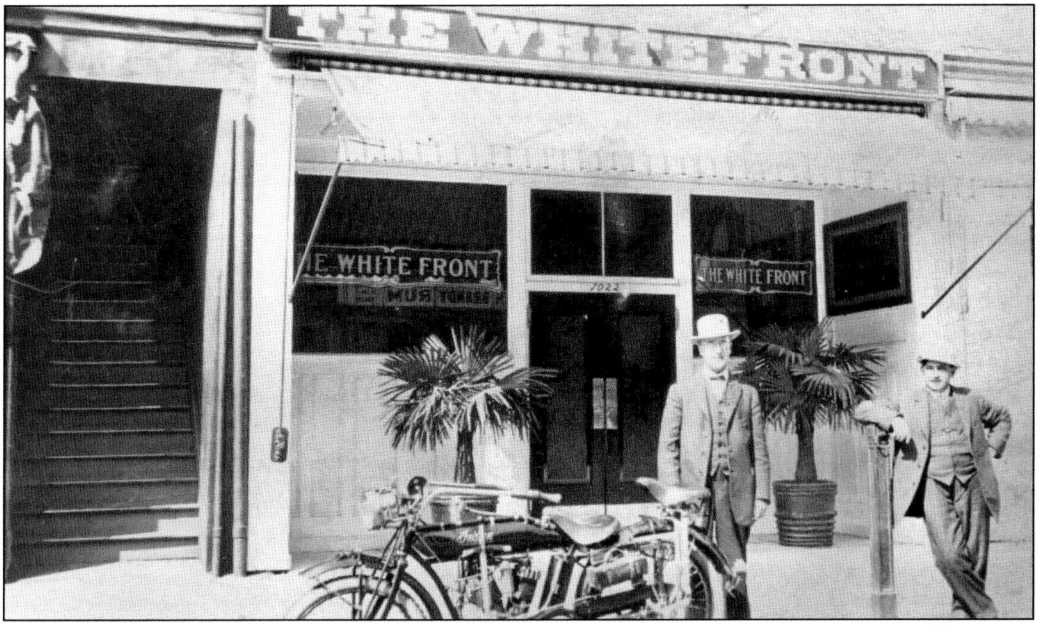

The White Front Café was owned by Mike Ignacio, also known as Mike Silva, until 1916. Mike is leaning on a hitch in this 1914 photograph. The White Front had a succession of owners, including Domingos and John Silvey from 1916 to 1927, Tony Lewis and Manuel Paulino between 1927 and 1933, Manuel Paulino and Manuel Dias 1933–1938, and Joe Corey from 1938 into the 1940s. (Portuguese Cultural and Historical Society.)

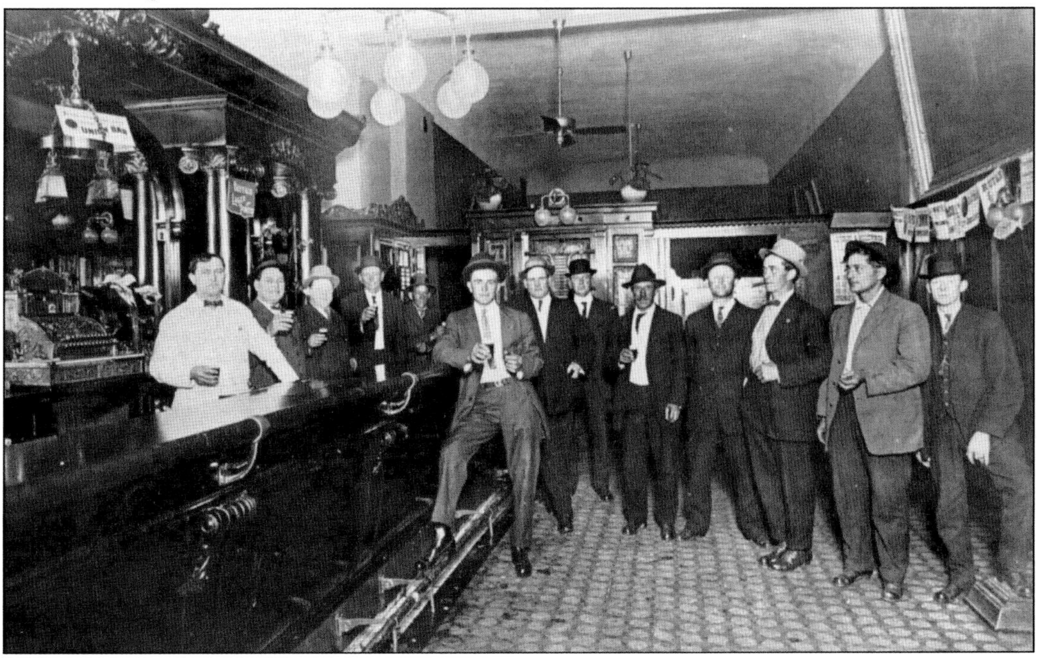

In this era, bars like the White Front Café were entirely men's domain, and women were seldom seen. This 1916 photograph captures the interior of the bar. Antonio Balshor, older brother of Al Balshor, was shot and killed in the White Front Café in 1923, just shy of his 20th birthday. (Portuguese Cultural and Historical Society.)

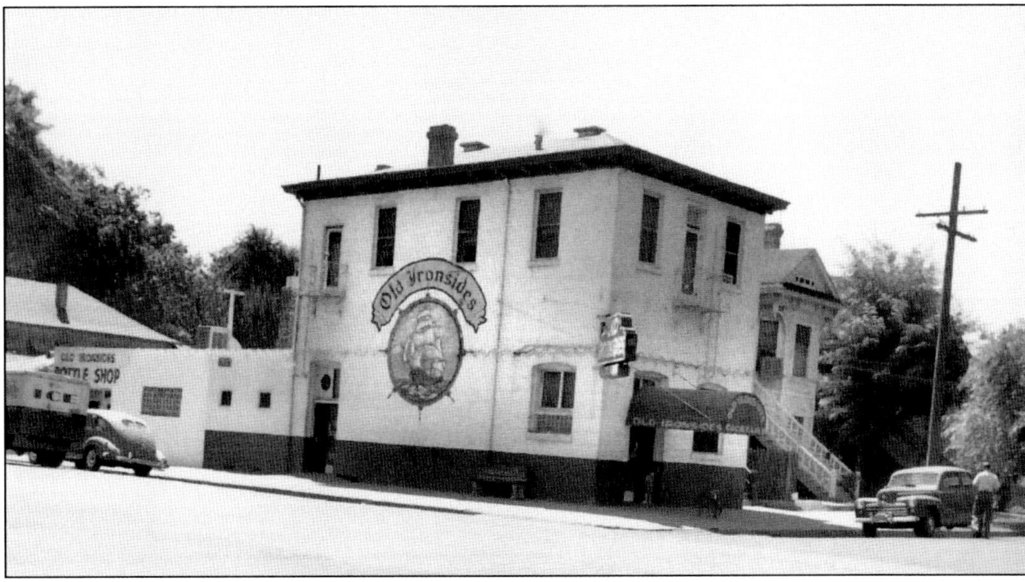

Old Ironsides was the first bar in Sacramento given a liquor license after the end of Prohibition, in 1934. The bar was opened by Bill Bordisso and his brother Lou. The name was suggested by the children of the previous owners of the building, the Ryan family. At the time, schoolchildren were encouraged to contribute pennies to a national fund to restore the USS *Constitution*, "Old Ironsides." (Kanelos family collection.)

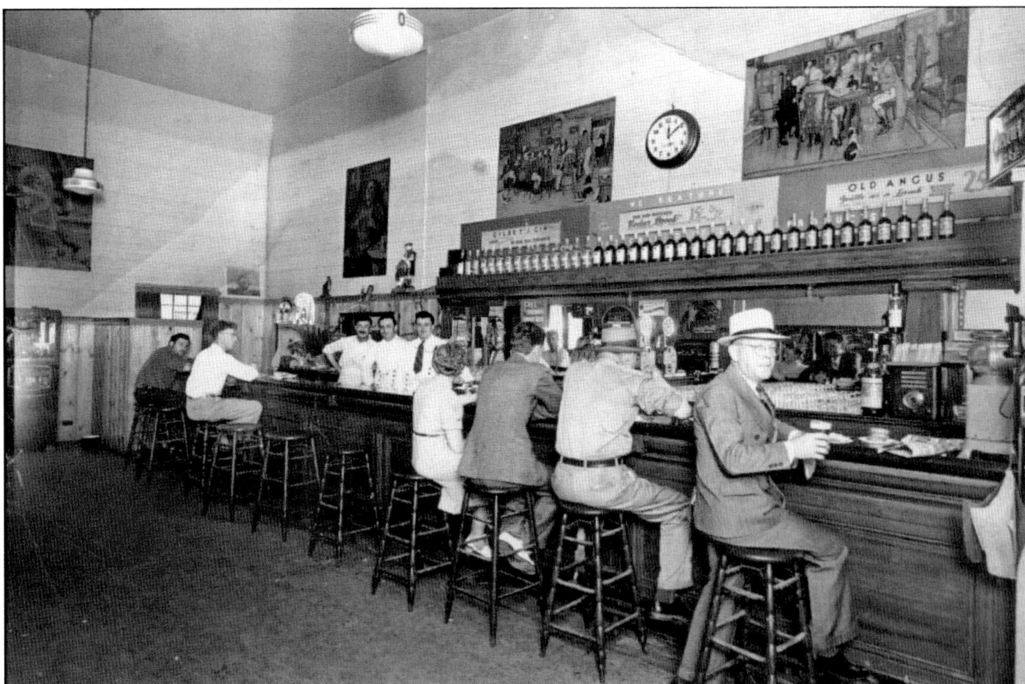

Bill, who was a former baseball player for the Sacramento Solons, and Lou tended bar at Old Ironsides and also served lunches. Rather than offering a full menu, only one item was served each day: spaghetti with meatballs on Monday, short ribs on Tuesday, swiss steak on Wednesday, and so on. Eventually, they offered a full menu. (Kanelos family collection.)

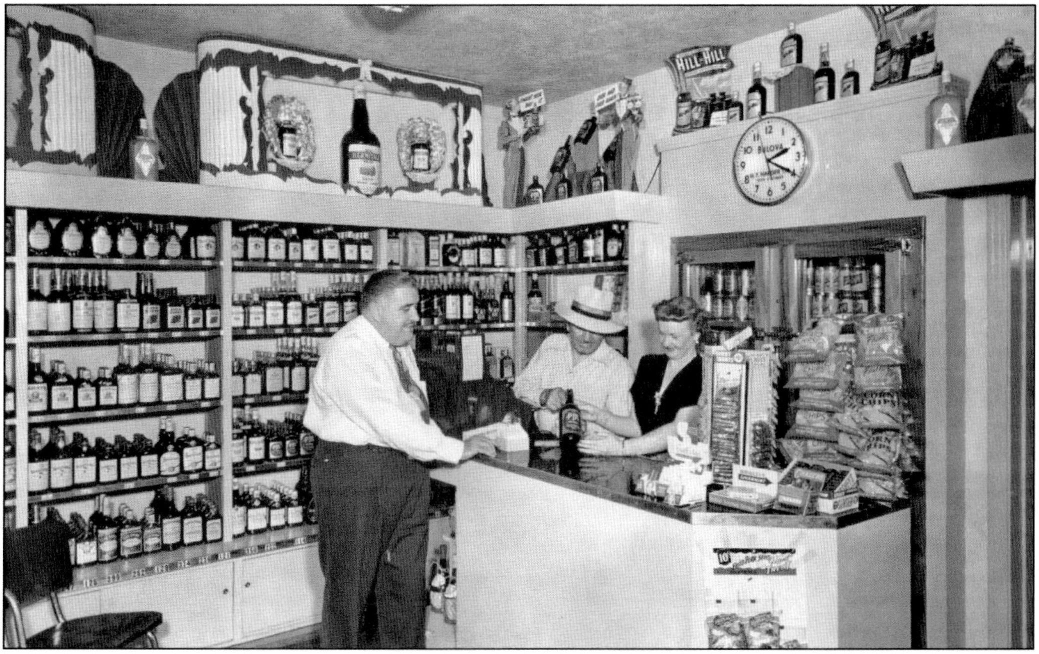

Next to the bar on S Street was the Old Ironsides Bottle Shop, also owned by the Bordisso family. Rose "Sunny" Bordisso, sister of Bill and Lou, was in charge of the bottle shop. The store was a favorite of lobbyists, who often came to purchase a bottle of expensive wine or liquor as a present for a legislator they wished to impress. (Kanelos family collection.)

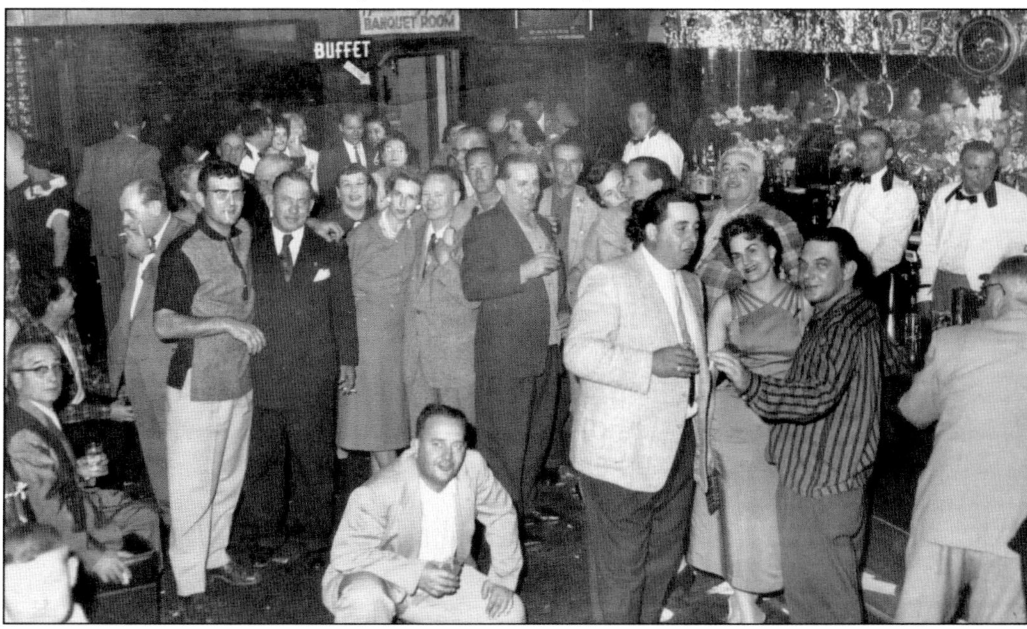

Old Ironsides became a popular destination for baseball players, state employees, nearby workers, and neighborhood residents. In 1959, a 25th anniversary party was held. A lively crowd turned out to celebrate. In 2007, Old Ironsides is approaching its 75th anniversary and is operated by Bill Bordisso's daughter Billie, her husband, Sam Kanelos (who also played for the Solons), and their three children. (Kanelos family collection.)

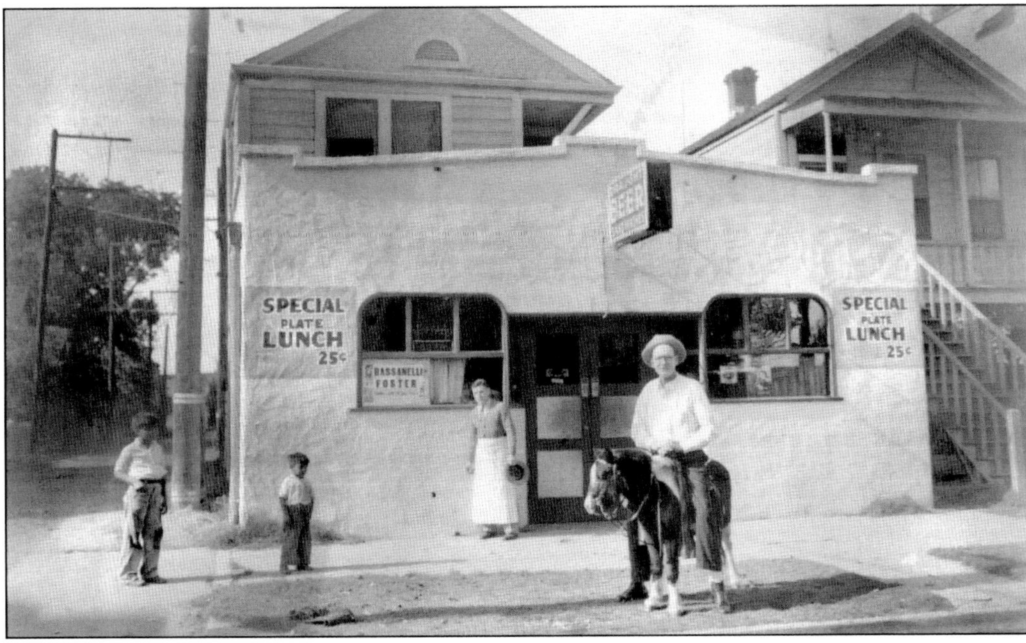

Manuel J. Viera, son of Arizona Gang member Manuel Vierra, opened a bar on Third Street, known as Viera's Tavern. In 1939, during Roaring Camp, many local businesses redecorated or even renamed themselves in order to attract tourists. During that summer, Viera's was repainted to resemble the Roaring Camp buildings and was renamed "Manuel's Likker Palace." (Manuel Viera collection.)

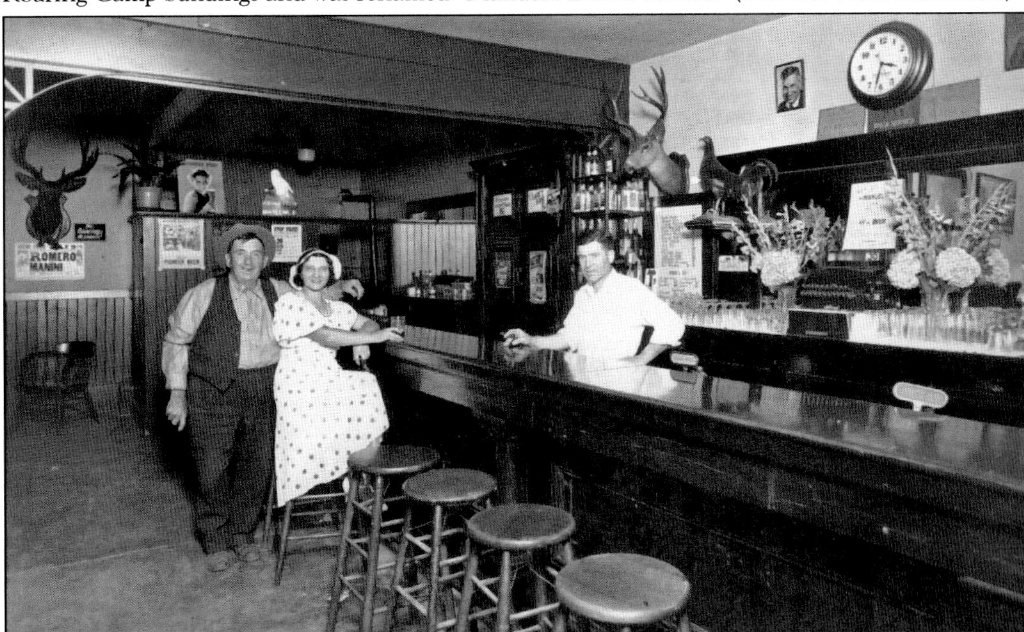

Located between S and T Streets, Viera's was a popular lunch spot for employees of the Western Pacific freight office and other industries on R Street. It, like Old Ironsides, opened soon after Prohibition ended. When Manuel grew ill and died, his son worked the bar in the evenings to help his mother. The bar was purchased by the state and demolished to make way for Interstate 5 in the early 1970s. (Manuel Viera collection.)

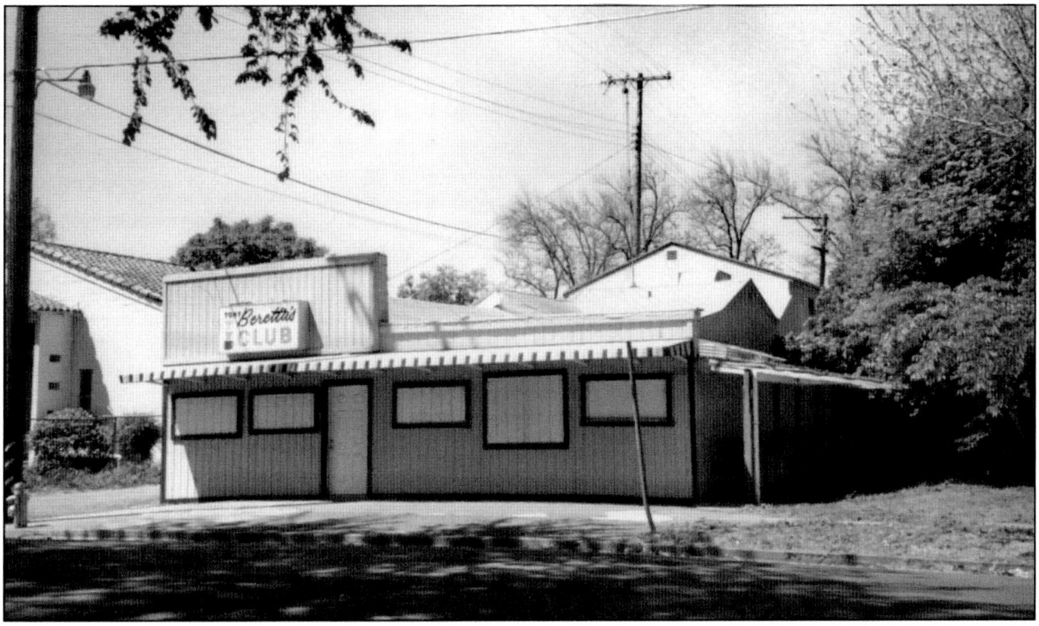

Tony Beretta's was located right next to Southside Park, on Sixth Street between V and W Streets. Beretta's served beer and wine to the older generation and was legendary among the kids for their delicious snow cones. Copious outdoor seating made it a popular summertime spot, where one could enjoy a drink or a snow cone and watch whatever was going on across the street in the park. (Author's collection.)

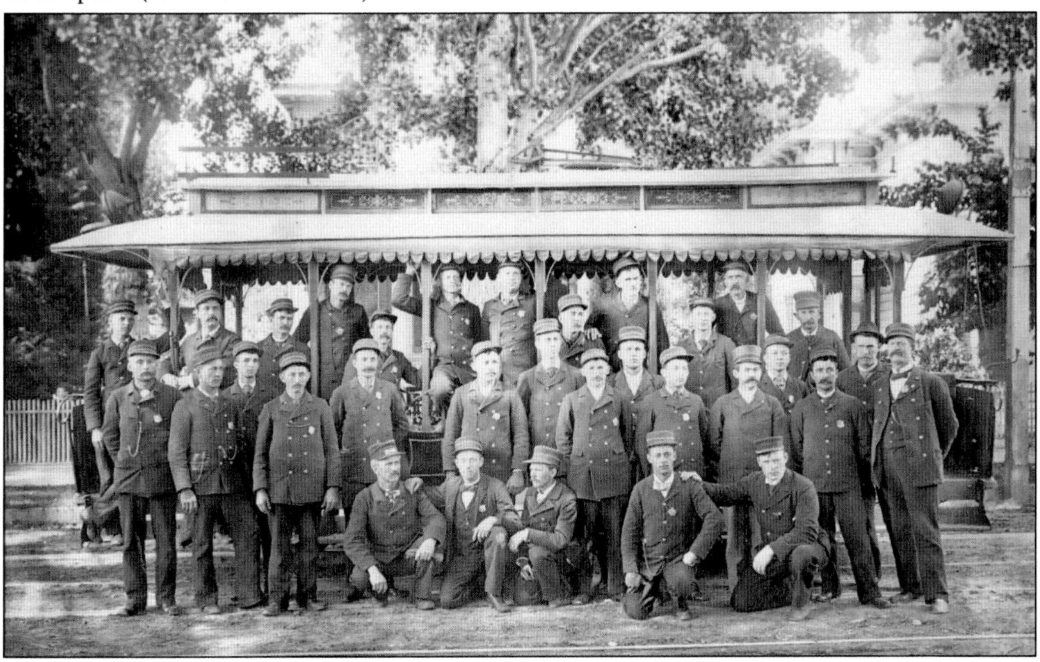

Southside was originally not well served by streetcars. The Tenth Street line ran to the city cemetery but was not convenient for those on the outskirts of the neighborhood. Cars like this single-truck Central Street Railway car operated in Sacramento in the 1890s, but most of the lines ran through the northern half of town. (California State Library.)

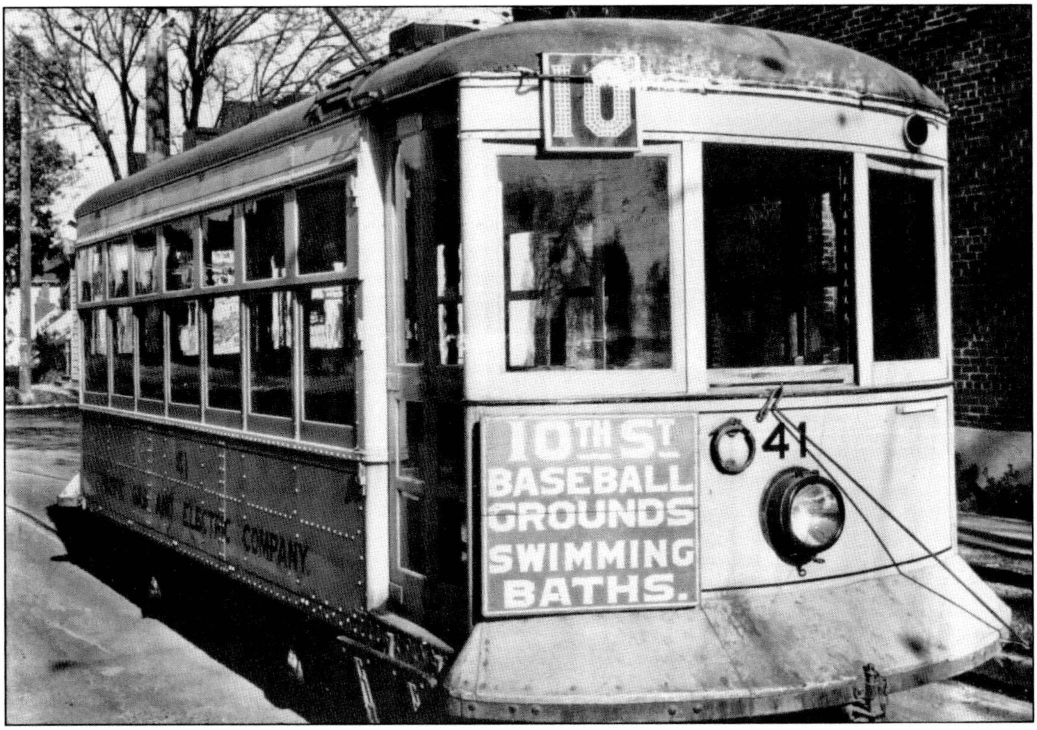

Pacific Gas and Electric operated Sacramento's main streetcar system from the early 1900s until 1943. Starting in 1909, they operated several routes into Southside, originally at the request of the Southside Improvement Club. Eventually, cars ran on Third, Seventh, Tenth, Twenty-first, P, and T Streets. This car ran on Tenth Street, with stops at the city cemetery, the baseball field, the Riverside Baths, and William Land Park. (Western Railway Museum Archive.)

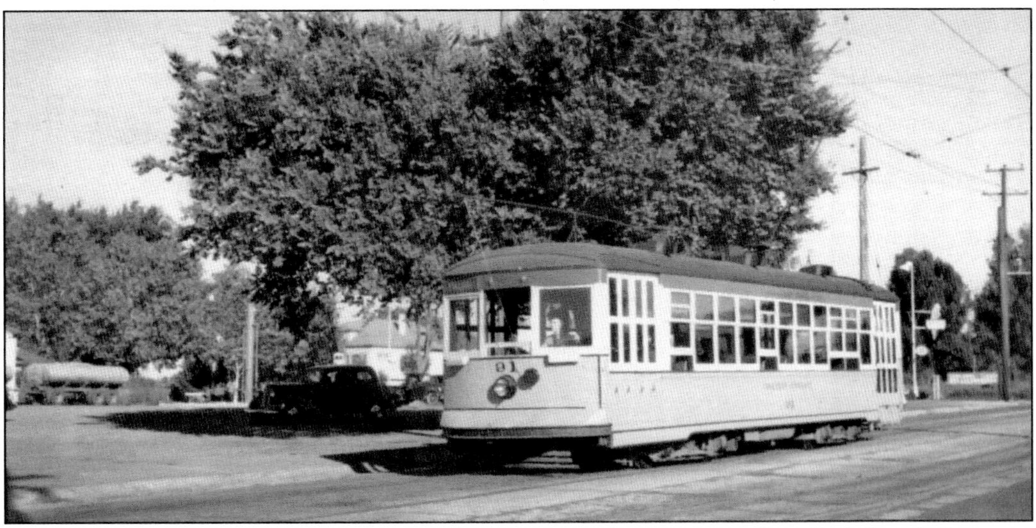

Central California Traction also operated a local streetcar line. Starting from Eighth and K Streets, it ran directly past Southside Park before turning left onto X Street. It then passed through Oak Park, stopped at the state fairgrounds, and continued down Stockton Boulevard through Colonial Heights and Colonial Acres. In 1943, Sacramento City Lines acquired both of these streetcar systems. The streetcars were replaced with buses in 1947. (Western Railway Museum Archive.)

Downtown Sacramento was the place to go for movies at the Senator Theater or dancing at the Trianon Ballroom on K Street, live jazz at the Mo-Mo Club on M Street, or fine dining at La Rosa on L Street. Manny and Alicia Viera encountered a street photographer on K Street *c.* 1950 who took this photograph. Manny bought a print as a reminder of a great night on the town. (Manuel Viera collection.)

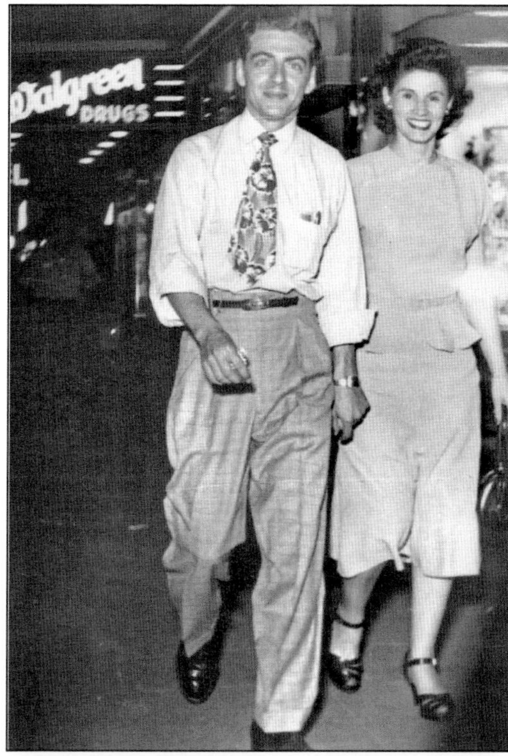

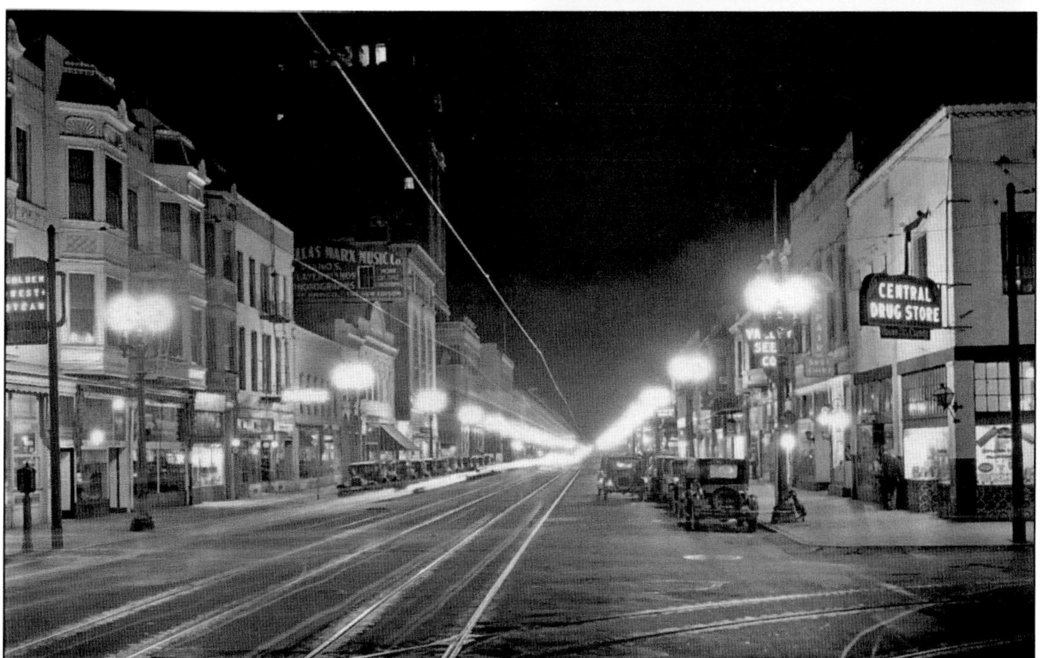

When Billie Kanelos was a teenager, fine dining meant the Country Maid ice cream parlor on J and Eleventh Streets: "They had a banana split that was *unbelievable*." She and her friends often went there after an evening movie, sometimes at 11:00 p.m. or later. Many businesses were open late, especially in summer when temperatures dropped at night. (California State Library.)

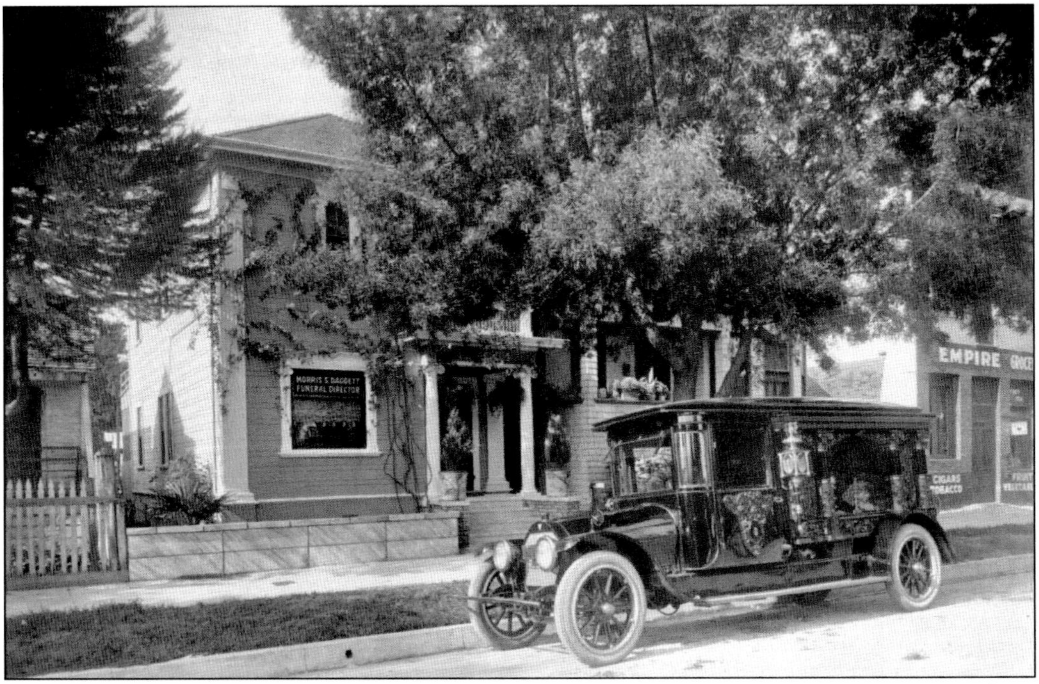

Morris Daggett Funeral Home was located at 506 O Street. Daggett's company motto was "Where Courtesy Prevails." (Portuguese Cultural and Historical Society.)

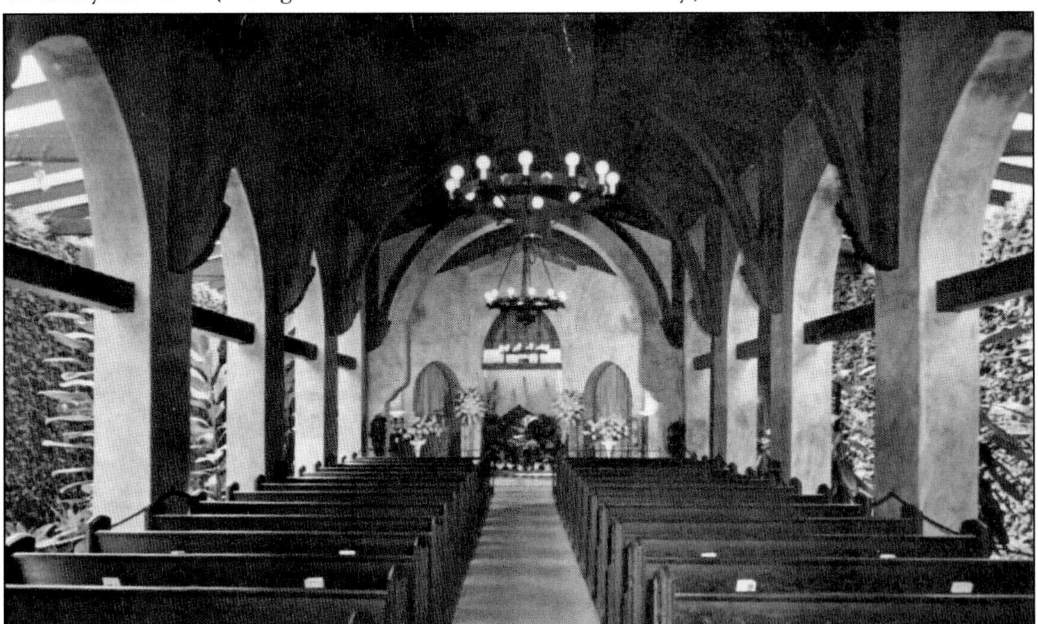

George Klumpp's Chapel of Flowers at 808 O Street opened its doors in 1939. Klumpp began his career as an embalmer in 1916. He died in 1971, but his associates Arthur Barnard Jr. and Robert Oehler purchased the business. The State of California purchased the building in 1972, but Klumpp's relocated to Riverside Boulevard. The original building still stands, as a health club. (Oehler family collection.)

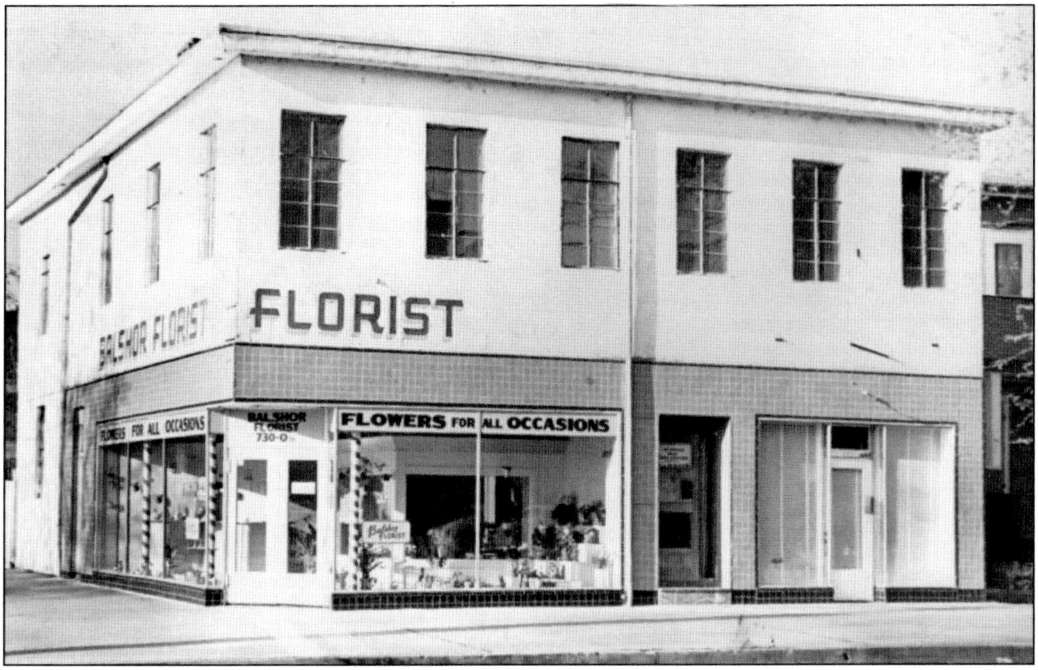

After being discharged from the army, Al Balshor apprenticed as a florist for Relles Florist on J Street. In 1950, he opened his own shop across from Klumpp's Chapel on Eighth and O Streets. (Portuguese Cultural and Historical Society.)

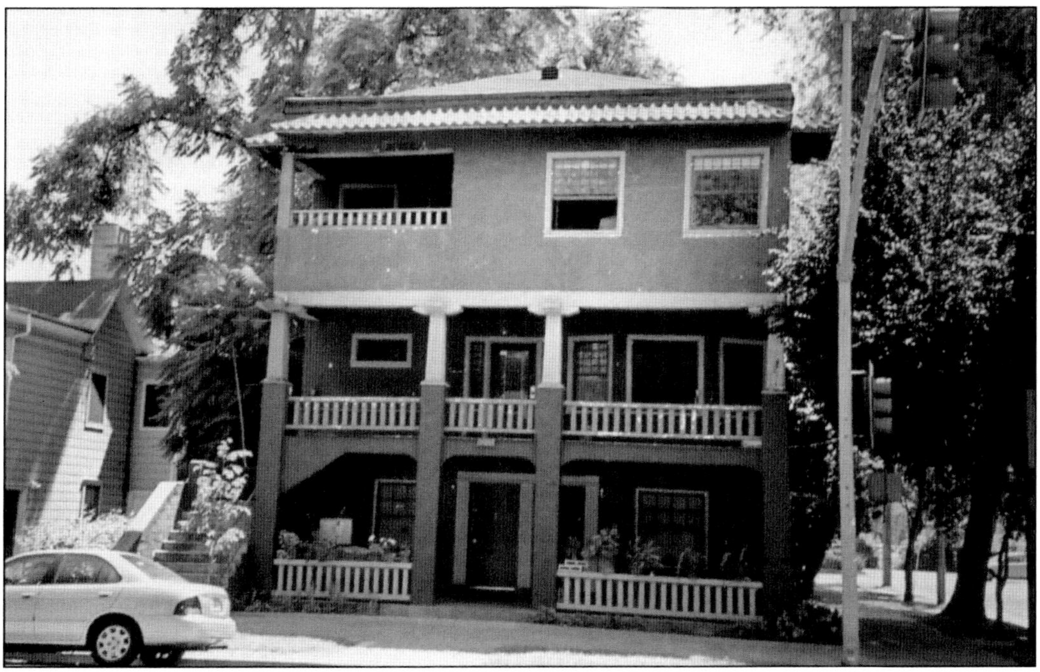

Morgan and Jones Mortuary, owned by Grace Morgan-Jones, was one of two African American–owned mortuaries in Southside. The other was Thompson Funeral Home at 1411 Seventh Street. Morgan-Jones was also an active member of the Women's Civic Improvement Club. Her mortuary was located at 1200 Q Street. (Author's collection.)

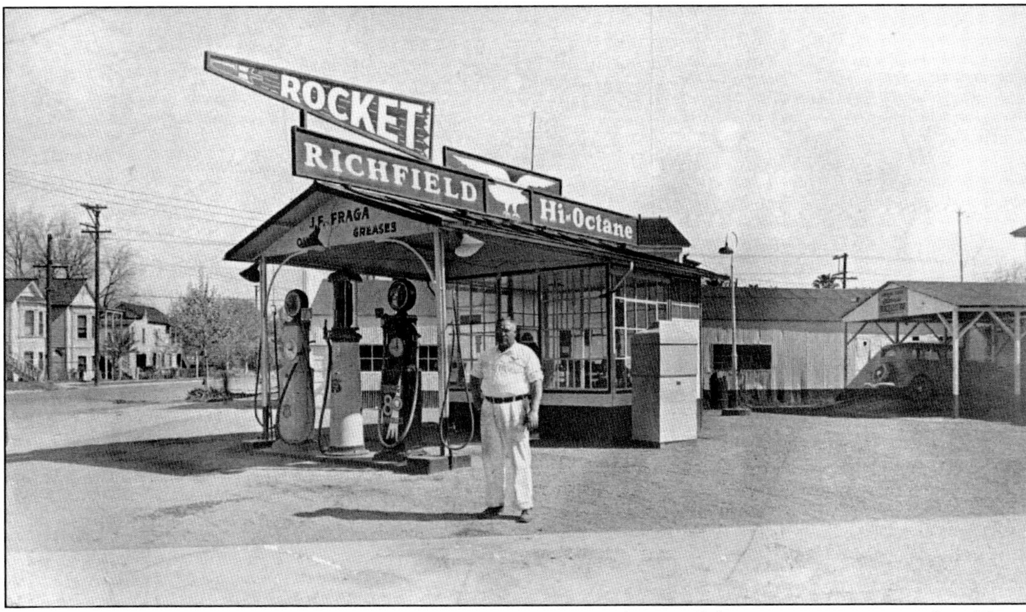

With the growing popularity of the automobile came a demand for service stations. Joe Fraga opened this Richfield gas station on the corner of Fifth and T Streets in 1927. (Portuguese Cultural and Historical Society.)

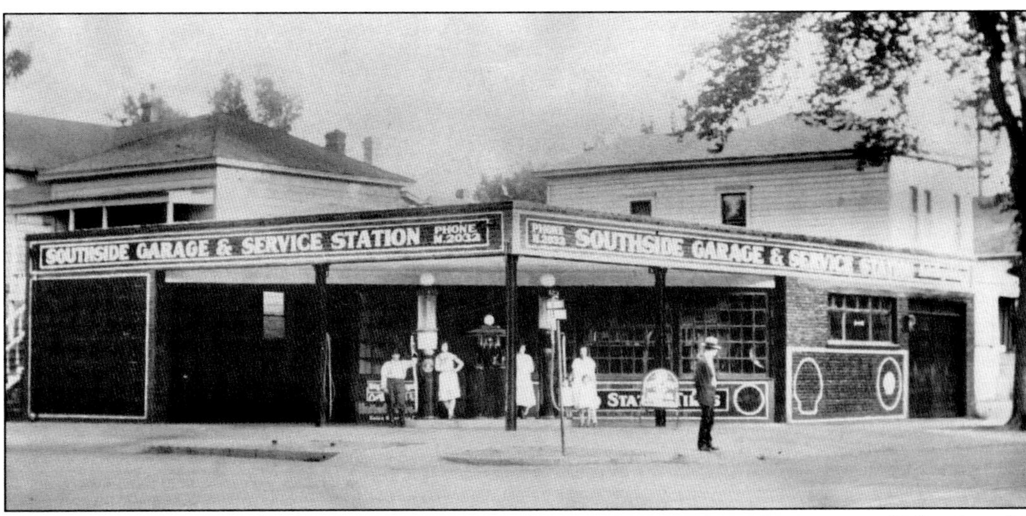

Manuel DaPonte's Southside Service Station and Garage opened on the corner of Third and S Streets in 1921. (Portuguese Cultural and Historical Society.)

Six

THE KNOTHOLE GANG

Baseball was a highly popular sport throughout Sacramento, and Southside Park was no exception. There were leagues for children and adults. Sacramento's parks and recreation department and private businesses in town sponsored neighborhood leagues for various age groups, and they played throughout the year. Thanks to Sacramento's generally sunny climate, baseball could be played nearly year-round. There was even an indoor baseball field, in the PG&E gymnasium on Front Street. Three baseball diamonds were located on the two-block area across X Street from the main portion of Southside Park. The great objective of any ballplayer in Southside Park was to send a home run from the ball field into Southside Park's lake.

Professional baseball in Sacramento was also wildly popular. The construction of Buffalo Park at the corner of Riverside Boulevard and Y Street (later changed to Broadway) in 1911 marked the beginning of half a century of baseball on the southern edge of Southside Park. The park was named after the park's sponsor, Buffalo Brewery, although the name was changed several times over the years. In 1922, it became Moering Field, after new team owner Lew Moering. When the St. Louis Cardinals made Sacramento their farm team, the name became Cardinal Field. In 1935, the name was changed again to Doubleday Field. In 1945, the name became Edmonds Field, named after KFBK sportscaster Dick Edmonds. This field was home to the Sacramento Solons, originally known as the Sacramento Senators. The baseball field had a special club for local kids, known as the Knothole Gang. Members were reserved bleacher seats for games at the stadium.

In addition to baseball, boxing was popular among Southsiders. The sports arena at Second and L Streets was the most popular spot for boxing matches. Many were amateur boxers in their spare time, but a few strove to become professional pugilists.

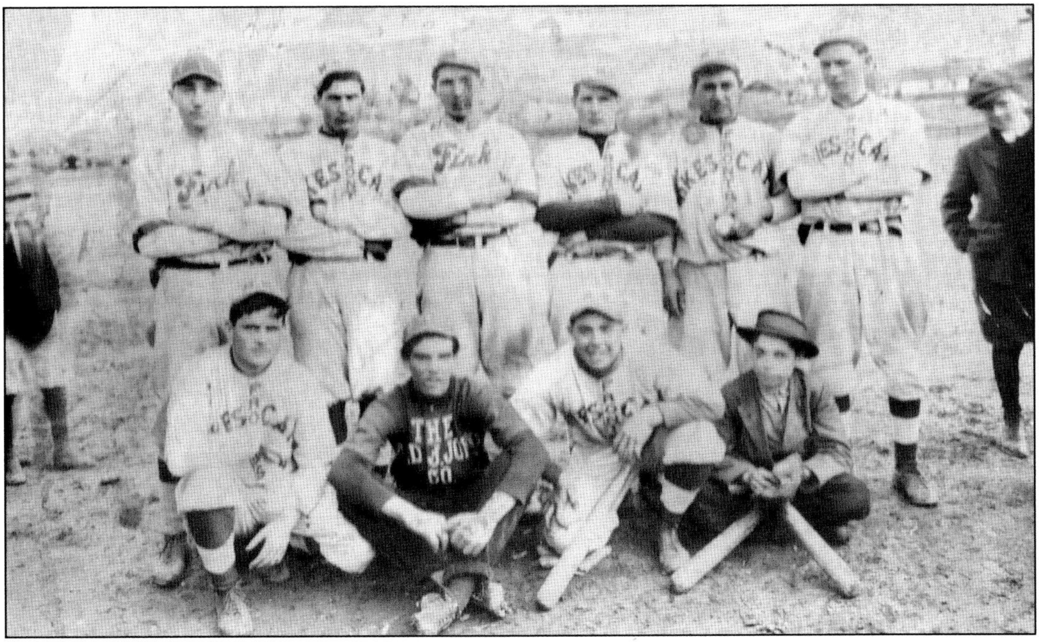

This photograph of the Mike's Café baseball team was taken on December 6, 1914. (Manuel Viera collection.)

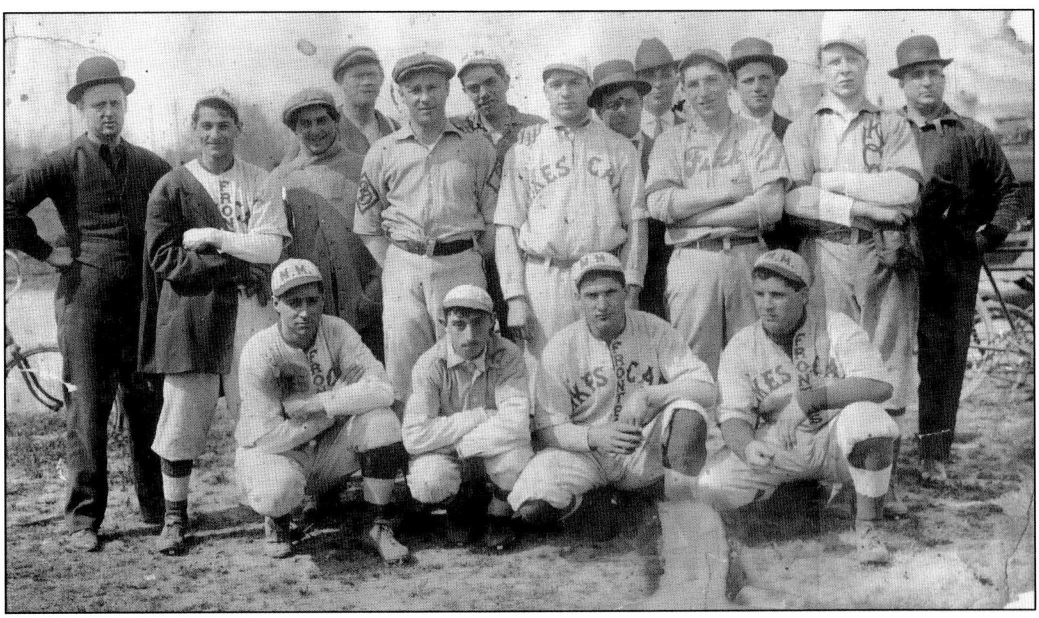

This photograph shows a similar group of players in assorted uniforms, possibly taken on the same day as the photograph above. The bare trees and the presence of heavy coats on a few people indicate that it could well be December and certainly indicates the readiness of Southsiders to play baseball at any time of year. The body of water behind the players is probably Southside Park's lake. (Manuel Viera collection.)

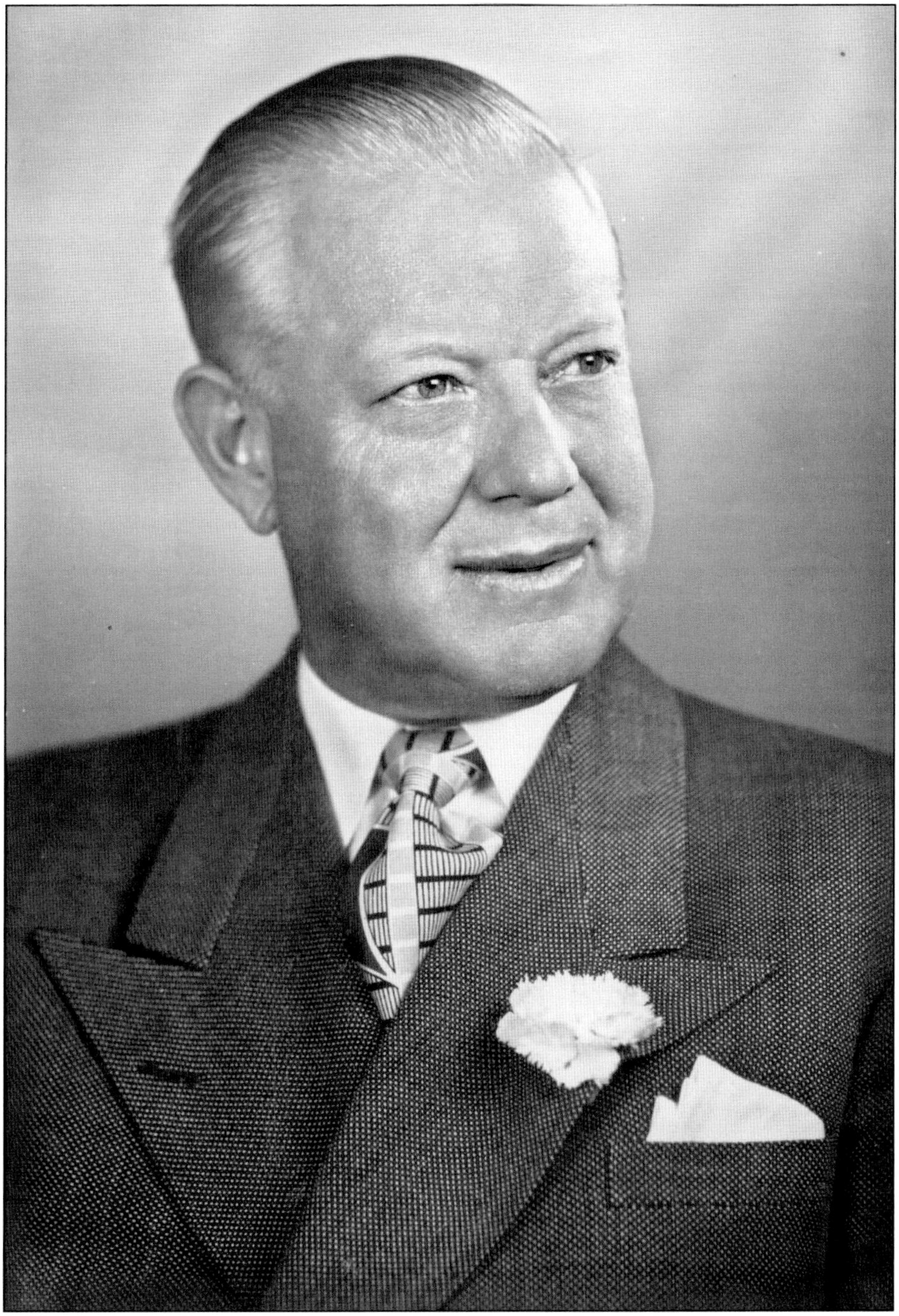

George Klumpp, whose Chapel of Flowers is shown on page 96, played many other important civic roles in Sacramento. He first ran for the office of county coroner in 1926. He was elected to city council in the early 1940s and served several terms, including a term as mayor of Sacramento from 1946 to 1947. He was not a baseball player, or even an enormous baseball fan, but he was instrumental in saving baseball in Sacramento. A disastrous fire destroyed Edmonds Field on July 11, 1948. Klumpp, along with Harry Devine and Ed Sparks, helped create a plan to reconstruct Edmonds Field and bring back the ball game. (Oehler family collection.)

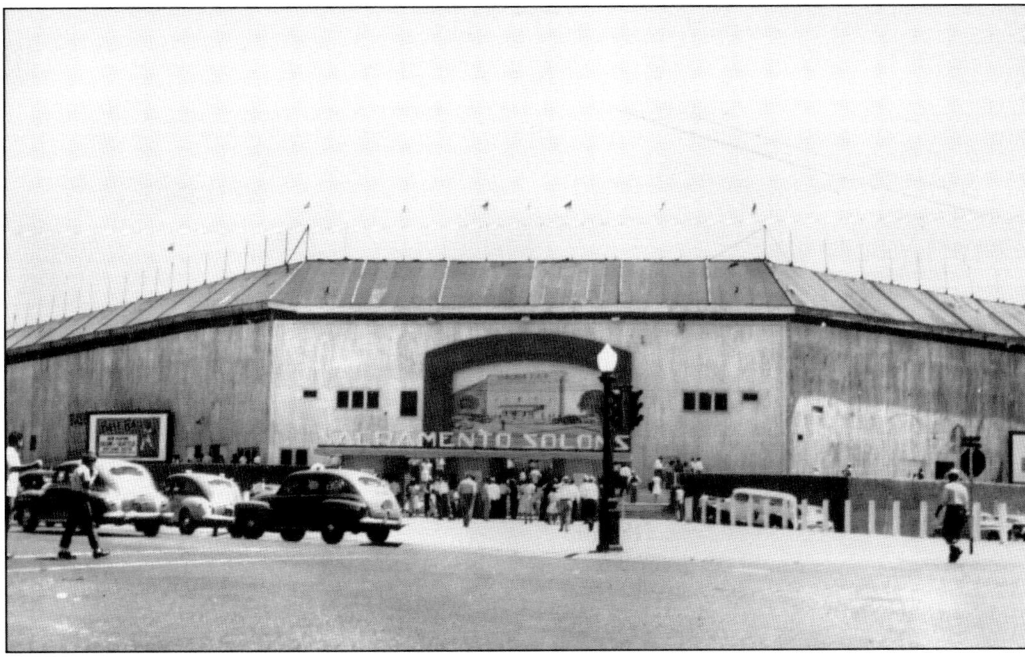

Edmonds Field reopened in 1950, bearing a painting of its wooden predecessor, but this version was made of fireproof concrete. Ten years later, the field went quiet again when the Solons disappeared in 1960, and the field was demolished in 1964 to make way for a Gemco department store. (Sacramento Archives and Museum Collection Center.)

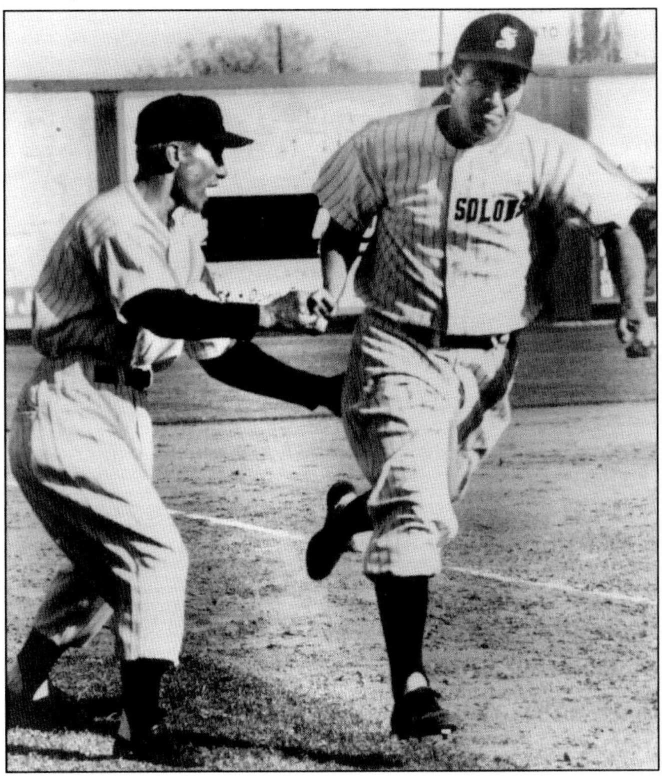

Tony Freitas was the pitcher of the 1942 Pacific Coast League championship game against Los Angeles. Ron King, a batboy at Edmonds Field, had iced champagne ready for the Los Angeles team, which was expected to win, but Freitas pitched a shutout game that gave Sacramento the championship. After their defeat, the Los Angeles team was in no mood for champagne. (Sacramento Archives and Museum Collection Center.)

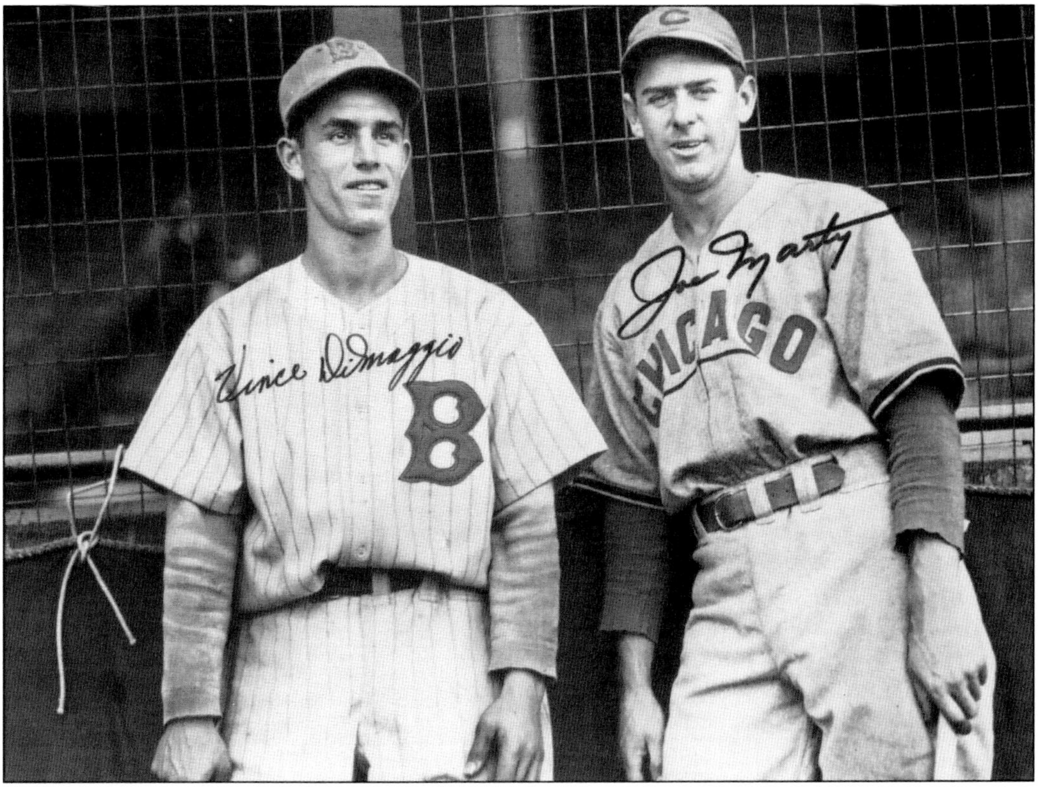

Some Sacramento Solons went on to join the major leagues. Standing next to Vince DiMaggio (Joe DiMaggio's brother) of the Boston Braves is Southsider Joe Marty, who was recruited by the Chicago Cubs after playing for Sacramento. He later returned to Sacramento to open Joe Marty's El Chico on Broadway. (Ron King collection.)

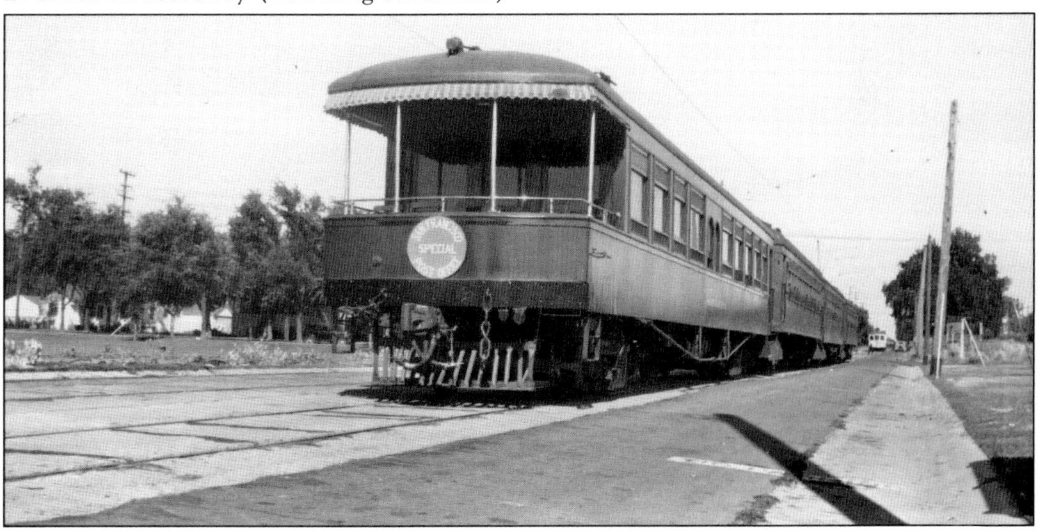

Sacramento Northern sometimes chartered special trains for sporting events. Here an SN interurban train, pulling deluxe parlor car *Sacramento*, is carded for "The S.F. Post Office Special." The train is parked on X Street next to Southside Park while the passengers enjoyed a baseball game at Edmonds Field, a few blocks away. (Western Railway Museum collection.)

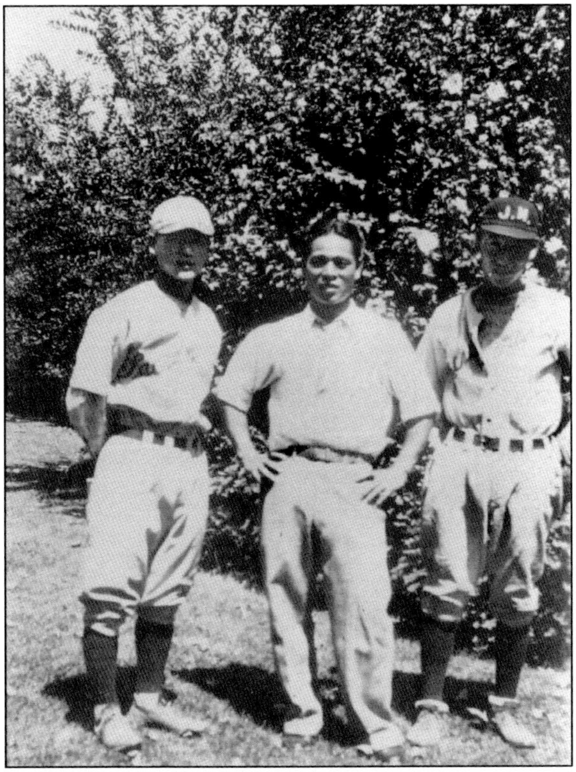

Sacramentans in Japantown were generally as fond of baseball as any other Southsider. Pictured here are (left to right) Frank Sawamura, George Nishimura, and Yoshio Nakagawa, from the Sacramento High School Dragons baseball team, in 1928. In an effort to appeal to Japanese baseball fans, Solons owner Lew Moering signed Kenso Nushida to play with the Solons. (Sacramento State Archives and Special Collections.)

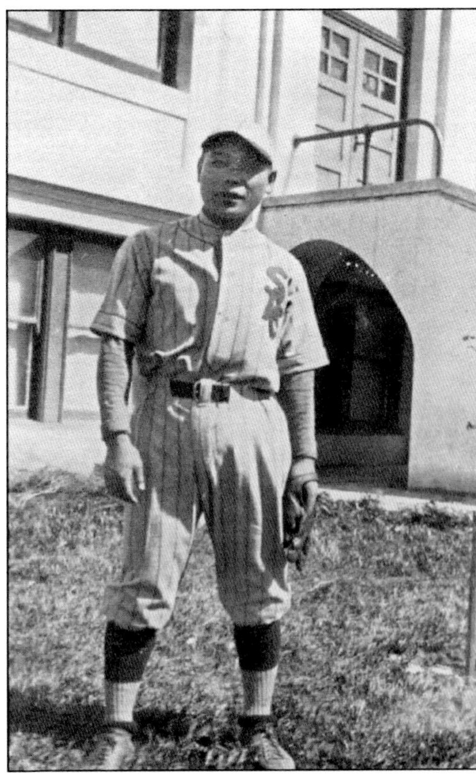

Pictured here is George Kawasaki, a member of the Nippon Stars, Sacramento's Japanese American baseball team. (Sacramento State Archives and Special Collections.)

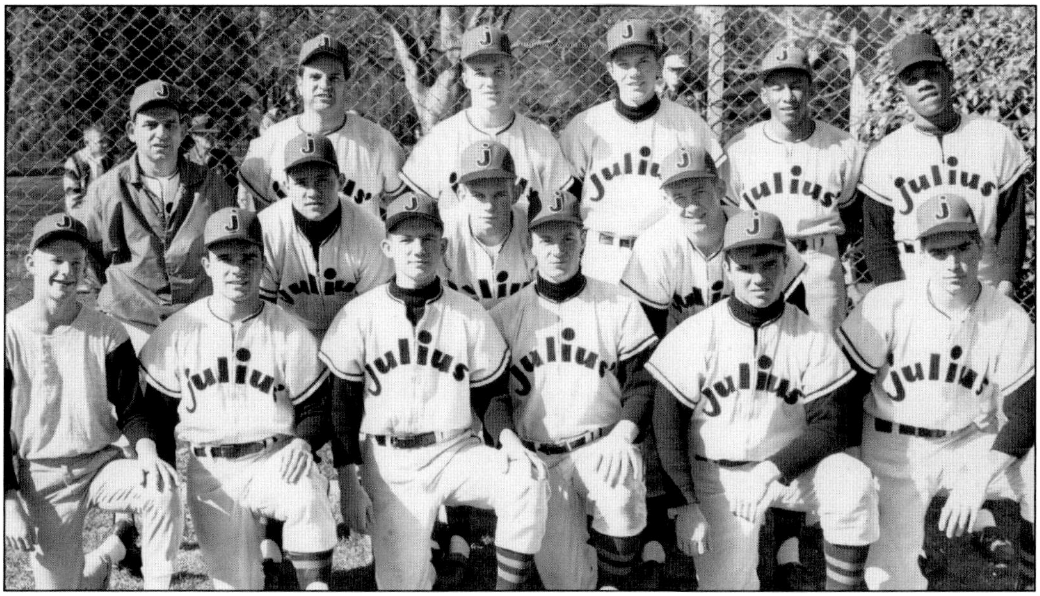

Ron King, the batboy at the 1942 championship game, was recruited to play Major League Baseball in 1946, at the age of 18. He later coached and scouted for baseball teams and eventually returned to Sacramento. In the 1960s, he coached for a Little League team sponsored by Julius, a men's clothiers on K Street. Nine of the young men in this photograph went on to play professional baseball. (Ron King collection.)

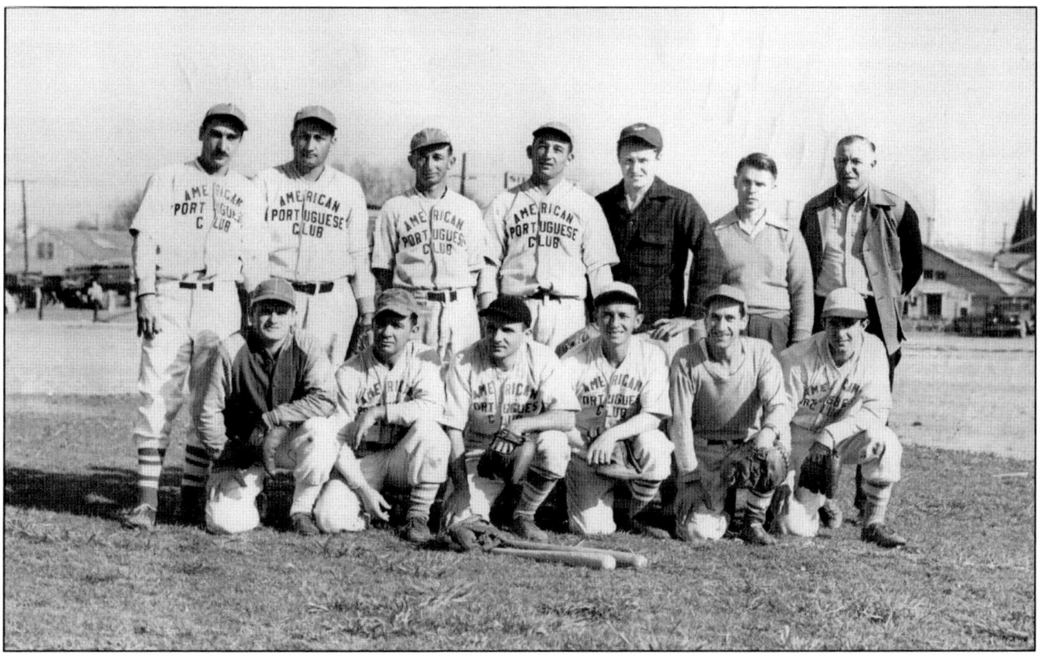

The American Portuguese Club was Sacramento's 1947 amateur baseball club champion. From left to right are the following: (first row) Vince Slivich, Wilbur Azevedo, Norm Silva, Clyde Soto, Joe Nevis, and Larry Bowa; (second row) Al Nevis, Al Serpa, Lou Soto, Bob Soto, Jo Franzoia, Bud Parker, and Louis Perry. The photograph was taken at the baseball field at Twenty-eighth and C Streets. (Steve Silva collection.)

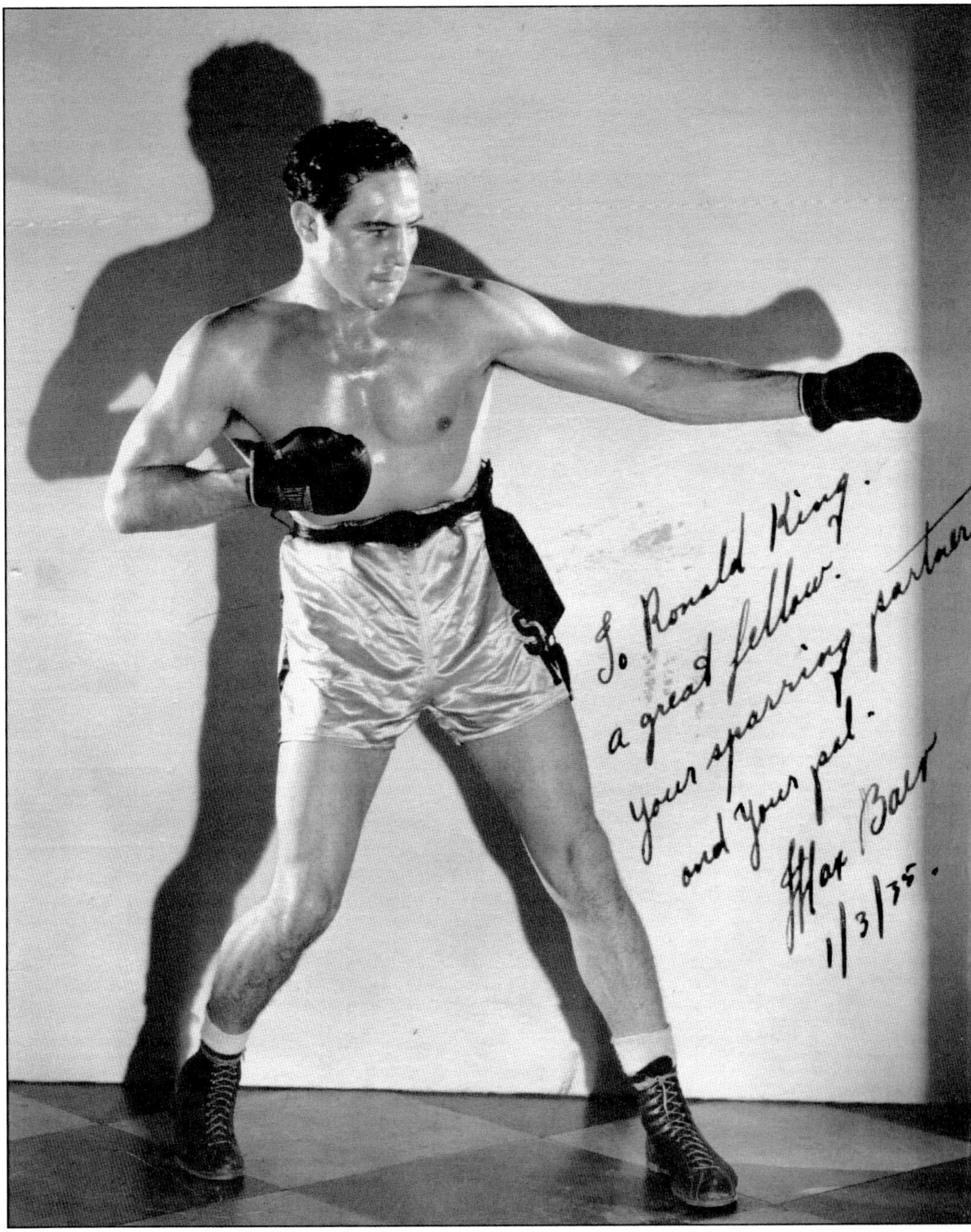

Max Baer was a legendary boxer who lived across from the Riverside Baths near Land Park. When a young Tony Lopez and some friends visited a candy shop near the baths, they recognized Baer. He greeted them warmly and bought them all candy bars. When Lopez explained that they were not allowed to swim at Riverside Baths because they were Mexican, Baer took them to the baths and demanded to see the manager. At Baer's insistence, Lopez and his friends were admitted to the pool, but as soon as Baer left, the management forced them to leave. (Ron King collection.)

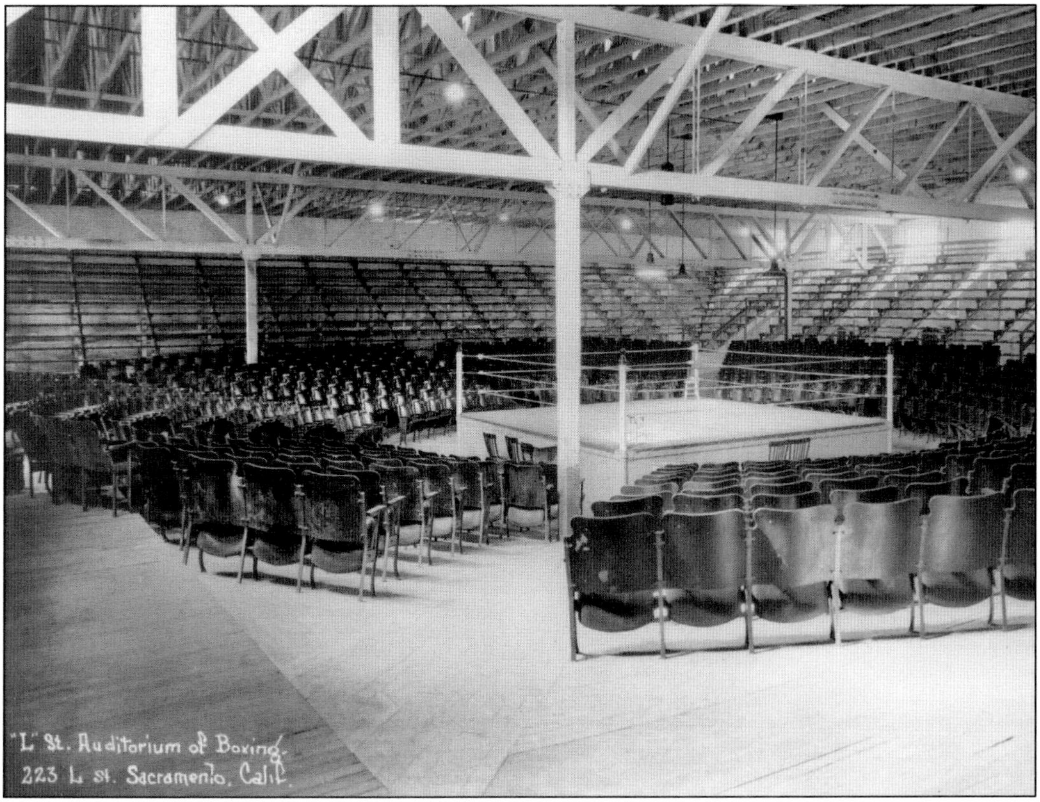

The L Street Arena was located at Second and L Streets. It was commonly used as a boxing ring but was also used for other sports like sumo wrestling. Every Fourth of July, the Tokyo Club held a sumo tournament at this arena. Ed Mores recalled that cigar and cigarette smoke was often so thick that one could not see the ring from the back bleachers. (Al Balshor collection.)

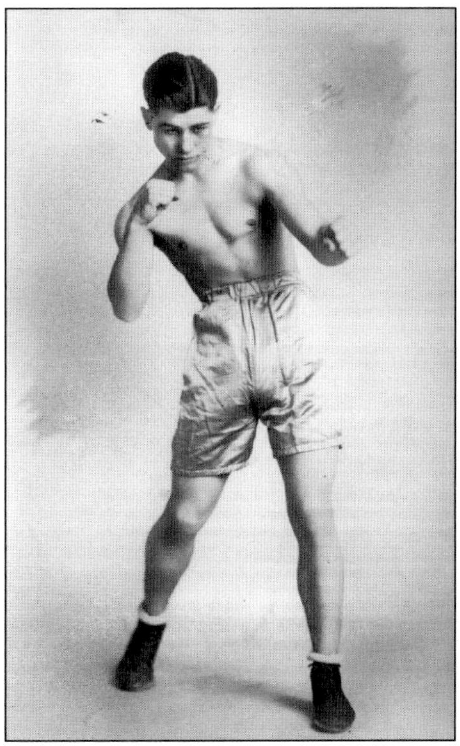

Marshall Vierra, son of Manuel S. Vierra, was a skilled prizefighter, but he did not want his mother to know he was a boxer, so he fought under the name "Jimmy Marshall." Eventually his reputation as a boxer grew enough that he had to come clean to his mother about his profession. (Manuel Viera collection.)

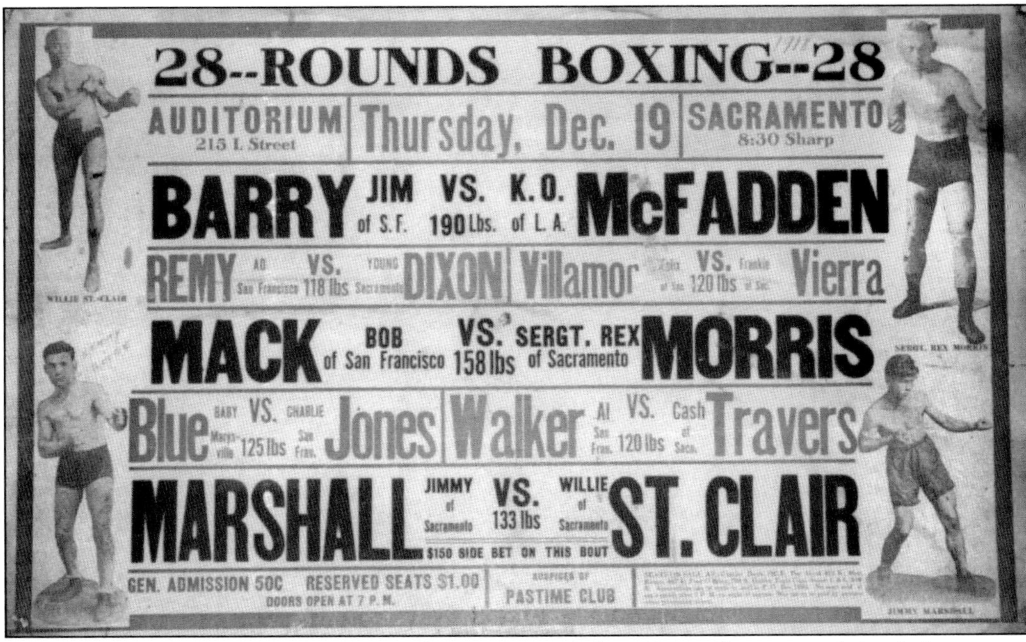

Boxing posters like this one were used to promote fights. Typically, most of the fighters were local amateurs, with more experienced fighters at the top of the card. This fight was held at the L Street Arena. (Manuel Viera collection.)

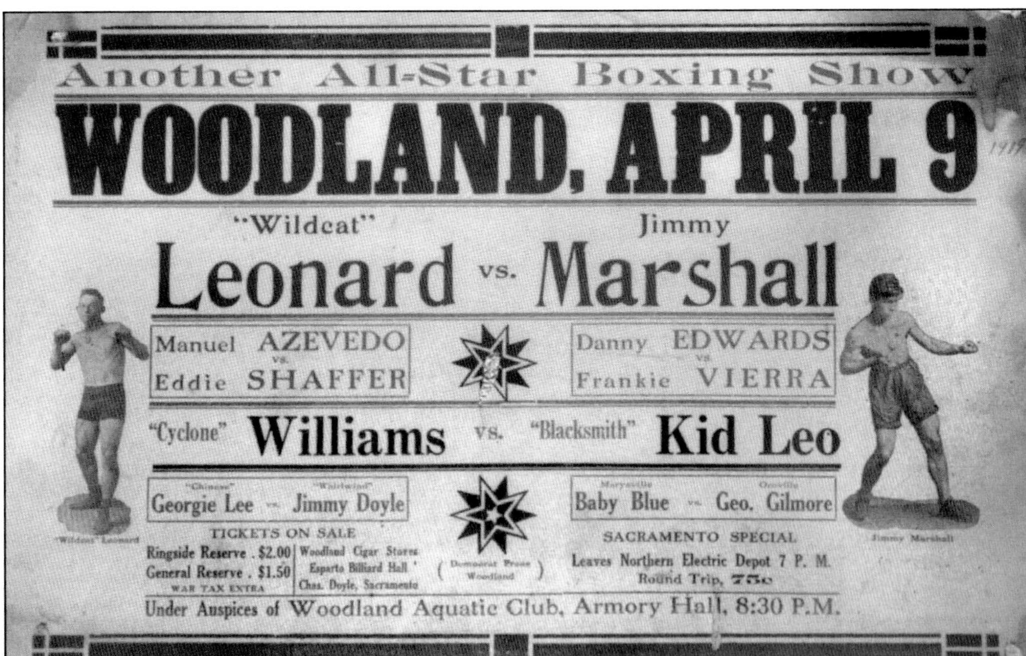

As noted above, railroads sometimes chartered special trains for sporting events. This match in Woodland was advertised in Sacramento, and the interurban railroad line Northern Electric (which later became Sacramento Northern) advertised a special 75¢ round-trip fare to see Jimmy Marshall fight "Wildcat" Leonard at Woodland's Armory Hall in 1919. (Manuel Viera collection.)

Seven

Southside Improvement

The Southside Improvement Club was responsible for much of the civic progress in Southside Park. Their first action, asking for removal of the R Street levee in 1902, promoted the city's growth and encouraged new housing in the neighborhood. Calling for a streetcar line into Southside and improved road paving gave the neighborhood better transportation to the central city and remote workplaces. Their best-known campaign, the creation of Southside Park, created a cultural center and recreation area that could be enjoyed by all Sacramentans. Southside was the first park in Sacramento created largely because of public demand, rather than beginning as a city planner's concept or an amusement park built by a private developer intent on drawing investors.

The club was formally incorporated on November 10, 1913, although it had already been active for over a decade. Dues were 25¢ a month and are still 25¢ a month after 95 years. This has led to the club's nickname, "the two-bit club." In addition to neighborhood advocacy, the Southside Improvement Club helped support the neighborhood with regular events like the Fourth of July fireworks show.

The Southside Improvement Club was one of many organizations in the neighborhood. Organizations like the Dante Club, the Sacramento Valley Japanese Association, the Women's Civic Improvement Club, the Centro, and many others held meetings, supported communities, and called for change. This interest in civic participation and community involvement served the Southsiders well, in good times and bad.

Southside Park is currently represented by the Southside Park Neighborhood Association, which is open to anyone who lives or owns property in the neighborhood, or who is simply interested in the neighborhood's issues. Formed in the early 1990s, the association provides an organized voice for the community, represents the neighborhood's interests at city hall, and hosts social events in the park. It has carried Southside's legacy of civic involvement and diversity to the present day.

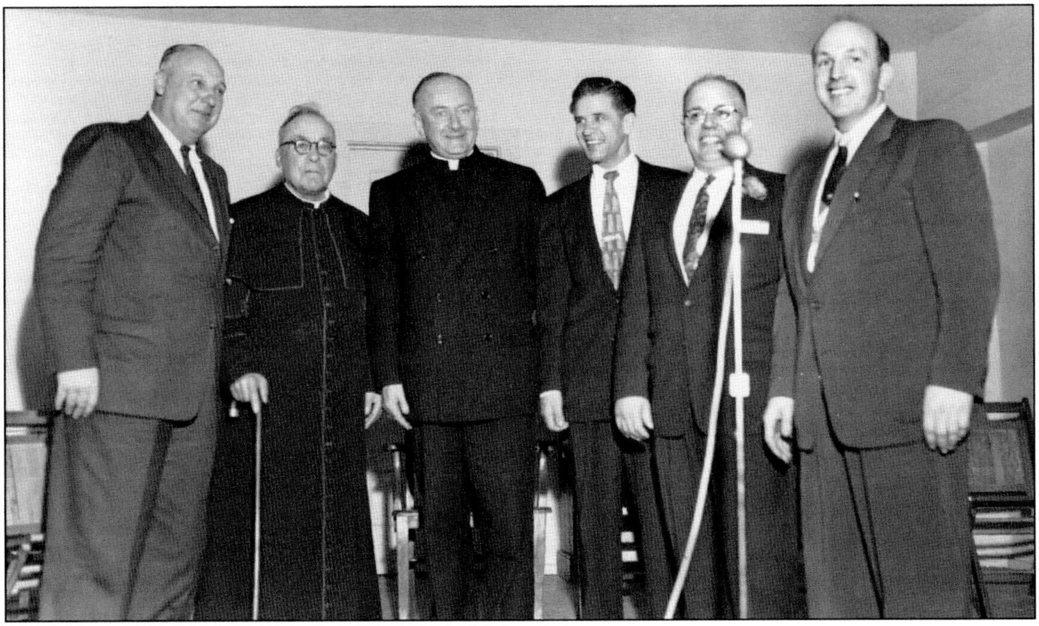

Southside Improvement Club members came from all walks of life. Club membership was considered a necessity for a career in local politics. In this photograph, taken in approximately 1957, (left to right) an unidentified county supervisor, Monsignor Azevedo of St. Elizabeth's Church, Bishop Joseph McGucken, and Mayor Clarence Azevedo join club president Al Balshor on the podium at St. Elizabeth's Church. (Al Balshor collection.)

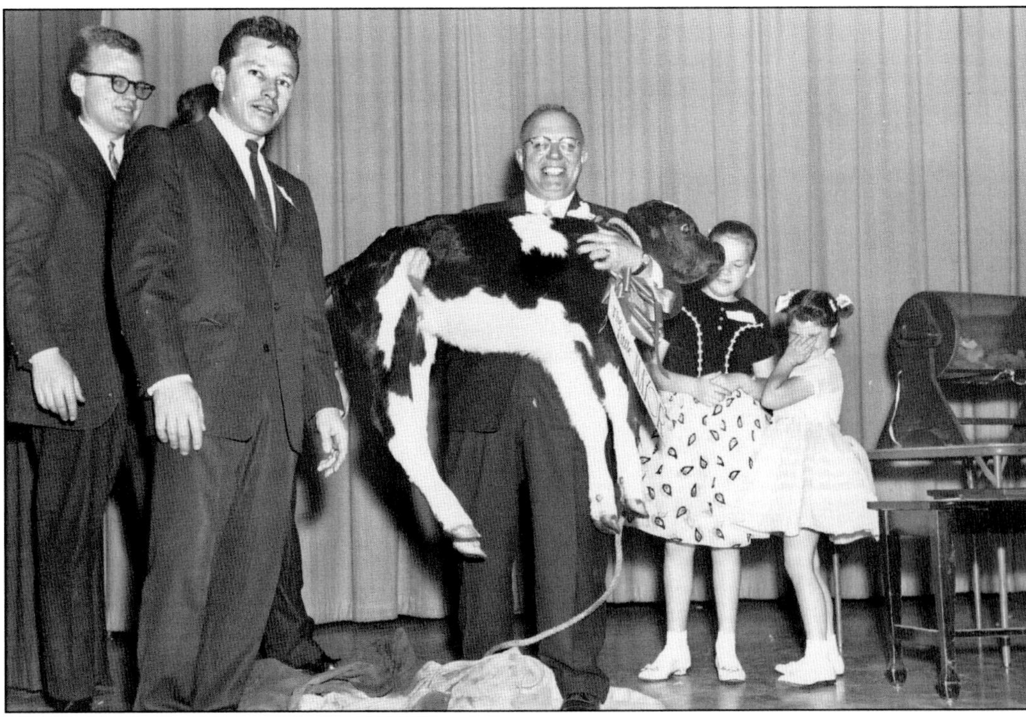

At this meeting, the Southside Improvement Club gave Mayor Azevedo a small Holstein cow. Standing to the left of the mayor is Kenneth B. Cayocca. (Al Balshor collection.)

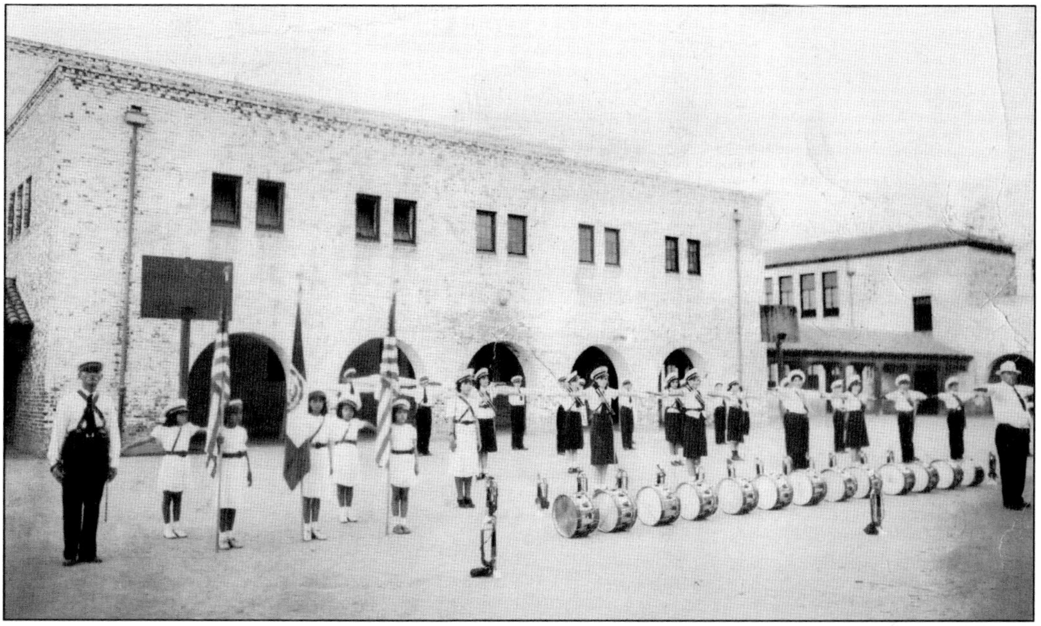

Honorifica was an organization founded by Southside Park's Latino community. In the 1930s, Honorifica sponsored a children's drum and bugle corps. Bandleader Juan Perez, a veteran of the Mexican army, provided instruction in music, maintenance of instruments, and parade drills. Here the corps practices on the grounds of the Lincoln School. (Herlinda Herrera.)

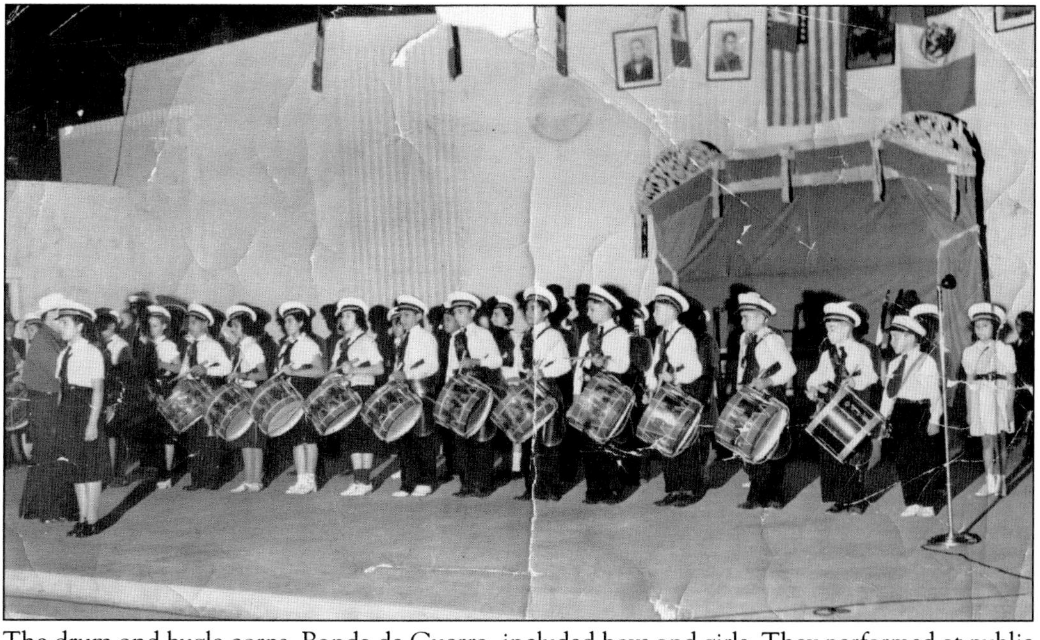

The drum and bugle corps, Banda de Guerra, included boys and girls. They performed at public functions, like Cinco de Mayo and Mexican Independence Day (September 16), at the Southside Park bandstand. Banda de Guerra also entered, and won, statewide drum and bugle corps competitions. According to band member Herlinda Herrera, their performances emphasized precision and synchronized movement: "You could only see one body, one drum and one bugle." (Herlinda Herrera.)

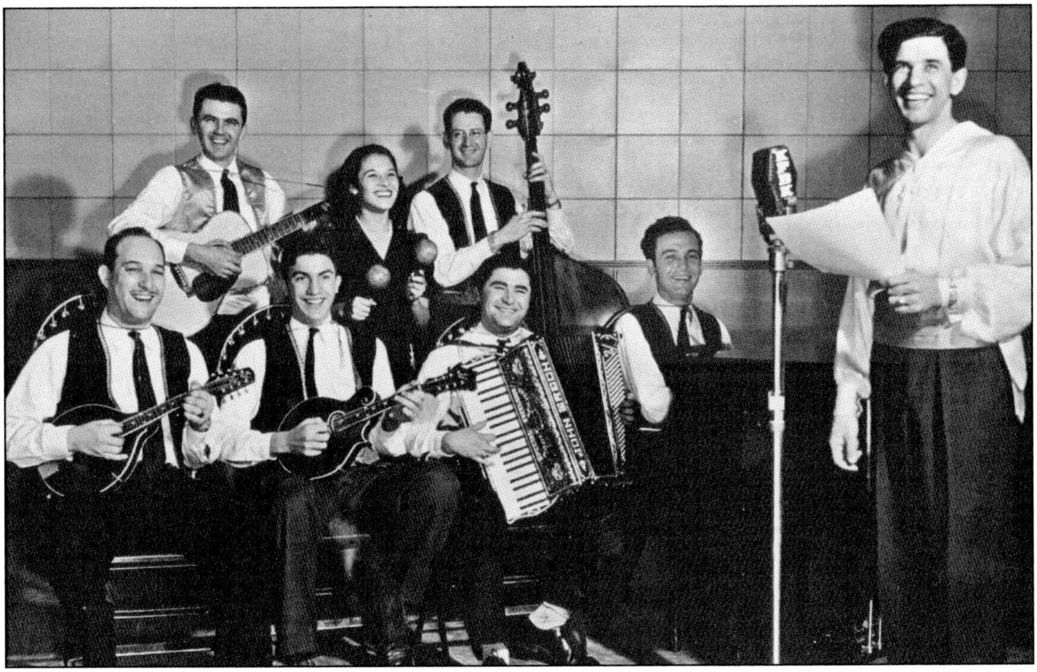

Gabriel Silveira was a Southsider with many talents and a long history of civic involvement. He was born in 1907 on the island of Pico in the Azores and came to Sacramento about 1917 with his mother. A musically talented young man, he composed music and performed plays in the basement of St. Elizabeth's Church. In 1934, he hosted a radio program called *Memories of Portugal* on KROY. (Portuguese Cultural and Historical Society.)

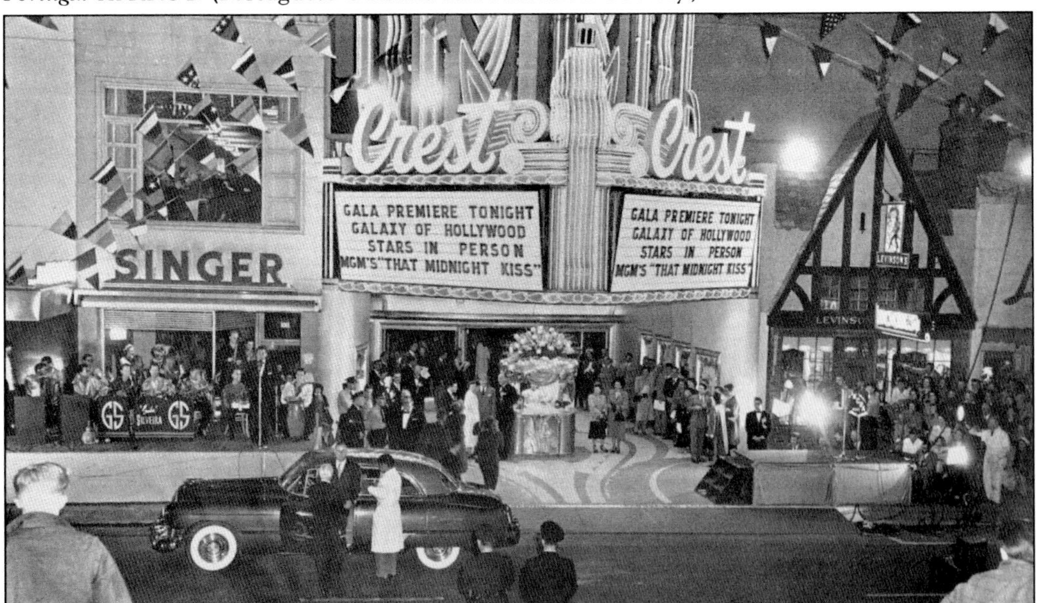

On October 6, 1949, Gabriel Silveira and his orchestra performed outside of the new Crest Theater for a gala opening. His band is visible to the left of the Crest's marquee. Later that evening, his band performed at the post-premiere party at the Senator Hotel's Empire Room. (Portuguese Cultural and Historical Society.)

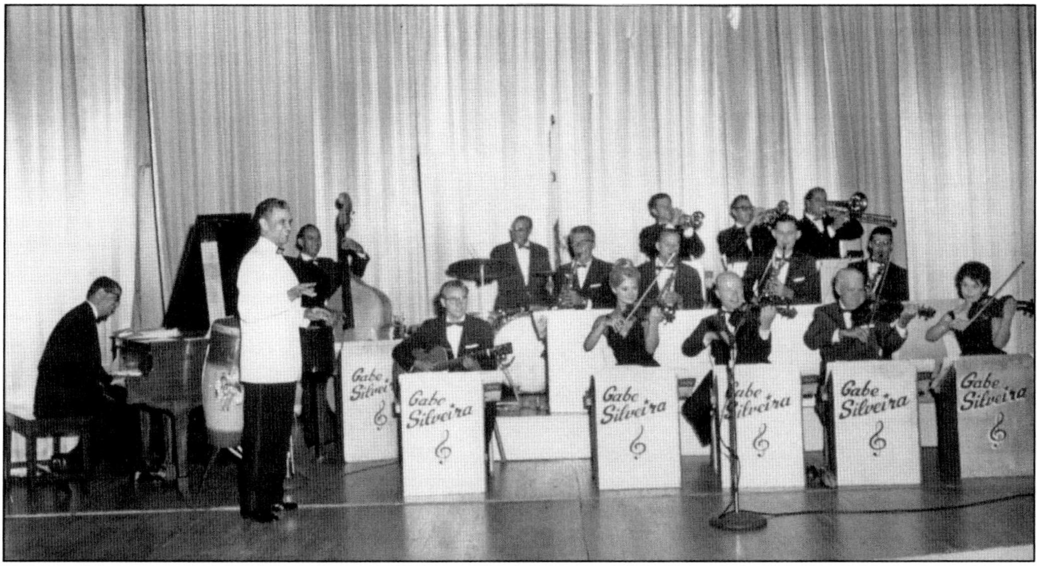

Here Silveira's orchestra performs at the El Dorado Inn, now known as the Woodlake Inn. After World War II, he formed a band called the Lost Gaucho and directed a television program called *Music in the Latin Mood* for KFBK. He also owned a furniture store at Twenty-first and X Streets and later opened two more stores. (Portuguese Cultural and Historical Society.)

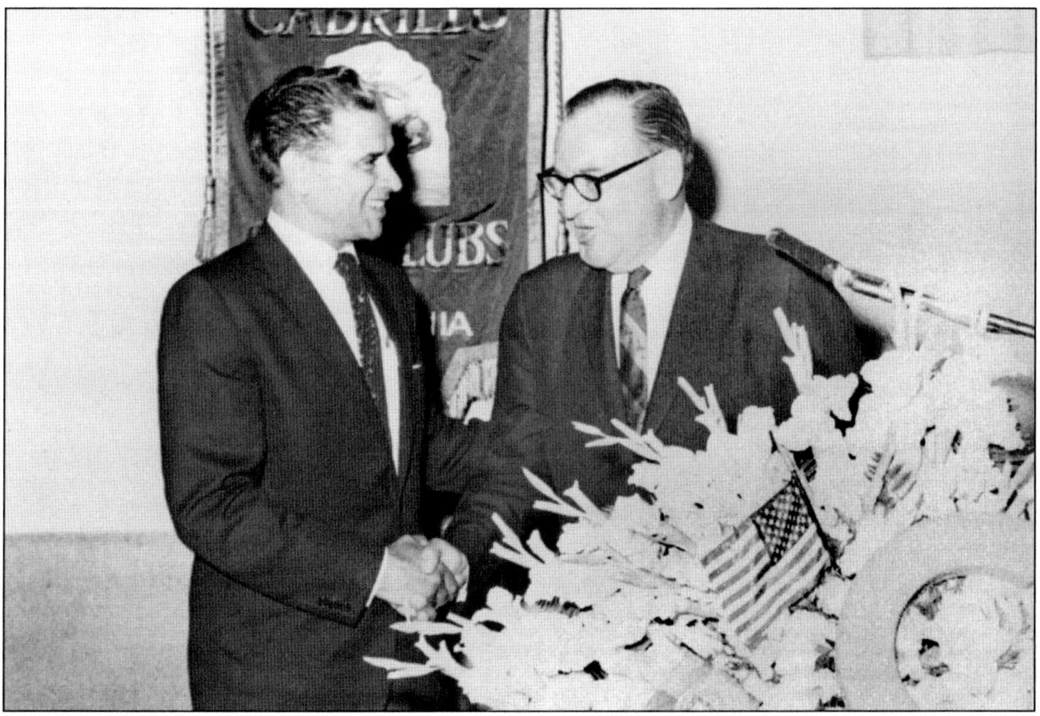

Gabriel ran for city council in 1961 on a platform of opposing the routing of Interstate 5 through the residential neighborhoods between Second and Third Streets. Despite the fact that he barely had time to campaign, he came close to winning a seat on the Sacramento City Council. Here he shakes hands with Gov. Edmund G. "Pat" Brown (right) on Cabrillo Day at the California State Fair in 1960. (Portuguese Cultural and Historical Society.)

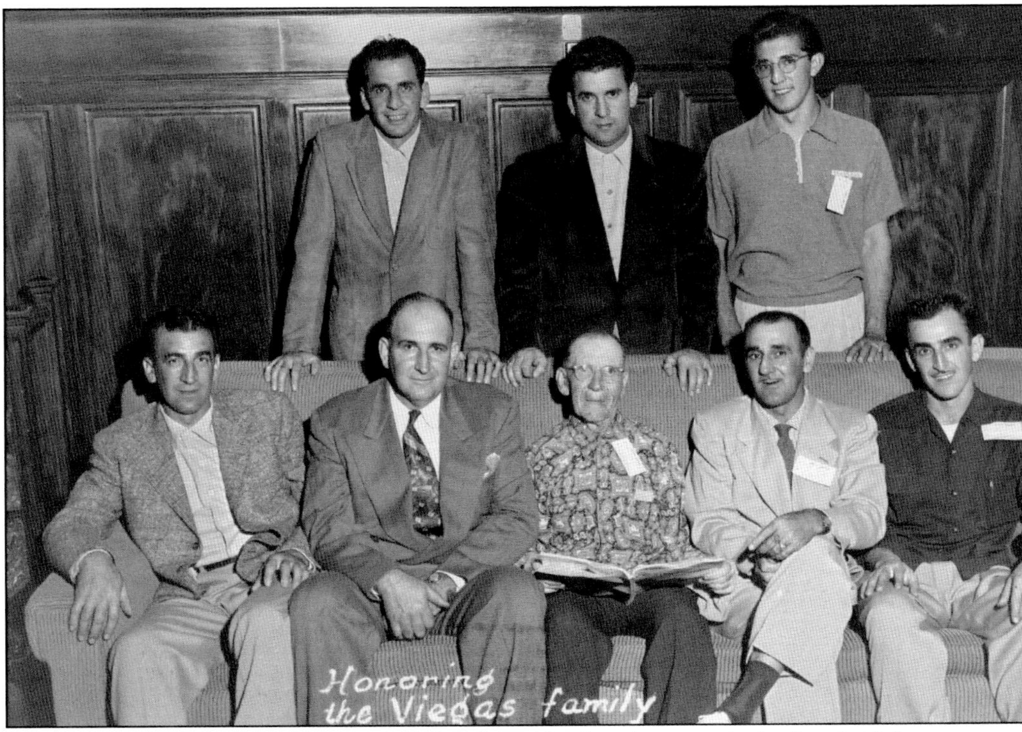

Civic participation was a multigenerational tradition. In this photograph, the Southside Improvement Club honored the Viegas family, with three generations of members. Pictured from left to right are (seated) Clark, Gus, Frank, Val, and Danny Viegas; (standing) Tony, Eli, and Ted Viegas. (Al Balshor collection.)

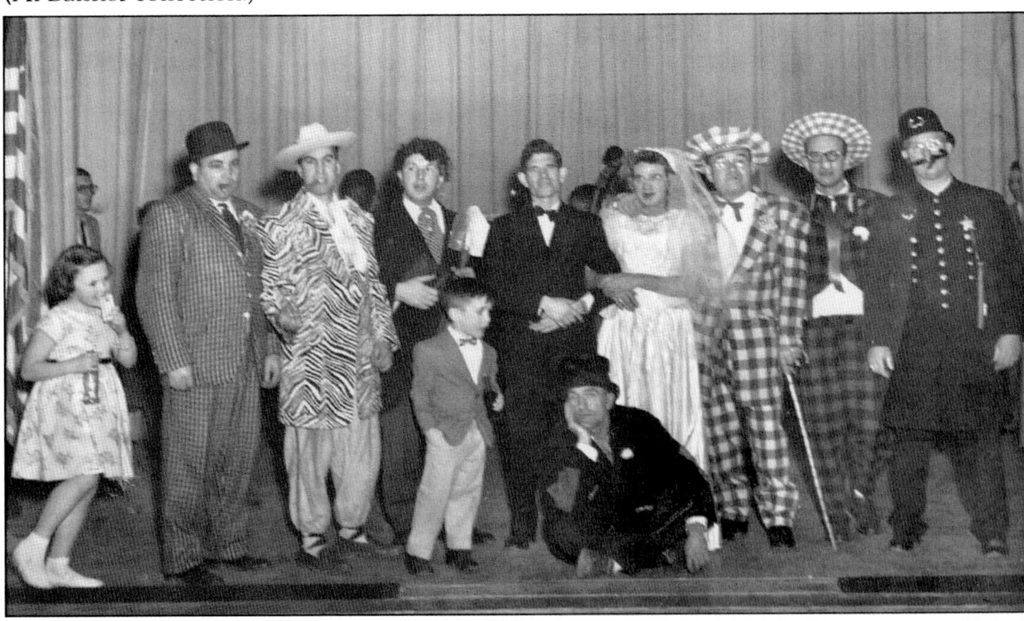

Sometimes civic participation got a bit silly. Here the Holy Angel Men's Club put on a "Men's Fashions" show to raise funds for the Holy Angel School. Admission cost a $1 donation, and the door prize was a 21-inch television. (Al Balshor collection.)

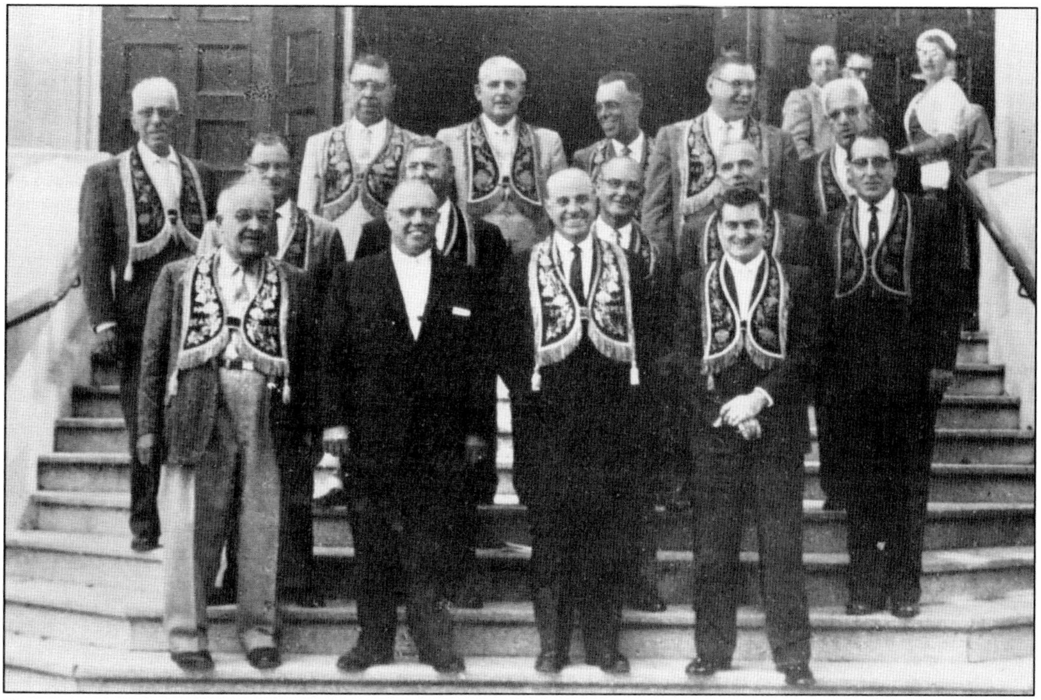

Some civic organizations were focused on particular ethnic communities. Here the second annual meeting of UPEC (União Portugesa Estado da California, or Portuguese Union of the State of California) poses on the steps of St. Elizabeth's Church in 1959. Mayor Azevedo is in the first row, second from the left. (Portuguese Historical and Cultural Society.)

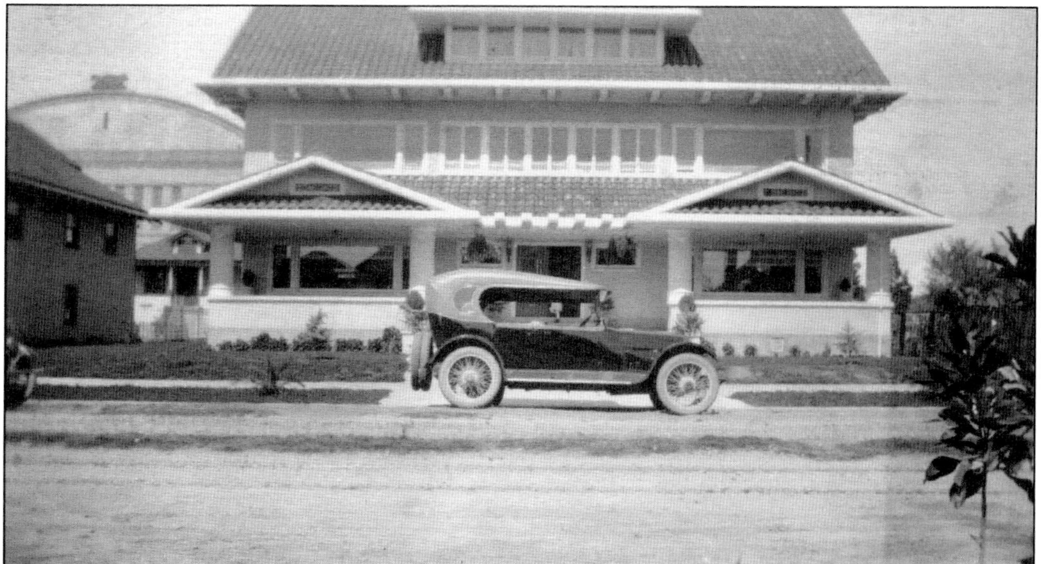

This house was originally the home of Manuel Machado, known as the "Bean King." In the 1950s, the home was a boardinghouse for single African American women. Housing choices for these women were often sharply limited because of housing discrimination. It was also a gathering place for the African American community, including the Women's Civic Improvement Club, and a site for wedding receptions and other public events. (Portuguese Historical and Cultural Society.)

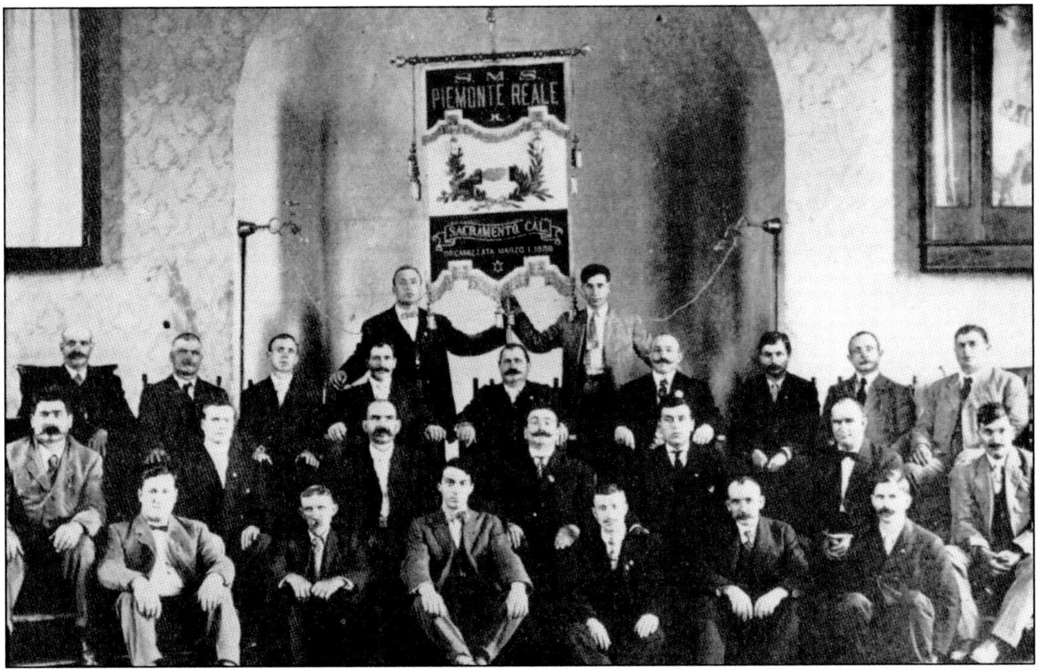

The Piemonte Reale was Sacramento's oldest continuous Italian American association, originally founded in 1888. Organizations like this provided members with medical assistance, financial help in times of unemployment, social activities, and even job placement. These groups were found among all of the different ethnic groups in Southside, and some can still be found today. (Italian Cultural Society.)

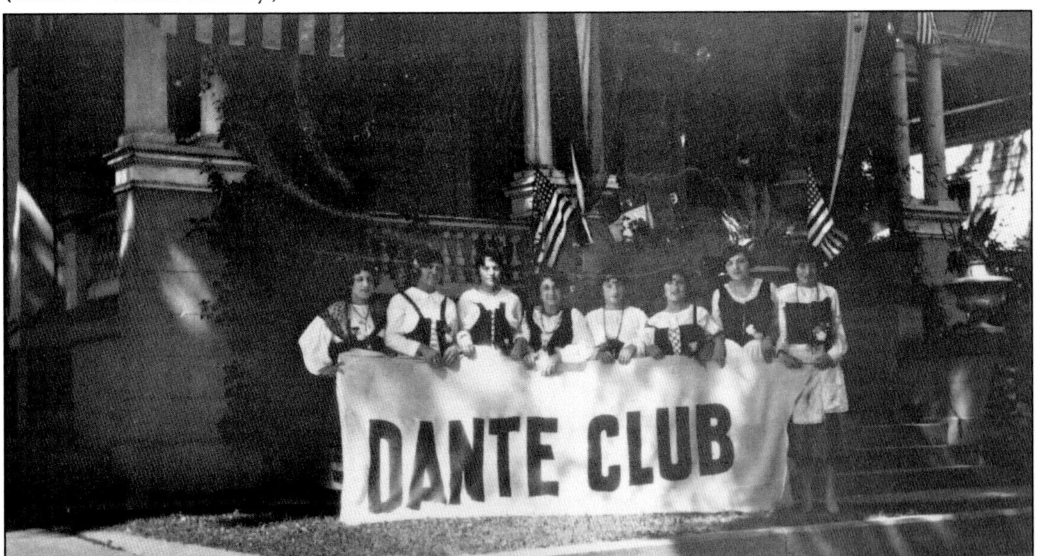

The Dante Club was established in 1923 as a way to encourage music, drama, art, literature, athletics, and social activities among the Italian American community. In 1926, they bought this building at 1511 P Street for use as their community center. They also had a women's auxiliary and a baseball team. Cultural organizations like this helped ethnic groups maintain cultural identity while encouraging new immigrants to learn American ways. (Italian Cultural Society.)

Eight

BLIGHT AND RENAISSANCE

In the 1950s, Sacramento's population expanded rapidly into new suburbs. Many Southsiders moved out of the central city to new suburban neighborhoods like Land Park, East Sacramento, or the Pocket area. For some, this was a natural progression out of their parents' homes. For others, moving out was not easy because racial exclusion laws were still in place. Some nonwhites had white friends purchase lands for them, but many remained in the neighborhood.

In the business district and city hall, however, the outlook was grim. Few new buildings were being constructed downtown, and businesses were suffering. Those who lived in the suburbs preferred new shopping malls like Town and Country Village or Country Club Center to driving downtown to shop on K Street. Sales and property tax revenue sank, while the costs of city services rose. To city planners and businesspeople, state and federal urban redevelopment programs presented a potential solution.

Redevelopment programs were developed by the federal government to replace substandard housing for the poor with new, high-quality housing. However, most cities, including Sacramento, used these programs to expand the central business district. New housing units produced by the programs were far fewer than the number of units destroyed during redevelopment, and often the replacement units were far more expensive than the neighborhood's original housing. Additionally, the city development authority did not consider the thousands of single men staying in hotels and boardinghouses near the waterfront to be permanent residents. Thus, the city was able to justify greatly reduced estimates for replacement housing.

The City of Sacramento needed to borrow money to fund redevelopment and asked citizens to approve Measure B, a public bond measure, in 1954. Measure B failed to pass, but the city council decided to borrow the needed funds by issuing bonds to be repaid by the increased property tax value of the planned development area. This method, known as tax increment financing, was used in redevelopment districts around the country. By demolishing neighborhoods and building businesses, higher city tax revenue would pay back the bonds. This plan was successful, and tax valuations for the redeveloped blocks went beyond the city's expectations. But the neighborhoods, and the people who lived there, were gone.

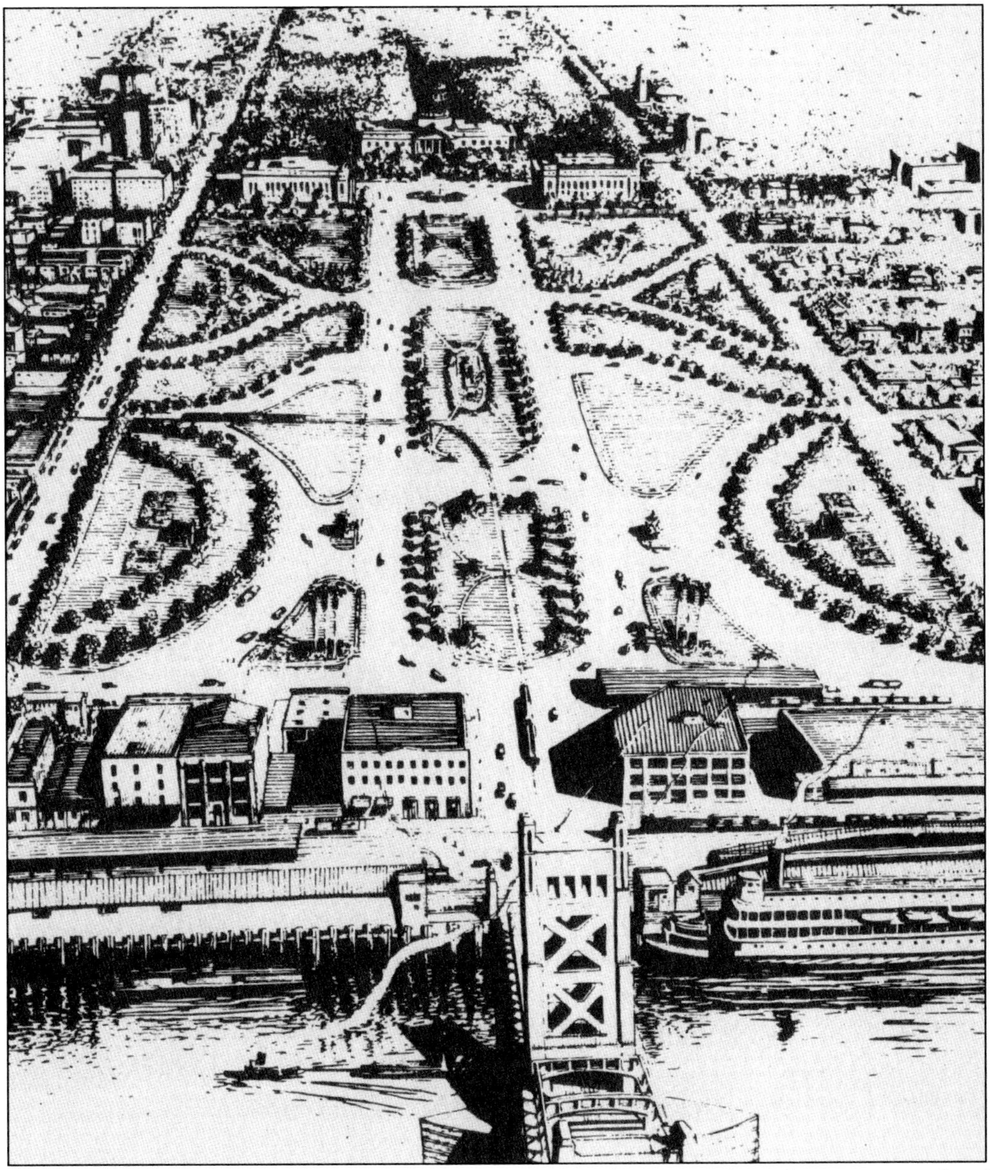

There were many plans to renovate or otherwise improve the approach to the state capitol on M Street. On June 24, 1908, civic planner Werner Hegemann was quoted in the *Sacramento Union*: "Leading toward the bridge as it does, M Street will more and more become very important as a thoroughfare. If properly treated and protected it may, with the capitol in view, become one of the most beautiful streets anywhere. If not properly protected nor properly developed it will become as meaningless and vile in appearance as K Street with its lack of shade and mix-up of competing structures." In 1934, the Sutter Club urged the Downtown Association to consider a beautification plan on M Street to complement the new Tower Bridge, then under construction. City manager James Dean called for improved lighting and regular tree planting, and John Skelton of the Downtown Association recommended that property owners in Japantown decorate the fronts of their structures "in an Oriental manner." The 1935 plan, shown above, would have removed Japantown entirely, forming a gigantic parkway from L to N Street. (Sacramento Public Library, Sacramento Room.)

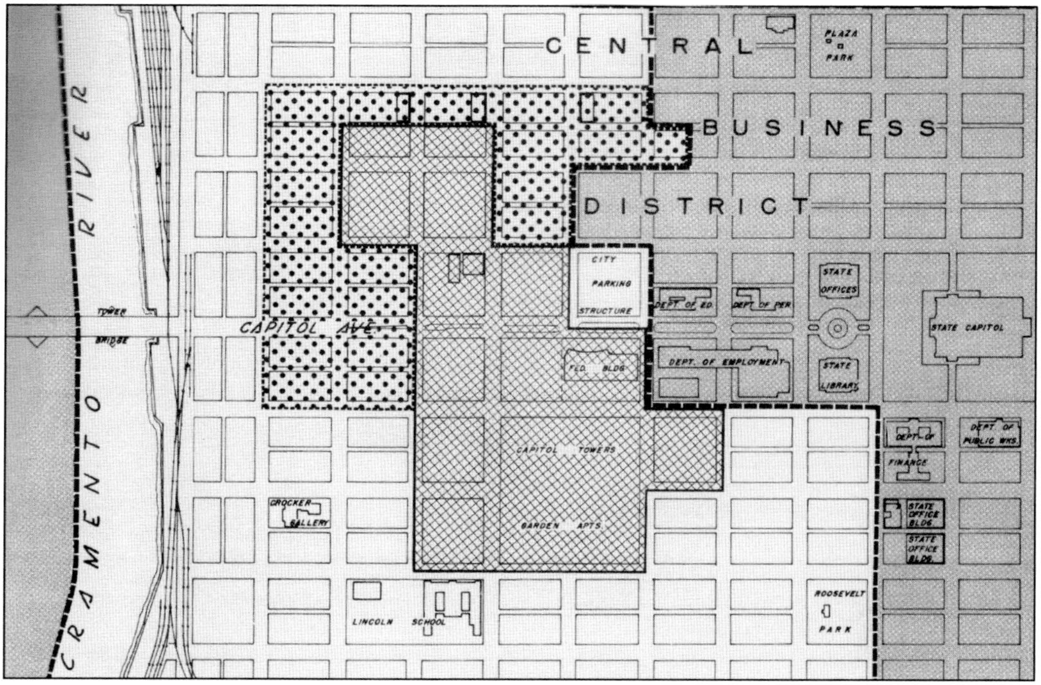

The California State Capitol urban renewal plan was executed in three stages: Project 2-A, a 15-block area along M Street; Project 3, called the "Capitol Mall Extension Project"; and Project 4, the Riverfront Project, which encompassed the waterfront from the Southern Pacific shops all the way to S Street and east to Tenth Street. This included much of the northern half of Southside and all of Japantown. (Sacramento Public Library, Sacramento Room.)

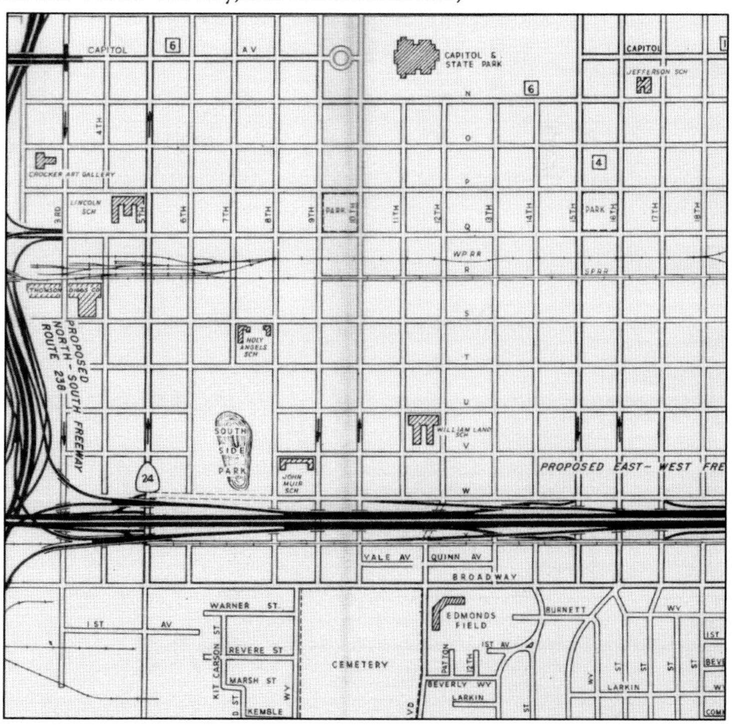

Another federal project considered a solution to city problems were interstate freeways. Two major projects passed through Southside: Highway 50, which occupied the block between W and X Streets through the entire length of the central city, and Interstate 5, whose path triggered considerable public debate. Highways, some argued, would help keep downtown accessible to suburban dwellers. Highway 50 passed directly through Southside Park, eliminating 25 percent of the park. (Sacramento Public Library, Sacramento Room.)

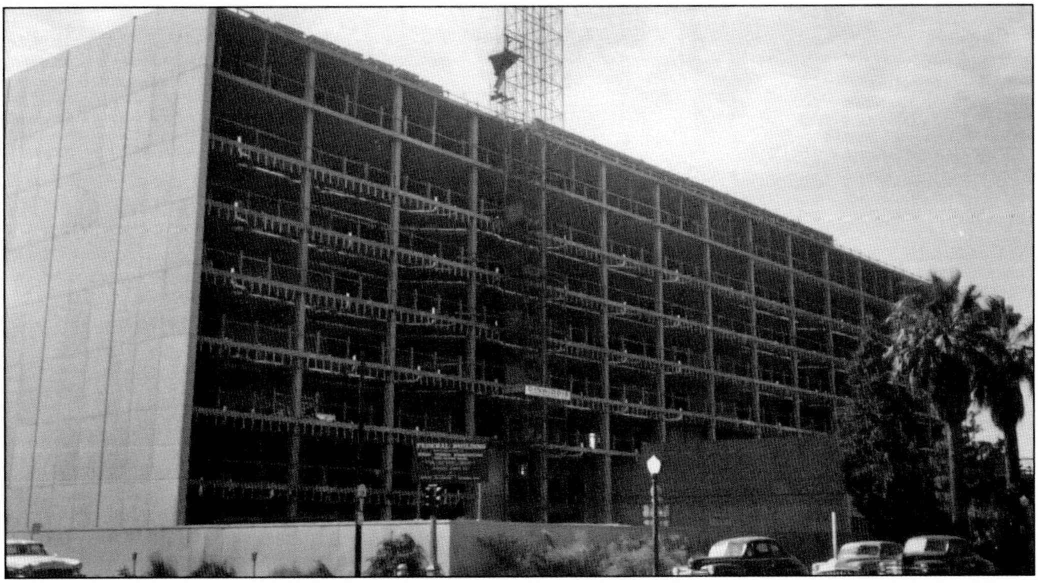

The Capitol Mall extension projects replaced homes and businesses with large office buildings along the length of M Street. The street was expanded into a boulevard with a grass median. Early plans projected similar widened boulevards along I and Q Streets and large-scale integration of city blocks into larger "superblocks." The Capitol Towers apartment complex used the "superblock" concept, as did the pedestrian malls along K and O Streets. (Sacramento Archives and Museum Collection Center.)

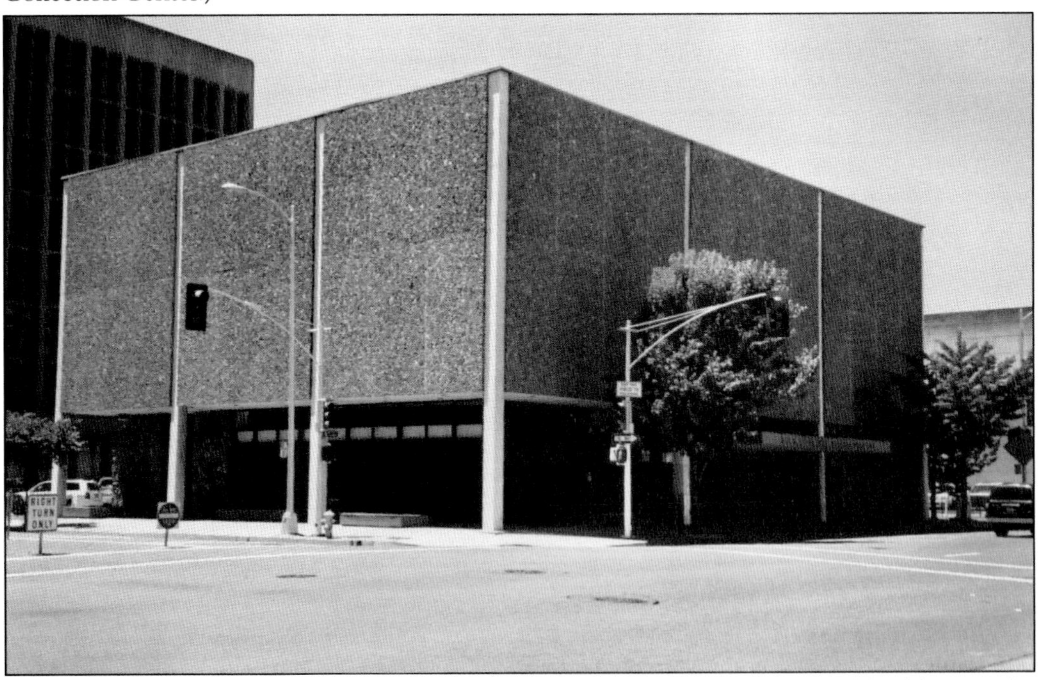

Some of the blocks cleared were sold to private developers for commercial buildings. The Sacramento Savings building at Fifth and L Streets was the first completed commercial structure as a result of the redevelopment program. Ironically, this building is vacant and dilapidated in 2007. (Author's collection.)

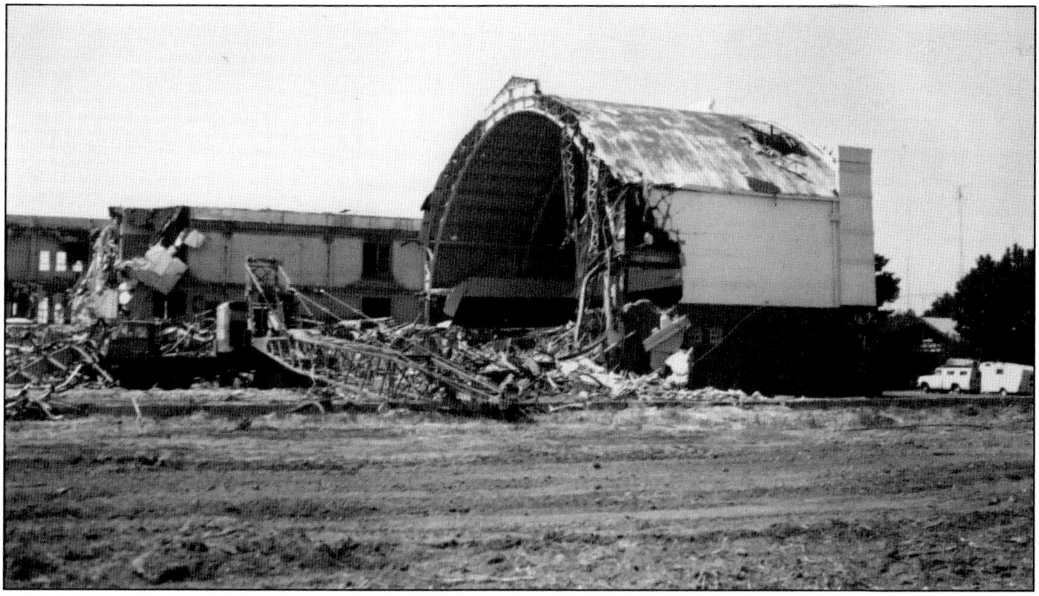

Here the National Guard armory on W and Twelfth Streets is being demolished to make way for Highway 50. The Manuel Machado house, later home of the Women's Civic Improvement Club, has already been demolished. Four blocks away, the Southside Park clubhouse and ODES hall were demolished, and a quarter of the Southside Park lake was filled in. (Sacramento Archives and Museum Collection Center.)

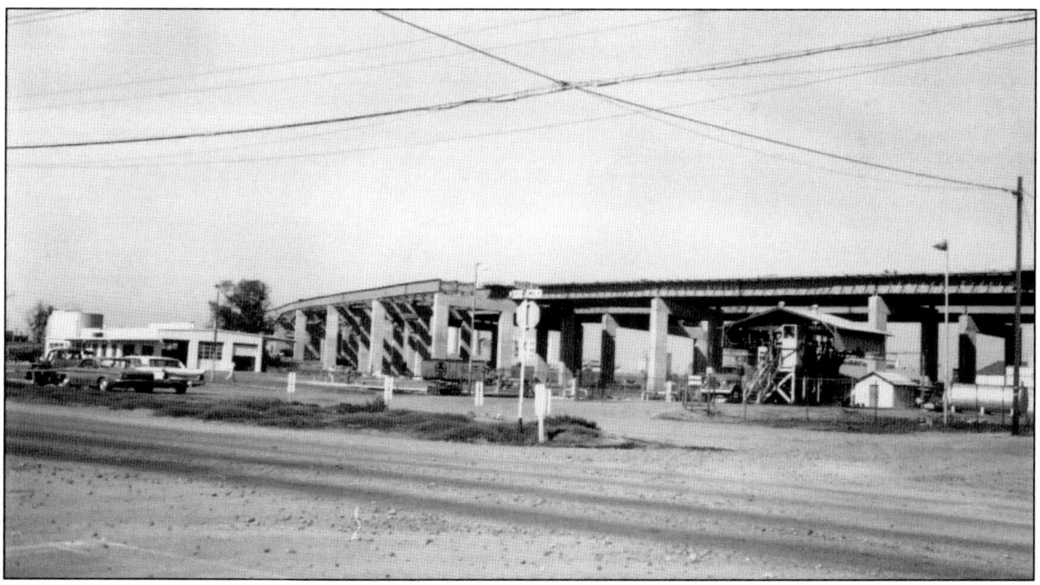

Highway 50 and Interstate 5 made use of land adjacent to the Sacramento Northern belt line along X and Front Streets. Sacramento Northern and Central California Traction abandoned the belt line in 1966. Since they had switched to diesel locomotives, they were able to make use of existing Southern Pacific and Western Pacific tracks to reach their remaining customers. (Sacramento Archives and Museum Collection Center.)

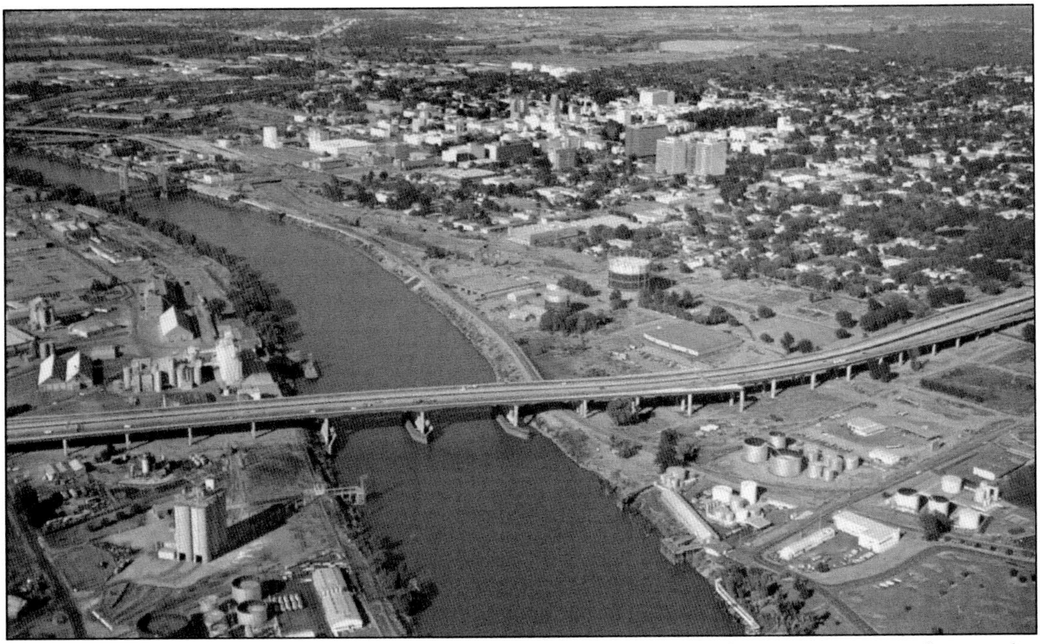

The route of Highway 50 meant that the Tower Bridge and Capitol Avenue were no longer the main entrance to the city. The grand boulevard, with its majestic view of the capitol, is not visible from the highway. In this photograph, land clearance for Interstate 5 is clearly visible in the dirt swath that weaves from Third to Second Street and back again before passing over the rail yards. (Author's collection.)

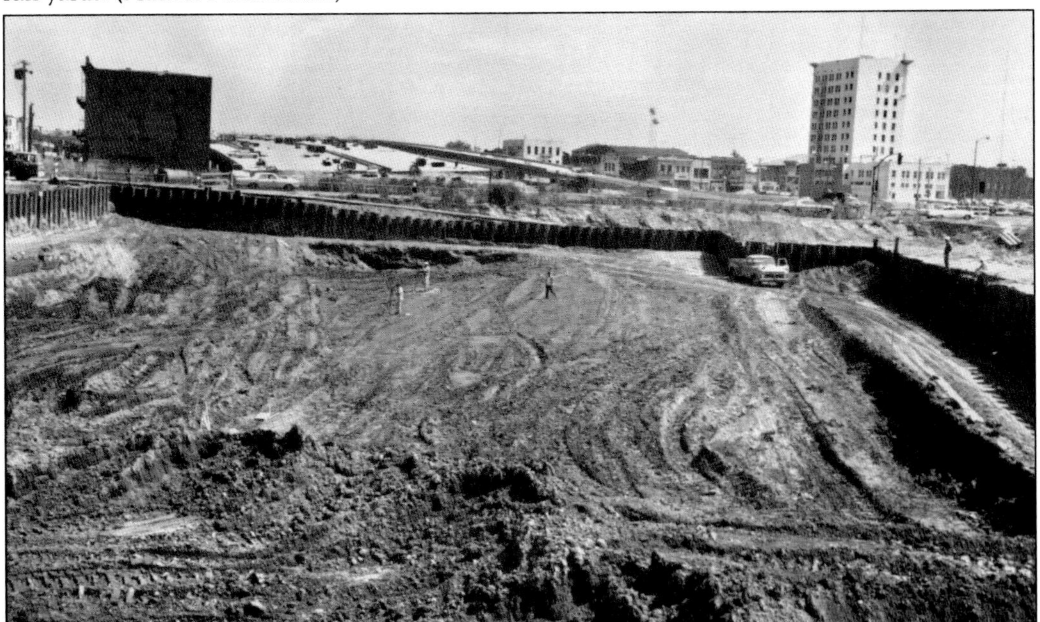

Here Interstate 5 passed through the land once occupied by the L Street Arena. To the left are the remaining blocks along the river that would become Old Sacramento. Even today, many Sacramentans consider the interstate to be an uninviting moat surrounding an otherwise exemplary historic district. (Sacramento Archives and Museum Collection Center.)

Prostitutes who once worked downtown moved their business to Southside Park. Fourth and T Streets, once the heart of the Portuguese neighborhood, became an infamous prostitute's stroll. This button, produced in the 1960s or 1970s, jokes at the hazards of the neighborhood, but sometimes the dangers were very real. Some sympathized with the prostitutes, but pimps and drug dealers wanted to dominate the neighborhood by force. (Author's collection.)

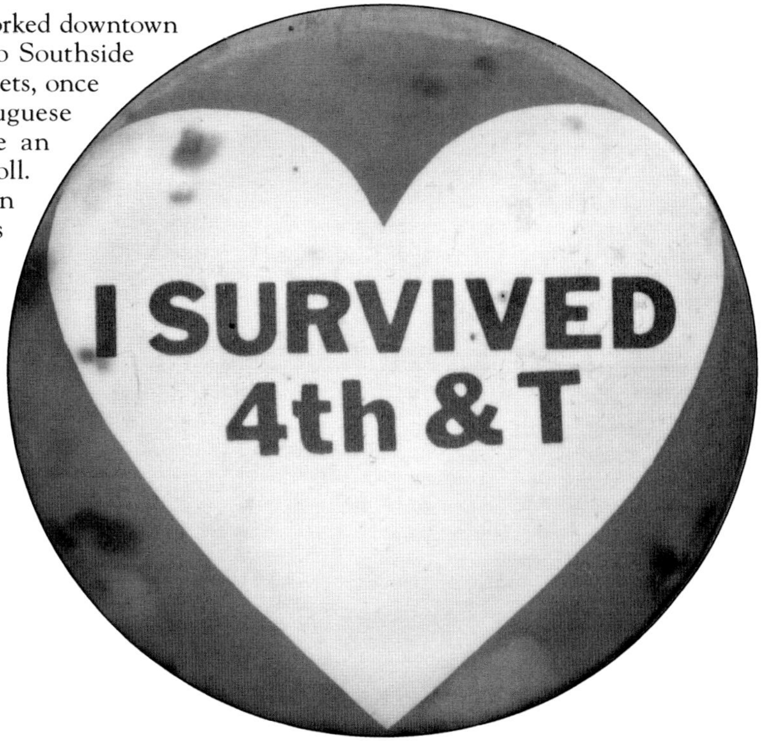

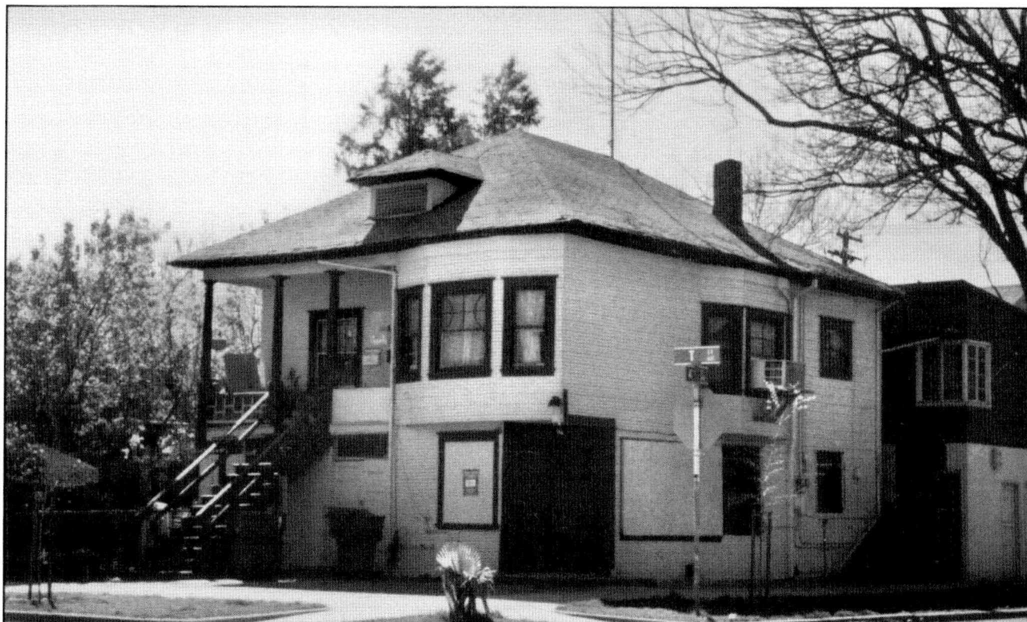

Once again, neighborhood activists in Southside demanded change. Volunteers like Marie Balshor organized groups who followed prostitutes with signs, deterring customers and bringing police attention to the area. It took a great deal of work and time, but neighborhood action drove prostitution out of the neighborhood. Today the corner of Fourth and T no longer bears the moniker "Hooker Hollow." (Author's collection.)

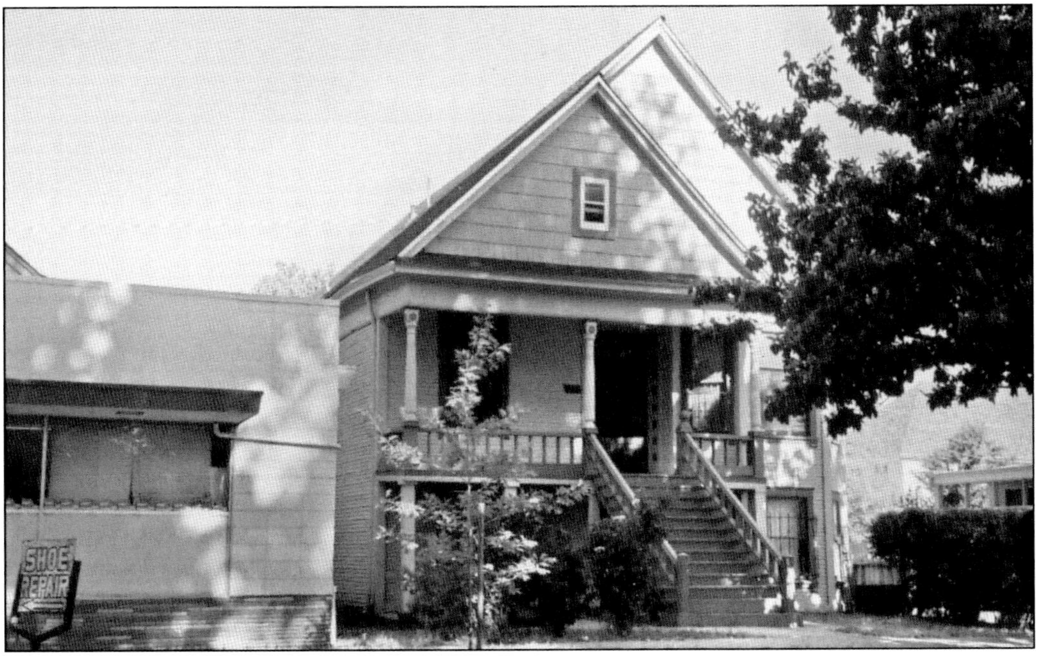

In more recent decades, Southside and other central city neighborhoods attracted students and bohemians. Relatively inexpensive housing, inviting trees, and historic architecture had an appeal to many that superseded previous generations' concerns about the dangers of cities. Often like-minded friends would share the rent on a large house that had previously been a family home. (Author's collection.)

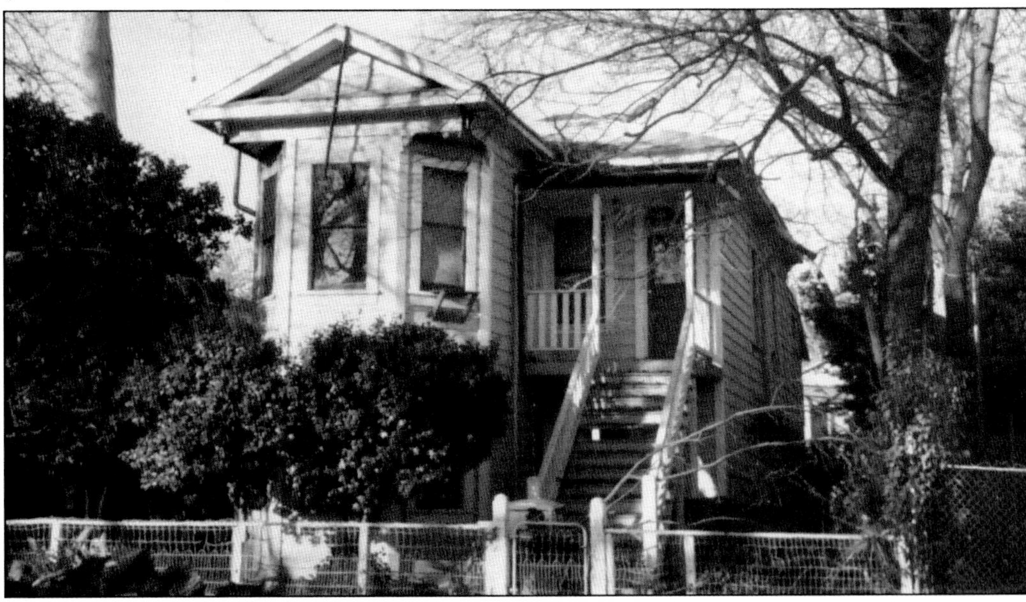

While many properties in Southside Park are still dilapidated and awaiting repair, there are signs of change. New infill projects are making use of existing vacant lots, and homeowners with an interest in rescuing classic homes from decay and dilapidation are making changes in the face of the neighborhood. Historic preservation efforts in conjunction with the city of Sacramento help preserve architecture and reverse the effects of neglect. (Author's collection.)

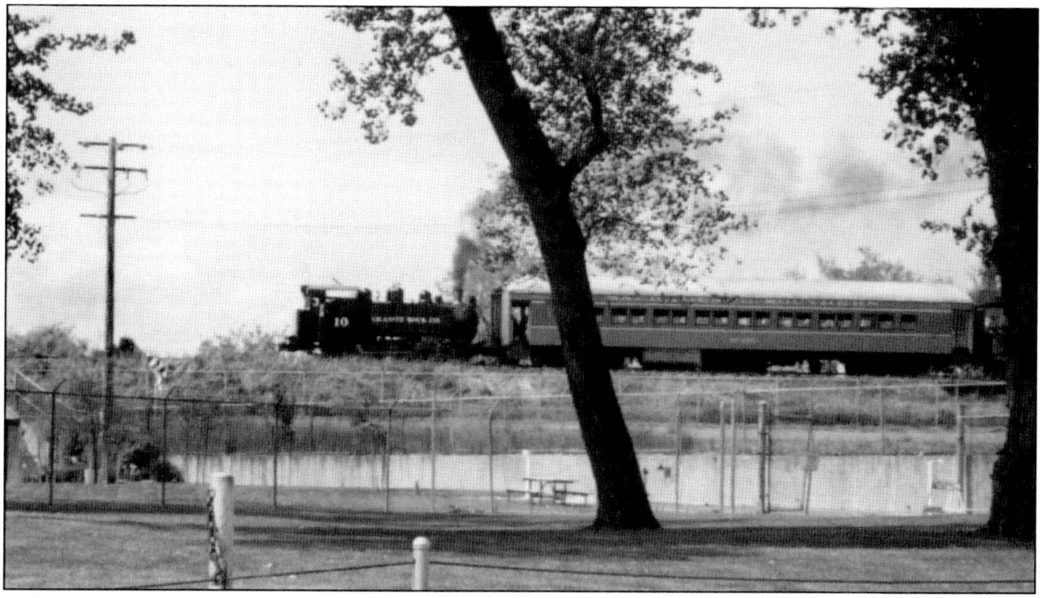

There are still railroads operating along Front Street, although rail traffic is limited to the Sacramento Southern Railroad, the California State Railroad Museum's tourist line. It does serve one remaining industrial customer, Setzer Forest Products, south of Broadway. The Towe Auto Museum still occupies the produce warehouse on Front Street, although plans exist to redevelop the neighborhood where it sits. (Author's collection.)

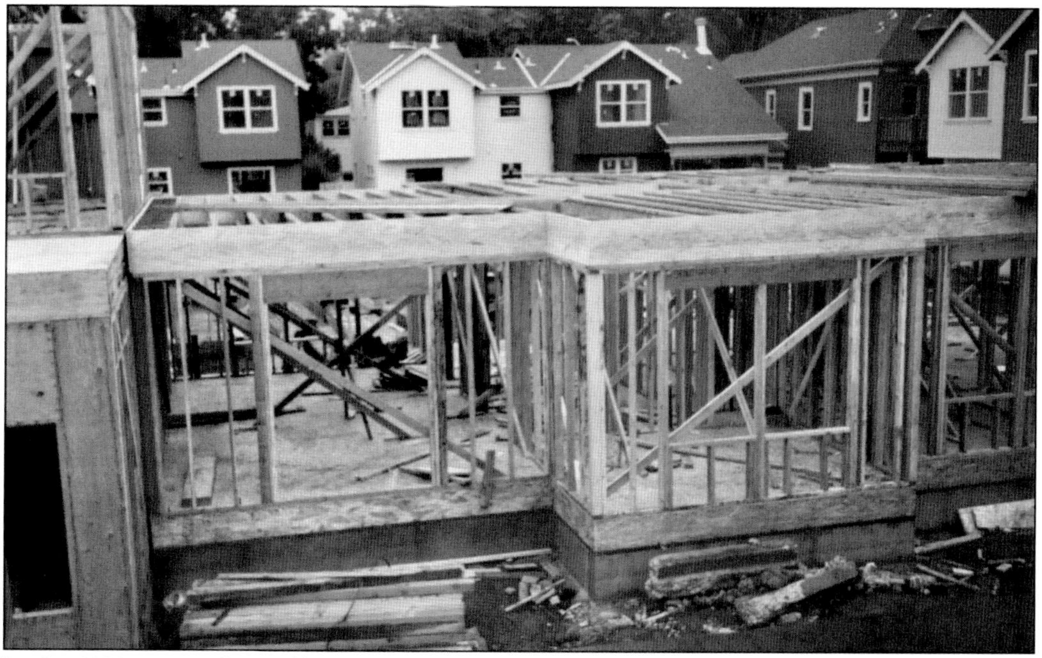

In the 1990s, a new form of housing appeared in Southside Park. This cohousing project is based on closely set individual homes, with a shared communal space in the middle and a community dining and multipurpose hall. Residents share meals on a regular basis and cooperate in decisions affecting the whole cohousing project. In many ways, projects like this reflect the community traditions of Southside Park that date back a century. (Paul Trudeau collection.)

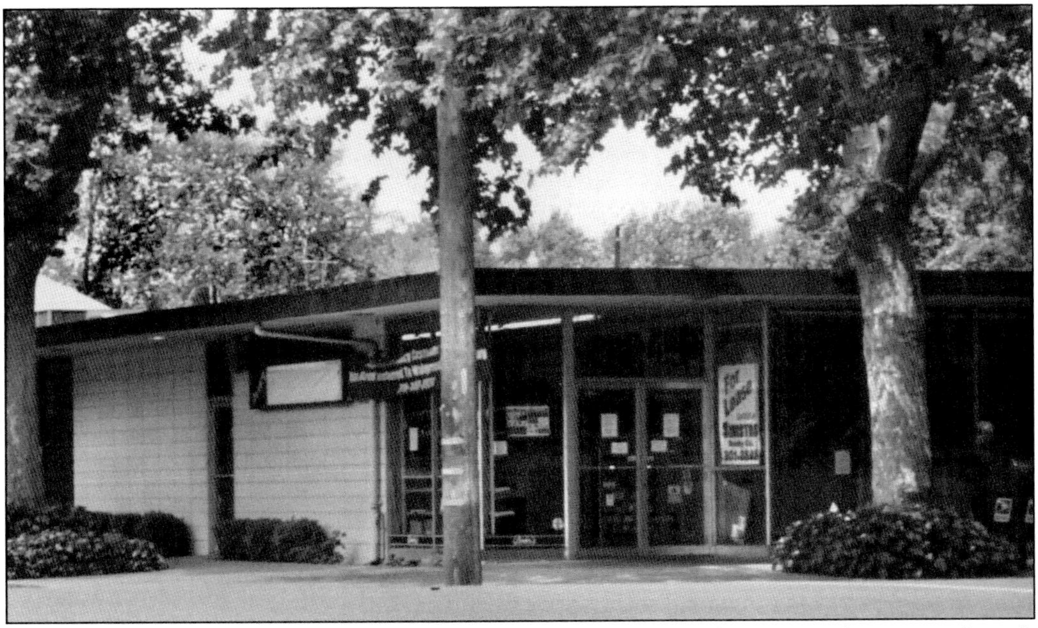

When Japantown and the Chinese neighborhoods were eliminated, many residents moved south into the remaining neighborhoods of Southside, and there is still a strong Asian presence in the neighborhood today, including businesses and community organizations. Ouye's Pharmacy, formerly located at 400 L Street, relocated to Tenth and V Streets in 1959 because of redevelopment. Its doors finally closed in 2007. (Author's collection.)

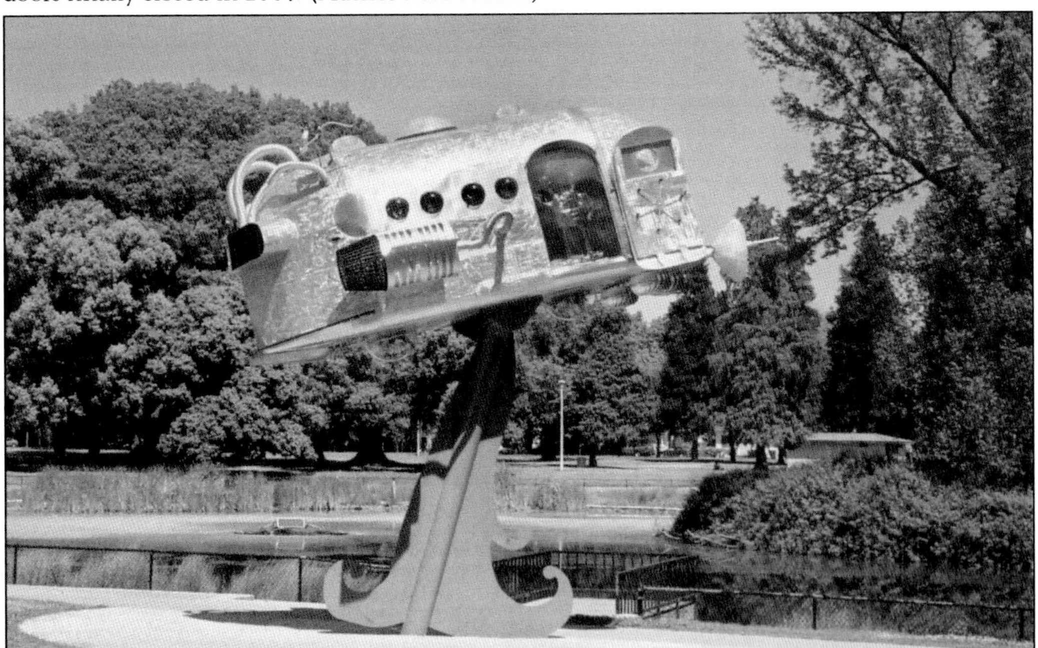

Southside Park still provides a pleasant oasis in the middle of the city. It is still the site of many annual celebrations, including Cinco de Mayo and Mexican Independence Day. Recently its playground was rebuilt and expanded, complete with this imaginative statue. Southsiders today can still stroll among the trees and enjoy the breeze down in Southside Park. (Author's collection.)

BIBLIOGRAPHY

Fogelson, Robert. *Downtown: Its Rise and Fall, 1880–1950.* New Haven and London: Yale University Press, 2001.

Galarza, Ernesto. *Barrio Boy.* Notre Dame, IN: University of Notre Dame Press, 1993.

Holmes, Lionel and Joseph D'Allesandro. *Portuguese Pioneers of the Sacramento Area.* Sacramento, CA: Portuguese Historical and Cultural Society, 1990.

Jackson, Keneth. *Crabgrass Frontier: The Suburbanization of the United States.* New York: Oxford University Press, 1985.

Lastufka, Ken. "Redevelopment of Sacramento's West End, 1950–1970: A historical overview with an analysis of the impact of relocation." Master's thesis, California State University, Sacramento, spring 1985.

Maeda, Wayne. *Changing Dreams and Treasured Memories: A Story of Japanese Americans in the Sacramento Region.* Sacramento, CA: Sacramento Japanese American Citizens League, 2000.

Monkkonen, Eric. *America Becomes Urban: The Development Of U.S. Cities And Towns, 1780–1980.* Berkeley and Los Angeles, CA: University of California Press, 1990.

Pierini, Bruce. "*Gli Italiani di Sacramento:* The Italians of Sacramento." *Golden Notes* Vol. 37 No. 2, summer 1991.

Roberts, Brian. "Redevelopment at the crossroads: How Sacramento City chose between priorities in the 1950s." *Golden Notes* Vol. 35 No. 2, summer 1989.

Sacramento Branch, American Association of University Women. *Vanishing Victorians: A Guide to the Historic Homes of Sacramento.* Sacramento, CA: Fong and Fong, 1981.

Stanley, David G. and Jeffrey J. Moreau. *Central California Traction: California's Last Interurban.* Wilton, CA: Signature Press, 2002.

Wright, George F., ed. *History of Sacramento County, California.* Oakland, CA: Thompson and West, 1880.